"In an era where many people are crying for a return to sacred experience, James Swan's book could not be more timely. The readers of *Sacred Places* may be motivated to embark upon a quest that will bring them in closer contact with the land, with history, and with people who felt close to the earth. The global ecological crisis demands respect and reverence for Nature before it—and the humans who are a part of it—are irreparably devastated."
—Stanley Krippner, Ph.D., professor of psychology at Saybrook Institute,
coauthor of *Dreamworking*

"By focusing on the often ignored spiritual and aesthetic riches of the endangered natural world, psychologist Jim Swan puts the battle to save the environment in a fresh and invigorating perspective."
—Winifred Gallagher, senior editor of *American Health*

"*Sacred Places* mirrors the growing consciousness in humanity today of our inseparable connection to the earth and to the value of the teachings of ancient and traditional cultures in this regard. A wonderful book for our times."
—Paul Horn, recording artist and originator of the "Inside" series

"There is no more important topic than the relationship of mankind and nature. Our western culture took God out of nature and put [God] in the sky, leaving nature open for pillaging and despoiling. We have built a world upon that. The task now is to put God back into nature. Finding sacred places is a way. . . . If nature is sacred, then our own human nature—reflective of the grand nature—is sacred. Armed with the view that our own nature is an emanation of the godhead, we can finally and truly coordinate our activities with nature's and heal the earth."
—Jeff Cox, West Coast editor for Rodale Press,
gardening editor for the *San Francisco Chronicle*

"*Sacred Places* is an extraordinary book to read and a challenge to absorb; it is a rich, complex work that breaks many current and centuries-old taboos concerning the value of personal experience, dreams, visions, and voices. The unitary consciousness of its author challenges our learned behavior about separation and division from all that is. In this pioneering volume, a labor of love, Jim Swan offers up a host of soul-stirring ideas, insights, and helpful suggestions as to how to improve our relationship with nature. He gives us a program for re-education, a new way of seeing/visioning reality, and becoming co-creators with nature. *Sacred Places* is a must for all those interested in Native American studies, Native American worldviews, and Native American sacred places."
—Nancy C. Zak, Ph.D, Native American studies scholar;
professor at the Institute of American Indian Arts, Santa Fe

"*Sacred Places* . . . feels good to me—bringing wonderful memories of experiences in the beauty of Father Spirit's aliveness in Mother Earth, as well as giving information new to me. I learned more about my own inner experience and also about the sacred energies of Earth as perceived by other cultures."
—Brooke Medicine Eagle, native Earthkeeper, healer, teacher, and ceremonial leader

"Jim Swan's book brings us insights into the importance of sacred places in nature. These places have had a deep psychological and spiritual meaning for people from earliest times, and they work on us individually as well as on a tribal or communal level. This book describes how these meanings transcend our current emphasis on ecology, pollution, and the preservation of species—it extends to the more tenuous (but no less vital) humanistic concerns of mysticism and our spiritual connections to the earth. This book is a plea for conservation: a spiritual conservation of the environment."
—Lawrence Halprin, landscape architect

"The sacredness of landscape is as difficult to capture as the beauty of sunsets or the power of wild mountains. Jim Swan in this wide-ranging book brings us one step closer to realizing, appreciating, and hopefully protecting the sacred sites where our earth seems to sing."
—Jeff Rennicke, Northwoods editor of *Backpacker Magazine*

"Full of challenging connections and hypotheses. Opens the reader to much that is intuitively important and to realms beyond the senses. I don't know if researchers can explain the basis of folk wisdom, but they should try."
—Robert Sommer, professor of psychology at the University of California at Davis and author of *Personal Space: The Mind's Eye* and *Social Design*

"Jim Swan has devoted a lifetime to the study and the experience of sacred space. This book distills the essence of what he has learned. Based on a tradition that stretches back beyond ancient Greece to the lore of primal peoples, his work is also as contemporary as the latest court case involving threatened Native American holy places. If you have the feeling that some locations in nature have a special power, whether you can explain it or not, you will find this book full of surprises that link science with the spirit of place."
—J. Donald Hughes, Ph.D., professor of ancient history at the University of Denver, author of *Ecology in Ancient Civilizations*, and member of the advisory board of *Environmental History Review*

SACRED PLACES

SACRED

HOW THE LIVING EARTH
SEEKS OUR FRIENDSHIP

PLACES

JAMES A. SWAN

introduced by
James Lovelock

BEAR & COMPANY
PUBLISHING
SANTA FE, NEW MEXICO

LIBRARY OF CONGRESS CATALOGING-IN-PUBLICATION DATA

Swan, James A.
  Sacred places : how the living earth seeks our friendship / by James A. Swan.
      p.   cm.
  Bibliography: p.
  Includes index.
  ISBN 0-939680-66-1
1. Sacred space. 2. Sacred space—United States. 3. Indians of North America—Religion and mythology. 4. Indians of North America—Freedom of religion. I. Title.
BL580.S92 1990
291.3'5—dc20   89-33139
                                                                CIP

Copyright © 1990 by James A. Swan

Bear & Company, Inc.
Santa Fe, NM 87504-2860

Cover illustration: Richard Fields, "Morning Owl," 1987
Back cover photo: Michael Powers © 1990
Cover & interior design: Angela C. Werneke
Editing: Gail Vivino
Typography: Buffalo Publications
Printed in the United States of America by R.R. Donnelley

9 8 7 6 5 4 3 2 1

To the Earth

At least 50 percent of the author's profits from sales of this book goes to support the participation of traditional peoples in the annual Spirit of Place symposium, which seeks to build bridges between ancient wisdom and modern science and design, and to assist the efforts of traditional peoples to preserve their cultures and sacred places.

CONTENTS

ACKNOWLEDGMENTS

This book arises from over fifteen years of study of sacred places, a topic which found me more than I found it. My quest to understand the power of place in modern society has been aided by many, many people in several different cultural settings, and it would be impossible to mention everyone here, although I have tried whenever possible to give them credit in the text.

My early love of nature was nurtured by my parents, Donald and Evelyn Swan. They helped me develop my first set of ''eyes'' by giving me the chance to grow up in and around the marshes of Lake Erie in a way which few children today know.

My second set of ''eyes'' has come through my contacts with Native American people. Some of my most cherished teachings have come from the Alaskan Inuit, the Klamath and Modoc tribes of southern Oregon, the tribes of the Pacific Northwest, especially the Lummi people, medicine men Rolling Thunder and Sun Bear, the people of American Samoa, José Lucero from Santa Clara Pueblo, William Fields, and the many shamans whom I have come into contact with while working with *Shaman's Drum* magazine. The trust and faith which these people have given me have been a root for making this book possible, and I am deeply grateful to them and all their families and ancestors for what they have shown me.

I also appreciate the guidance and support shown by Stanislav Grof. His pioneering work on mapping out the realms of the mind and its potentials for experiencing has been crucial to formulating much of the research shared here. Stanley Krippner has also been very helpful to my understanding of shamanism and parapsychology, which helped build bridges between my experiencing and my being able to conceptualize what I had come to find and know.

James Lovelock's foreword for this book is deeply appreciated. His pioneering spirit has many times helped remind me that I needed to be willing to say what I felt in my heart about new directions for science as well as our caring for the Earth.

Also crucial to the completion of this book have been Norman Gilroy and The Institute for the Human Environment, Mike Cohen from the National

9

Audubon Society Expedition Institute, John Hunting and Judy Donald and the Beldon Fund, Joshua Mailman, Sidney Lanier, and Laurence Rockefeller, for they have enabled me to pay the bills while going where few others seem to want to journey.

A special thanks also goes to Timothy White and *Shaman's Drum* magazine for giving me the chance to write and edit for them. This enabled me to keep abreast of shamanism and traditional cultural matters all around the world.

Throughout the process, my wife Roberta and my son Andrew have endured my labors, inspired me, and consented to allow our home and lives to be taken over at times by various spirits of places. Their love, support and critical reviews of my work have played a major role in shaping what follows on these pages.

Sacred places best speak to us through their presence and images. The contributions to this book of photographers Cindy Pavlinac, Michael Powers, and Dan Budnik are sincerely appreciated, as well as the willingness of Guenn Nimue, Master Thomas Yun Lin, Bill Corliss, and the Ohio Historical Society to provide images to help make the places come more alive through these pages.

Also, a special thanks goes to Barbara Clow, Angela C. Werneke and Gail Vivino at Bear & Co. for their skillful editorial work and cheerful spirit. And Linda Allen, my agent, who always seems to know what I should be writing better than I do, has been a real joy to work with.

FOREWORD

On the way home from Tavistock, the road rises from the Tavy valley and, at the crest, the view straight ahead is dominated by a strange conical peak, a remnant of a fiery volcanic time long ago. The peak is surmounted by an oblong building that, as the distance closes, resolves into a church with a square tower. The road skirts the rocky hill and goes on to the village that lies in its shadow to the north; the village and the hill share the same name—Brentor. I often stop at the foot of the hill and walk the short, steep, rocky path to the church at the top.

It is the highest place for miles around, and in the winter the winds are so fierce that to stand up is to risk being blown off. The rain driven horizontally penetrates any clothing, yet villagers attend the services in the unheated church of St. Michael de la Rupe. At other times and on quiet sunny days the prospect is one of the most pleasing that I know. There is a view to the ocean, both to the north and to the south; to the east and west rise the granite massifs of Dartmoor and Bodmin moor. Everywhere in between is the garden-like patchwork of green fields bordered by hedgerow and small woods.

On some days, when I climb to the church, there is a sense of presence. Not extrasensory, but something perceived by one's senses that can be neither seen, heard, nor felt in the usual way. It would be easy to attribute to this sensation the recognition of something sacred. A momentary contact with some entity larger and outside of the mind.

Brentor is by no means the only place that has this special ambiance. I have felt it on other hilltops, especially those shaped as pyramids and with a clear view of the lower ground on all sides. It comes upon one in some churches and cathedrals, especially when there is near silence. It also can be felt in forests; a place near Salisbury in Wiltshire especially comes to mind. It is called the Great Yews and is an old plantation of yew trees that have grown so large and so dark that the cavern-like spaces between their branches fill one with that familiar sense of presence.

My calling is science, and I believe that nature is objective. My image of the world is made according to the strict rules of science. Surely you may think an acceptance of the idea of sacred places and such a way of life can never go together. Those with faith are repelled by the reductionist, atheistic values of science; the scientist has no time for a belief that is based on faith alone.

It is true that a few poor souls try to keep their science and their faith in separate mental compartments, the one opened on weekdays and the other on the Sabbath. To me this is near to madness and unnecessary; theology is a part of science and was only recently separated from the rest of it. To be sure the divorce was messy and motivated on both sides by narrow selfish interests. It was the nineteenth-century development of expertise and professionalism that turned both science and religion away from vocation and into greedy pursuit of narrow self-interest—a way of life so well described by the word "career"; a word that reminds me of the porcine plunge of Gadarene.

If you believe the Earth to be alive, or even if, as a reductionist scientist, you consider such a possibility as a theory, your way of viewing the world will be changed. There will be space in that picture seen by the soul on the screen of the mind for sacred places. There will be other channels than the single one viewed by those unfortunates trapped in the paradigm of spaceship Earth. They see only an old and rusty ship made of dead matter, with life in separate cabins and humans and crew on the bridge.

To think of the Earth as alive brings the realization that life can only be fully expressed on a planetary scale. It is not so surprising then that a scene or a place, part of a living planet, can have a sacred beauty. In some natural wilderness; or where people live in harmony with the planet and with themselves; there is a sense of seemliness. Wherever the Earth is fit and wholesome it is beautiful like a young animal in the glory of its perfection.

I suppose that our feelings about a place depend upon how well our mental images map on to the input of our senses. It is easy then to understand why Dr. Johnson, like the denizen of any other city, should have said of the countryside: "One green field is like another." I think he would have understood that I feel just the same about city streets.

Most of us lead our lives in cities and therefore have only the two-dimensional view of nature portrayed by photographs or on the television screen. Imagine a world where men and women were raised separately until adulthood. It would not make loving relationships easy. The fact that the Earth is more raped than loved may come from our unnatural separation from her in the cities.

Is it possible to love the Earth and yet be scientifically curious about her? Perhaps invention and motivation make the difference between loving and exploiting. Victorian reductionism and vivisection seem to go together, and there would be something very unseemly about taking an electrocardiogram on a honeymoon to keep check on the feelings of the heart.

I am similarly repelled by the thought of climbing the hill to Brentor laden with instruments to measure magnetic field fluctuations or local radioactivity—an expedition to discover the connection between the feelings of sacredness and these physical variables. I do not know why this is repugnant to me; all I do know is that it would feel wrong to do it. Yet I readily admit to going to other beautiful places to measure the composition of the atmosphere to learn more about Gaia.

My friend Peter Fellgett, the physicist, has discovered that ambiance can be expressed in scientific terms. The senses convey to the operating systems within our heads far more than we are aware. The conscious expression of the totality of these inputs is ambiance. Could it be that there is a special quality of ambiance attached to Brentor and other places that feel sacred? I hope so, for this is a more gentle and less invasive way to get to know Gaia.

Curiosity stays unrequited and just as well. I look forward to joining with you in reading this book, and am grateful and honored to have been asked by Jim Swan to write this Foreword.

James Lovelock

LIST OF ILLUSTRATIONS

SACRED
HOW THE LIVING EARTH
SEEKS OUR FRIENDSHIP
PLACES

Photo 1. *Red Rock, Sedona, Arizona. Photo © 1990 by Cindy A. Pavlinak.*

INTRODUCTION

"Science is based on human values and is itself a value system."

ABRAHAM MASLOW[1]

In 1969 I completed my Ph.D. at the University of Michigan in a program officially titled "Resource Planning and Conservation," but which my committee agreed was "environmental psychology" since half of the committee was from psychology and half was from natural resources. I had begun in 1961 as a wildlife management major, intending to become a game biologist. My motivation for changing my major was that I am one of those people who likes to get down to the roots of a problem, and along the way I came to the realization that all environmental problems arise in the human mind.

As Earth Day 1970 arose from the collective unconscious of the nation and the world, seemingly triggered by the hideous oil spill off Santa Barbara, California, the University of Michigan became a focal point for action. The campus had been well-schooled in social protest by earlier waves of demonstration against racial inequality and the war in Vietnam. One afternoon in 1969, a group of graduate students and faculty met to work on developing a definition for what "environmental education" should be. We all shared our views and looked at what had been written on the blackboard. Everyone agreed that people needed to be informed about the problems of the times, concerned about the state of the environment, and able to take positive steps toward solving problems. In our agreement, there was a moment of silence. Somewhere deep inside of me a thought arose that had to be spoken. "Places feel different, and that's important too," I said, not really knowing quite why.

Everyone around the room looked at me as though I had let out a well-kept secret. Then, slowly, heads nodded "yes." In a few minutes we had added the idea of "environmental sensitivity" to the list of what environmental education should do.

The thoughts of that meeting were written up by Bill Stapp, the faculty member in charge of developing the new environmental education program at the University of Michigan.[2] He shortly published them, and people eager for direction picked them up almost verbatim and began to use them all around the United States. Then, a couple of years later, Stapp left Ann Arbor to direct environmental education for UNESCO. He took the definition with him, and today you will find countries all around the world talking about the need for "environmental sensitivity," although just what that means is not really that clear.

When I began working in the field of environmental psychology, it was not even an official discipline within the American Psychological Association. APA formed a division of environment and population psychology after 1970, as a result of many people calling for psychology to become more relevant.

There were few behavioral scientists interested in ecology at the time of Earth Day 1970. As a young faculty member with this unique specialization, I spoke at 22 teach-ins across the United States around Earth Day, hosted three documentary films about the environment, and received recognition for my research about how people develop attitudes about air pollution. My linear career projection at that time was to become a university professor with tenure, studying the social and political attitudes of people about pollution and other environmental problems.

However, in 1971, just as my new career was taking off, I went through a painful divorce. The emotional turmoil that resulted was something very new to me, and to understand my feelings I entered psychoanalysis.

I would not recommend analysis for everyone, but for me it worked, far beyond what I had expected. Lying on the couch twice a week, I sought answers to my feelings about relationships. Having studied psychology, I thought I had all the answers and just needed to clarify some things. But, after a couple of weeks of analysis, my analyst said a very devastating thing to me. He told me to stop reading about psychology. Shocked, I asked why. He replied that I was too quick to figure everything out. If you really want to understand yourself and human behavior, he said, live it, then try to figure it out.

Eight months later I left the University of Michigan to accept a teaching position at Western Washington State College. To see the country better, I drove out, and felt drawn on the way to visit the Black Hills of South Dakota. The crowds at Mount Rushmore overwhelmed me, and, feeling psychically wounded by the helicopters, honking horns, and bumper-to-bumper traffic, I headed south to look for a quieter place.

A few miles of lodgepole pines and granite cliff faces later, I felt better. As the Custer State Park border materialized, a buffalo crossed the road in front of me. Suddenly everything changed. I felt transported back in time as the dark brown animal lumbered across the road, and my driving pace slowed to a snail's pace.

A few miles further down the road, I came to a simple turnout. The place seemed no different than the areas I had just passed, but it felt different. I stopped, got out, and began to walk. The trail led me through a landscape of dark-green pine groves sprinkled across a golden grassland. I came to a meadow, and slumped down to eat lunch. Looking out across the waving prairie grasses, my stress washed away and things took on a sparkling clarity. Then—they appeared. Peeping, squealing, barking, and running, prairie dogs began to materialize all over the place. As I sat still, they came very near to me, and I found a closeness with them that I realized had been missing in my life. A tear rolled down my cheek, and I found myself thinking the words "We are all children of Mother Earth." I stayed in that field until dark.

The peace and calmness that I experienced in that field stayed with me for days, until the routine of a new job took over my consciousness. One day, several months later, I was reading the book *Black Elk Speaks* by John Neihardt, which details the life of a Lakota medicine man named Black Elk. I came across a reference to a certain sacred meadow in the Black Hills called Pe Sla. As I was reading this name, a strange chill shot down my spine, which was usually a sign that something important was happening. Further reading disclosed that at the heart of the Black Hills there is a sacred meadow where nomadic bands once gathered every summer. Before fences and roads had been constructed, the Lakota had gathered at Pe Sla to conduct a ceremony called the "Okislataya wowahwala," which means "Welcoming Back All Life in Peace."[3]

As I read those words, memories of that magical afternoon in the Black Hills filled my mind. The same tears I had known then filled my eyes again, and I felt a deep sense of peace enter me. I could not account for these feelings fully, and that bothered me, for I now was living in a land of great peaceful trees and soft ocean water. But at that moment my analyst's guidance came back to me about the need to experience first, and then to seek understanding. Not knowing quite why, I began keeping a journal about how I felt at various places.

Over the next five years I taught environmental studies and psychology, first at Western Washington State, then at the University of Oregon, and then at the University of Washington, while training to become a psychotherapist. I began asking my classes about places that felt special to them. It became clear that each person had one or two places that felt very special to them. When asked why, they might talk about special animals or plants, but most related their fondness for special places to the pleasant experiences they had there.

It was during this time that I became familiar with the applied kinesiology system of medical diagnosis.[4] This method of health evaluation involves testing the strength and weakness of various muscle groups, which in turn are associated with acupuncture meridians. If a certain muscle is weak, for example, it may be indicative of an inner organ weakness, rather than just muscle fatigue. By understanding which skeletal muscle or muscle group is associated with which organs, one can conduct a comprehensive physical examination without the need to master the delicate art of acupuncture pulse diagnosis.

Applied kinesiology experiments also show that memories can influence muscle strength. Recalling traumatic experiences, for example, will usually cause dramatic weakness in certain muscles, especially in those affiliated with the stomach, which is associated with emotions. If you ask people to think of various geographical places, the strength of their muscles may also be affected. Thoughts of favorite recreational places with which people have strong, positive memories will tend to leave their muscles strong, while thoughts of places where the people have had unpleasant experiences will weaken the muscle strength.

I was becoming quite confident about the association between people and their favorite places until I muscle-tested one woman who could find no place memory that could lift her spirits and vitalize her muscle strength. This very sensitive woman in her late twenties seemed depressed and weak, and I asked her if she was sick. She replied that she wasn't sick, but did feel listless. Then someone in the class called attention to the sweater she was wearing, which had metallic threads in it. She said she had just bought the sweater and was wearing it for the first time. Reluctantly, she took it off, and to her amazement, her muscle strength increased dramatically, and she could find her special place, too.

I then began experimenting with clothing and found that many people's muscle strength is significantly weakened by synthetic fabrics. In some cases, the overall mental-emotional feeling associated with weakness caused by clothing involves a difficulty in concentrating, and being spacey or ungrounded. One polyester body shirt had a particularly eery ability to weaken people, including weight lifters and professional athletes. I have yet to find a person who can be weakened by natural fabrics like cotton, silk, and wool, unless they have an allergy.

Using people who were wearing all natural clothing, I then experimented to see if people are affected by furniture, odors, and colors. Many people are, though the extent to which they are strengthened or weakened by these contacts varies considerably. For some people, muscle strength is also associated with mental clarity and the ability to concentrate, which relates to performance of skills and accident-proneness. The implications of this research are profound for workplaces, schools, and homes, as well as wardrobes. They also point to the need to expand our understanding of how people sense and feel to include awareness of the personal energy field. Modern science may not yet be totally comfortable with the concept of a life-force energy, for as yet there is no scientific data, replicable in different laboratories across the country, to validate the existence of superphysical energies.[5] But if people are aware of situations and conditions, and this awareness seems best expressed in terms of energetic interplay, then we need to take these impressions as a challenge for scientific research, and not dismiss them as superstition simply because we can't measure them. According to physicist David Bohm, the Western fall from holistic perception has its roots in ancient Greece, when measurement standards by which humans perceive the world were shifted from inner knowingness to external standards of authority.[6] The problem with this external scientific system is that if we can't measure something, then it supposedly doesn't exist.

The results of my research were presented at the First Regional Congress of the American Association for Social Psychiatry in 1977.[7] My paper was grouped in a special session of topics that didn't fit with conventional theory, which was organized by Dr. Stanley Dean of the University of Miami Medical School. When I finished my presentation, the next speaker was a Venezuelan psychiatrist, Dr. José Geller. Geller's presentation described a contemporary folk healing group in Venezuela, the Cult of Maria Lionza, which conducts healing rituals at Sorté Mountain, some 300 kilometers from Caracas. He reported that he first became interested in these rituals because some of his clients went to them and came back feeling much, much better. Then he showed a film of a healing, which was a little like everything you've ever wanted to see in terms of magic, sorcery, and witchcraft, all condensed into twenty minutes. He ended his presentation by saying that his contact with members of the Maria Lionza religion had moved him so much that he had been initiated by them as a shaman.

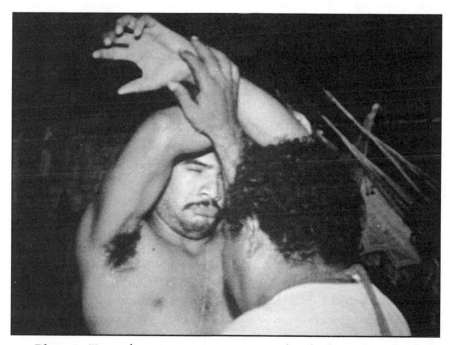

Photo 2. *Two mediums in trance communicate with each other in the midst of a healing ceremony at Sorté Mountain in Venezuela. Photo by Joaquín Cortés, courtesy of José Geller.*

That night I had a very vivid dream in which I was riding in a canoe down a jungle river with Geller paddling. We rounded a bend in the river and suddenly a giant jaguar jumped out at us, letting out a scream. The shock of this sight caused me to wake up with a start, only to hear the continued cry of a cat right outside my hotel room window. The next morning I discovered that a bobcat had been seen chasing mice in the hotel courtyard that night. Previous to that time I had always separated the dream world from the waking world. However, this encounter with a member of the cat family in my dream at the same time that a live bobcat was howling outside my window was my first inkling of how these two worlds can be very interconnected.

During the next several days José Geller and I became friends, and a few months later, in 1979, he came to Seattle, where I sponsored a workshop on psychodrama that he led. At that time I had a private practice as a therapist and also produced workshops and lectures on health-related subjects. During the previous two-week period we had been visited by the late Rev. Olga Worrall, Chippewa medicine man Sun Bear, and anthropologist Joan Halifax. At the climax of this intense high-energy period, Geller conducted a dream ceremony. That night I had a very vivid dream in which I met a regal-looking Indian named "Red Feather," who told me that I should "study the sacred places, as there is something very important there."

I began then to look at the anthropological literature on sacred places, finding references to tribes all over the world who had sacred places. During this time I also began to have dreams containing considerable imagery of the Northwest Coast Indians. I assumed that this was due to the reading I was doing, but found to my surprise upon mentioning this to my mother that members of her family from Canada I had never met had Indian blood.

Not long after the dream with Red Feather, I was approached by Sun Bear to produce a large public event based on a vision that he had had many years ago. In this vision, people dressed as animals came together and danced around a circle of stones.[8] Sun Bear said that he had waited for many years to bring this vision into the world and that he felt it was now time, based on a meeting of medicine people he had recently attended in Toronto chaired by the great Tuscarora medicine man Mad Bear Anderson.

Sun Bear called the festival the "Medicine Wheel Gathering." I said I would be delighted to be the organizer. He said that my response was good, but that we would have to ask someone else first. I thought he was going to call Mad Bear and offered him the phone. He said, no, we would have to ask someone before Mad Bear. I asked who. Sun Bear simply said, "The Great Spirit."

That night Sun Bear conducted a pipe ceremony before 65 people, using a pipe that had once belonged to "Nick" Black Elk, the Oglala holy man. He explained that the word "pow-wow" comes from the Algonquin root word *pauwaw*, which means "he who dreams." He talked about his vision and then prayed for dreams of guidance.

That night I had an extremely vivid dream. Sun Bear and I were walking along a road approaching a log cabin. The door to the cabin swung open, and when we walked inside, the room was filled with Indians, some of whom I recognized from old photos, including Wovoka—the Paiute who started the Ghost Dance—Sitting Bull, and Chief Joseph of the Nez Perce. They stared at us very intently and then a rear door opened. I walked through the door into a clearing surrounded by giant trees. I was given a wreath of holly leaves. Then I looked up at the trees and saw that three giant trees were not trees at all, but large forms with simple faces staring at me. The word "manitou" came to my mind, and I woke up with a start.

As I told Sun Bear about this dream the next morning over coffee, we began to plan the first gathering, making the call to Mad Bear to get the process underway.

In the spring of 1980, I had to go back to Michigan to help out with a family business. I knew I would be gone about a month, and the first Medicine Wheel Gathering would be taking place in September of that year. Then, about a week before I had to go, the place where we were going to hold the gathering suddenly became unavailable. Panicked, I called Sun Bear. He said, "Go ahead and have the posters made up. Just say that it'll be near Mount Rainier. If the medicine is right, the place will find us." I followed his orders and left for the Midwest.

Two thousand miles away in Michigan, I sat worrying about the thousands of posters going out for an event that had no place to happen. Then, one night, I had a very vivid dream. I was standing under a bridge over a rushing white-water river. A man wearing a green suit came over and we started talking. We shook hands and stepped back, as two beautiful snakes emerged from the ground where we had been standing. They began to writhe and coil and as they did, they grew larger and larger. Then they climbed up the bank and slithered off down the road. At breakneck speed, they raced up the road about 200 yards and then turned left. We followed them, and they almost flew down a dirt road with an open field on one side and a forest on the other. About a quarter of a mile down the road they came to a clearing ringed by trees. They rose up on their tails and began to dance in that clearing. Then they changed into two dancing rabbits. The next morning in the mail were the first set of posters for the Medicine Wheel Gathering.

When I returned to Seattle two weeks later, people told me they had found a place that might work out for the gathering near Mount Rainier. We climbed into the car and drove off to find it immediately.

Just before the national park boundary, we turned off the main road. Almost immediately we passed over a bridge crossing a white-water stream. A chill went down my spine. I had not told anyone about the dream. We drove about 200 yards and turned left, down a dirt road. To our right was an emergency airstrip for fighting forest fires. To our left was a stand of large cedars and Douglas firs. About a quarter mile down the road we came to a clearing that was used for overflow camping during the peak summer months. It was just like in the dream. We got out of the car. I was dazed. Two friends along with us went off to scout the place. They came back in a few minutes. One reported seeing some rabbits. The other asked if we'd seen the large snake at the edge of the circle. Three days later I met the man in the green suit. He was the U.S. Forest Service district ranger. This site became the place for the first Medicine Wheel Gathering, which drew some 650 people from all across the United States. Throughout the process of developing the gathering, I periodically had dreams in which Mad Bear would appear, dressed as a football coach, and give me directions in writing on his coach's clipboard. These directions included such details as whom to invite, how much to charge, and even some of the items to include on the menus!

During the gathering, Red Feather came to visit one night in a dream. He told me that by doing what I was doing, I was learning one way that Indian people used to find the right place to perform ceremonies, which was essential to my understanding of the power of place.

About one month after the Medicine Wheel Gathering, I had another vivid dream, as vivid as walking into a mythic setting for a feature movie. In the dream I was standing on the southern tip of an island in Lake Erie near where I had grown up. It was afternoon in the late fall. The wind was gusting from the west, driving up whitecaps on the dark gray water. Behind me to the west the sun was shining, but facing east there was a dark storm cloud over the lake. Then, from out of the eastern cloud, came a chain of white specks. They were coming toward me, bouncing on the wind. It soon became apparent that they were snow geese.

Slowly the flock came closer and closer, struggling against the west wind. Suddenly the geese set their wings and began to land in the waters right in front of me, which were sheltered. But just as they dropped their pink feet for the landing, they began to transform into short, dark-skinned, bare-chested, black-haired men wearing leather leggings. One man, who apparently was their leader, landed on the beach right in front of me. I will never forget the look on his face. An energy seemed to stream from his eyes that went right into mine and cleansed my soul. He was carrying a lighted white candle. With great seriousness, he approached me. He held out the white candle and I merged with it. Then the dream faded away and I woke up crying, knowing that something had happened that was more important than just what I had seen and experienced. My whole life had been changed.

A few weeks later I had the chance to share this dream with Rolling Thunder, a Cherokee medicine man whose extraordinary powers to heal and influence the weather have been documented by several researchers. Hearing my story, he leaned back in his chair and puffed on his corncob pipe for a few moments. Then he said, "Jim, you ought to go look up the Lapps—you might just find something very interesting there."

I went to the library and began reading. Geese in general are seen to be messengers of the gods all around the world, and in the mythology of the Lapps or "Saami" of northern Scandinavia the snow goose is a bird of mythic importance, as is the swan, my own family name. Prior to that time I had never bothered to look up the family tree, for I had always understood that the Swan side of my family simply came from Scotland. Checking on Scottish clans, however, I found that the Swans came to Scotland from the north, and one of their leaders was a short, dark-haired chieftain named Olaf the Black. In a flash I realized that I had dreamed of my own ancestry. As I thought of the dream and the snow goose people, a sense of peacefulness came upon me, for I knew in a deep, ancestral way that through honoring the power of place, I had stepped into harmony with my ancestors. After meeting James Lovelock, I shared this dream with him. We found to our great mutual delight that we apparently have common ancestry, for one branch of his family tree traces back to the Eskimos.

The power of these dreams did not fully become apparent to me until some time later, when I had a chance to talk about them with Rolling Thunder. He related some of his dreams in which the fiery Quetzalcoatl had entered him, and then he said, "There is a power to some places. This is a power which goes beyond the mind of modern man. It is a power to heal, to help others, and it can be misused too. Hitler wanted to use this to his advantage, but he was stopped.

"Your dreams have helped you to understand what this power is because you can know it only by feeling. The experiences you have at these places comes to you only when your thoughts and actions are right. You must experience the power of sacred places to understand them, and when they want you to know what they have to teach, they will let you know. When and how that happens is beyond your control."

It has been nearly eight years since Rolling Thunder told me this, and his words have proven true. At times I have wanted to give up this whole project because it seemed like it was fruitless and impossible to study something like sacred places when my research process was not something that I could control. But it has seemed that every time, just when I was about to give up, something would happen to breathe new life into the process. The spirit of my dreams has led me to see places from above the Arctic Circle to the Manua Islands of American Samoa, as well as all across the United States. This traveling has brought me into contact with every major group of Native American people. The more I have learned about sacred places, the more I have come to understand and respect the way traditional cultures experience place and nature, which is very different from the way modern society teaches us to perceive. There is value in both ways of seeing and being, but if people don't have the sense of knowing that comes first from feeling, then they have lost the root of being human, and application of the scientific method only tends to draw us further and further away from where we must go. Master Thomas Yun Lin, a Chinese *feng shui* geomancer who will be described in more detail in this book, insists that we have 100 senses by which to perceive nature in order to discern right action for each given place. These sensory processes are there, waiting for each of us, he asserts, if we only know how to develop them. Once we have these perceptions, we can test them out and see if they are valid or not. This is the proper place for science. It must work hand in hand with multi-sensory perception to guide us into living in harmony with nature.

> *"The dreams of magic may one day be the waking realities of science."*   SIR JAMES FRAZIER, THE NEW GOLDEN BOUGH[9]

ENDNOTES

1. A.H. Maslow, *Motivation and Personality*, 2d ed. (New York: Harper and Row, Inc., 1970), p. 6.

2. Wm. B. Stapp et al., "The Concept of Environmental Education," *Education Digest* 35, March 1970, pp. 8-10.

3. Ronald Goodman and Stanley Red Bird, "Lakota Star Knowledge and the Black Hills" (Sinte Gleska College, Rosebud Sioux Reservation, Rosebud, SD 57570, 1983).

4. John Thie, *Touch for Health* (Santa Monica, CA: De Vorss Pub., 1973).

5. Elmer Green and Alyce Green, "Biofeedback and States of Consciousness," chap. 18 in *Handbook of States of Consciousness*, ed. Benjamin B. Wolman and Montague Ullman (New York: Van Nostrand Reinhold Co., 1986).

6. David Bohm, *Wholeness and the Implicate Order* (Boston/London: Routledge and Kegan Paul, 1981).

7. James A Swan, "Environmental Energies: Effects on Health and Well-Being" (Paper presented at the First Regional Congress of the American Association for Social Psychiatry, Santa Barbara, CA, September 6-9, 1977).

8. Sun Bear and Wabun, *The Medicine Wheel* (Englewood Cliffs, NJ: Prentice Hall, Inc., 1980).

9. Sir James George Frazier, *The New Golden Bough* (New York: Criterion Books, 1959; New York: New American Library, ed. Theodore Gaster, 1964), p. 740.

Photo 3. *Delphi, 1976. Photo by Joseph Campbell, courtesy of ARAS, San Francisco, California, Campbell collection.*

ONE

The Dilemma of Sacred Places in a Modern World

The ancient Greeks sited a shrine at Delphi to honor the Earth goddess Gaia. Their choice was not by chance. The naturalist Pliny the Elder coined the term "geomancy" to describe the art of reading the subtle qualities of a place to discern what actions might best be conducted there. According to geomantic wisdom, Delphi was the place best suited to honor Gaia, goddess of the Earth and mother of the Titans. The "genus loci" or "spirit of place" at Delphi was especially powerful and favorable to prophecy due to an abundance of the mysterious Earth force called "plenum," which bubbled up from the ground there.

The temple at Delphi which housed the Pythia, or priestess oracle, was constructed around 1400 BC, and to this day millions of people report being drawn to Delphi by some mysterious magnetic force. Among those attracted to Delphi these days is a group of Greek government planners and industrialists who want to erect a new temple at Delphi: a giant aluminum plant. This 500-million-dollar Soviet-built plant is to be sited at the tiny hilltop village of Aya Efthymia, some seven and a half miles to the southwest of the ruins of the Delphi temples, which were the center of the Earth to the early Greeks. Mayor Elias Segounis of Delphi is outraged at these plans. He asserts that as the plant consumes from 800 to 1,000 tons of oil each day to power the plant's aluminum processing systems, the prevailing winds will shroud the ancient ruins in corrosive fumes. In addition, the plant will pipe between 3,000 and 5,000 cubic meters of tainted red mud into nearby fields daily, removing the fields from any other productive use and presenting the potential problems of both groundwater pollution and contamination of the nearby ocean from runoff.[1]

In the dusty outback of Australia, the striking natural monolith of Ayres Rock, or "Uluru" to the Aborigines, has a similar magnetic pull on people. Upwards of 500,000 tourists visit the area each year. To accommodate the visitors, the Australian government has had to carve holes in the rock for placing iron railings and fences to channel their visitations. Aborigine "clever man," or shaman, Burnam Burnam, remarks with disgust: "Just as white members of a church make their approach every Sunday in complete reverence, we would never climb over the sides and roofs of our church."[2]

Faced with a similar popularity problem, the British government has had to fence off Stonehenge to keep it from being "loved to death" by tourists. Some planners suggest erecting a concrete replica of the magical stone circle some distance away and directing sightseers there instead of to the real thing.

From the snowpacks of Mount Kalias to the Indian Ocean, the 1578-mile-long Ganges River of India is perhaps the most used and misused sacred shrine in the world. For centuries, wealthy Hindus have cremated their dead on the banks of the Ganges and then thrown their ashes into the river to ensure their succcessful journey to the next plane. Many poor people, however, cannot afford cremation rites. Instead, they simply drop dead bodies into the river, asking the mother river to take back her flesh. India's swelling population and poverty have resulted in these bodies becoming a monumental water pollution problem, so serious that Jayendra Saraswati, one of India's four Hindu spiritual leaders, has decried the practice of tossing dead bodies in the Ganges as a "social crime." Addressing pilgrims at the most holy city of Hardwar in the state of Uttar Pradesh along the banks of the sacred Ganges, Saraswati preached, "It will be futile to think of attaining salvation if we continue to pollute the holy river."[3]

From the jungles of West Africa, Voodoo priest Durbach Akuete from Togo worries about spirits angered by the destruction of the tropical rainforest and its various secret places of power. His concerns are shared by spiritual leader Bambi Baaba, Dr. J.K. Mugonza of Uganda, who fears for the stability of the entire Earth because of how modern people are treating sacred places.

For centuries, young Masai men in Kenya between the ages of fourteen and thirty have undergone the traditional initiation rite called Moranism, which culminates in a pilgrimage to their sacred center, Mount Kilimanjaro. Today, however, the Kenyan government has declared Moranism illegal. Should a young Masai dare to break the law, he may well be intercepted by a policeman who will shave his head, cropping off his distinctive red-mud-caked hair braids. The government, saying that such ritual behavior disrupts education and national development, seeks to confine the Masai to "native reserves" like Indian reservations.[4]

Closer to home, in an April 1988 five-to-three decision, the U.S. Supreme Court rejected a plea by the Karok, Tolowa, and Yurok Indian tribes of northern California to prevent the construction of a logging road through the rugged Chimney Rock section of the Six Rivers National Forest in the Siskiyou Mountains. The Native Americans assert that this area is their sacred "High Country" and is a stepping stone to heaven. In turning down the Indians' case, Justice Sandra Day O'Conner wrote for the majority view: "However much we might wish that it were otherwise, government simply could not operate if it were required to satisfy every citizen's religious needs or desires."[5]

There is trouble, too, in the land of the big trees of the Pacific Northwest. Fourteen tribes of Indians in western Washington are protesting Forest Service plans to log old-growth cedars in the Mount Baker-Snoqualmie National Forest.

Farther south, at Point Conception, just north of Santa Barbara, California, Chumash Indians worry about a liquid natural gas plant being built on the shoulders of the tawny brown hills which come tumbling down into the deep blue Pacific. In the view of the Chumash, Point Conception is the "Western Gate," a portal through which souls enter and exit from the earth plane.

To the east, in the Four Corners area of the American Southwest, the National Academy of Sciences has said that the sacred lands of the Hopi, Navajo, Ute, Zuni, and various Pueblo tribes should be declared a "National Sacrifice Area" to facilitate their easy development for harvesting uranium and coal.

And to the north in the Black Hills of South Dakota, the "Heart of the Earth Mother" to Plains Indian tribes, a dozen mining companies drool over the prospects of mining uranium and other precious metals from the oldest granitic-basalt uplift mountains in the United States.

In 1984 the First World Congress on Cultural Parks was held in Mesa Verde, Colorado. Some 350 delegates from 52 nations around the world attended this landmark gathering on preserving cultural heritage. A number of the participants represented indigenous peoples of the Earth, and, while they had many cultural differences, all the indigenous representatives agreed that they shared one common, serious problem: those lands which they considered to be sacred were in jeopardy due to the demands of modern society. Universally, these traditional cultural representatives said that the greatest obstacle to preserving sacred places was that modern people just didn't understand how or why these places were so special.

"The idea of a sacred place . . . is apparently as old as life itself," writes the late mythologist Joseph Campbell.[6] In the oldest epic poem known, which can be traced back to Sumeria some 5000 years ago, the hero Gilgamesh and his cohorts are described as approaching a sacred stand of cedar trees. Around the world, the Earth's surface is sprinkled with places whose names alone stir deep feelings in us: Palenque, Mount Omei, Mount Arafat, Mount Fuji, Lascaux, Iona, Jerusalem, Delphi, Mount Kilimanjaro, Mecca, Mount Sinai, Mount McKinley or "Denali," Chartres, the Great Pyramids, Stonehenge, Haleakala Crater, Mount Kalias, the Ganges River, Mount Katahdin, Machu Picchu, Lourdes, Fatima, and

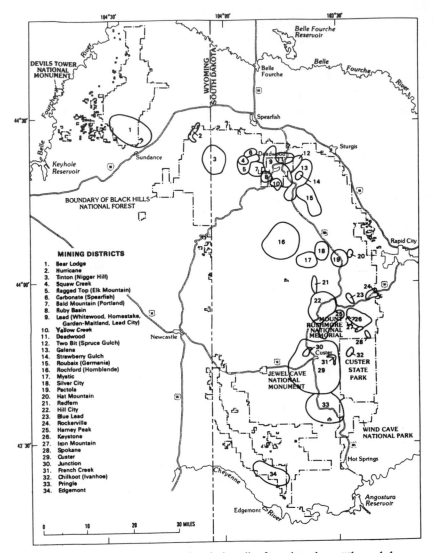

Figure 1. *Mining Districts in the Black Hills of South Dakota. The circled areas do not necessarily indicate where mining is actively occurring, but they do indicate areas which are zoned for mining and which contain precious minerals and ores. Reprinted from* Mineral Resource Potential and Geology of the Black Hills National Forest, South Dakota and Wyoming, *U.S. Geological Survey Bulletin 1580, Plate 2.*

the Sun Temple at Mesa Verde are among the most famous of the world's sacred places, but hardly the only ones.

Modern people may not understand why such places are sacred to ancient cultures, but we too are drawn to them like ants to honey. One of the keynote speakers addressing the 1984 World Congress on Cultural Parks was Lester Borley, director of the National Trust of Scotland, who described the dilemma of sacred places in a modern world quite well when he said, "The act of making pilgrimages to certain special or sacred places is probably the most popular of all world tourism motives, and the least understood." To support his point, Borley went on to quote a study of the English Tourist Board which found that an astonishing 72 percent of the tourists who come from abroad to Britain said that a prime motivation for their journeys was to visit various churches, cathedrals, and shrines. This was by far the most popular motive given for journeying to the United Kingdom.[7]

Viewing these mysterious, magnetic power spots collectively, there are to be three primary categories. One is the human-crafted building, which by its presence, and regardless of its form or size, marks a place as special for religious reasons. These churches, shrines, and temples make up the majority of sacred places in the modern world. In general, their siting is a matter of economics or convenience rather than having any association with the uniqueness of a specific locality.

A second type of sacred place is one where the larger whole has become condensed into a symbolic statement or form: a microcosm of the macrocosm, as Joseph Campbell called it.[8] Like a crystal in a radio set, these structures use sacred design to draw together the greater whole and magnify its magical nature, creating an ambient spiritual intensity like the heat and light formed under a magnifying glass aimed at the noonday sun. Typically such sites have an astronomical or astrological alignment aspect, such as Stonehenge, or the solar/lunar observatory on top of Fajada Butte in Chaco Canyon, or the Bighorn Medicine Wheel in Wyoming. By condensing the cosmos into a smaller sphere, its laws can be observed and experienced more clearly, and human lives can be placed more accurately in accord with them. These sacred places are a statement of how beauty and meaning can result when people and nature are working together in harmony. Their siting is linked to a system of subtle natural forces about which we understand very little and which we do not even have a good language to describe.

From our modern mindset, we can recognize the socio-political significance of a little white church, appreciate the majestic beauty of the sacred architecture of a cathedral or shrine like the Taj Mahal, and understand the significance of a cosmically ordered sacred site. There is a third category of sacred place, however, which is more difficult for modern minds to recognize as being sacred, but which is far more common among more primal-minded people. This is the place in nature which bears no special marking, except perhaps for a well-worn foot path.

The Earth's surface is dotted with special sacred groves, springs, caves, rivers, stones, meadows, mountains, valleys, deserts, and volcanos, which are rooted in the consciousness of early Earth worship. In Exodus 3:5 of the Bible the Lord says to Moses, "Draw not nigh hither, put off thy shoes from thy feet, for the place where one standest is holy ground." Today we interpret this as meaning the inside of a church or synagogue, but in earlier times, in many traditions including Christianity, there were also places in nature which were recognized as having a special spiritual quality. We flock to Lourdes in hopes of being healed, but forget that it was the natural spring there which drew Bernadette to the place before any shrine was built. In a similar fashion, most of the great cathedrals of Europe are sited upon the worship places of earlier religions.

In the United States we can also find examples of how newer religions have adopted the sacred sites of traditional peoples. For example, each Good Friday upwards of 10,000 pilgrims of all creeds and races converge on the tiny adobe Santuario de Chimayó near Española, New Mexico, sometimes called the "Lourdes of America." On a Good Friday in the early 1800s, a man from the family who built this church said that he saw a "burst of light" coming from the ground in the area where the Santuario now stands. He reported that he dug in the ground there and found a crucifix consisting of a dark green cross and a darkened Christ figure. When the church was built, this crucifix was supposedly placed in a small room to the left of the main altar called "El Pozito," which means the "little well room." When one walks gently into this hallowed tiny chamber, aside from the religious icons, the most striking sight is the huge pile of crutches, braces and canes which have been cast aside by those who say they have been healed by visiting the Santuario de Chimayó. On closer inspection of this room, an even more amazing sight is discovered. There is a hole in the floor exposing bare earth. For over 150 years people have been taking soil from this hole to ingest, rub on their bodies, and carry away in bottles and jars for shrines at home. According to most pilgrims, the soil holds the source of the healing power of the place. The Tewa Pueblo Indian word for this place was originally "Tsimayo," which means "good flaking stone," and presumably describes the obsidian which can be found there that was once used for making knives and arrowheads. However, a spring also bubbles to the surface nearby, and Indian legend says the spring and the earth around it have potent healing powers.[9]

In recent years we have seen important strides in medicine arising from the reassessment of ancient wisdom. One of the more prominent examples is the development of biofeedback, with which people learn to gain conscious control

Photo 4. *Santuario de Chimayó, New Mexico. Photo by J. Donald Hughes.*

over parts of the body which were previously thought to be uncontrollable. Biofeedback utilizes machines to tell people when they are gaining control over muscles and organs, but the same physical acts of voluntary control have been performed for centuries by yogis, dervishes, and shamans as a result of their practices of meditation, trance journeying, and martial arts. Similar breakthroughs have occurred in herbal medicine (such as those which appear to have promise as cures for AIDS), acupuncture, and the use of mental imagery in healing. As we face ecological problems of growing severity, perhaps a more objective evaluation of ancient Earth wisdom could lead to important new insights on living in greater harmony with nature, yielding something akin to a biofeedback system for evaluating environmental quality.

If one were to seriously approach glowing campfires around the world and ask traditional elders about the significance of sacred places to modern society, the answer which would be given time after time is that the sacred places of the Earth must be protected. One would be told that human structures, at best, are amplifiers of the energies that were there in the first place. The essence of the sacred spirit which manifests at a sacred place, the elders would say, arises from nature itself. And it is that spirit which is the key to recovering harmony with nature.

It is understandable that people do not like to be displaced from their homelands. Preserving cultural heritage artifacts also is not difficult to appreciate.

But the elders assert that these sacred places are numinous points of spiritual power which are the very core of our only chance to live in harmony with nature, not just for indigenous peoples, but for everyone. To quote a transmission from a Northern Cheyenne Elder's Circle delivered to the 1988 Spirit of Place Symposium by José Lucero, a trusted messenger for many Earth circles of wisdom, "Sacred sites and areas are protection for all people, for the four colors of man, black, yellow, red, and white."[10]

When asked why this is so, the elders speak in terms of visions, voices, encounters with animals, and "power," in a way very unlike how our modern dictionaries define the word "power." My friend Kenneth Cooper from the Lummi Indian tribe up near the Canadian border on Puget Sound says, "When we walk in the mountains, in some old growth stands of cedar, among the wise old elder trees, anything you want to know you can find there." And since I know Kenneth Cooper as a man who "walks his talk" and speaks from the heart with a spirit that seems to come from the very soul of Puget Sound where he fishes, I think he is speaking the truth in what he says about the power of place. I also know that modern psychology has no way to understand or appreciate what Cooper is talking about. The mind is an adaptation to an earthly reality, and has many possible ways of perceiving that reality at any one given time. So until one has tried walking in the shoes of a Lummi fisherman or a Hopi corn planter for a time, it is better to reserve judgment about what is possible to know from nature and what is not.

Since the development of the Industrial Revolution, humanity has embraced the Newtonian-Cartesian model of science to provide normative principles for ordering life and work, a stabilizing social role previously held by theology and philosophy. The result of this shift has been a massive transformation of nature and human society in countless ways which can be seen in the world all around us. Part of the power of the scientific method has been its ability to show flaws in the old thinking. The Earth isn't flat. There are no demons dwelling in the oceans. The sun doesn't revolve around the Earth. But this mechanistic model of reality in time becomes self-destructive, because life behaves according to organic, non-linear patterns, and there are many more dimensions to reality than fit easily within the physics and chemistry of the day, which is demonstrated by the work of many researchers in the fields of consciousness studies and transpersonal psychology.[11]

In the short run, problems can be solved with linear, mechanical methods and models. But these strategies ignore the systematic nature of life. One of the basic qualities of a system is that whenever any single part of it is changed, all the rest is also changed. Hence people can conjure up millions of chemicals, manufacture just about anything out of plastic, and devise electrical contraptions to do almost anything. With the degree of technological capability available these days, the most important question facing science and technology isn't what we as people *can* do, but rather what we *should* do. "There is no free lunch," as Barry Commoner has reminded us, and acid rain, Bhopal, Chernobyl, the Greenhouse Effect, depletion of the ozone layer, and mountains of garbage are the results of the myopic application of mechanical science at its worst.

In a modern society where science has replaced religion's original role of giving stability, comfort, and meaning to life, we find ourselves searching for new means to guide our lives as the weaknesses of the prevailing scientific paradigm become more and more apparent. We have churches for religious purposes. Museums and historical parks preserve antiquities. Within the boundaries of national parks, recreation areas, forests, and game preserves we also retain places of scenic beauty and biological significance. In no place in our lands or minds, however, do we have an expression of the spiritual values of nature. As a result of our modern mindset, according to our legal system in the United States today, white, black, and yellow people do not have any sacred places except houses of religious worship. Native Americans can have sacred places, but they only exist legally when one or both of the following conditions can be shown to exist: (1) they contain artifacts 100 years old or older; and/or (2) they can be shown to be necessary for the ongoing practice of a traditional religion as sites for ceremonies and rituals which have been conducted there for many generations. Proving the sacredness of such a place to a court or planning commission is very difficult, which is one reason why it is so easy for sacred places to be converted into aluminum plants, uranium mines, ski areas, reservoirs behind dams, liquid natural gas refineries, clear-cut forests, or parking lots.

The purpose of this book is to examine the concept of what constitutes a sacred place in nature, and what the modern relevance and value of natural sacred places to humankind are as a whole. The overall presentation of the book is patterned in the form of a hearing or trial, because modern land use is ultimately determined through such processes. By organizing the data in this fashion, hopefully the material will be of great help to those people who are working to preserve sacred places before they are destroyed forever.

> "*The sacred expresses itself according to the laws of its own dialectic, and this expression comes to man* from without." MIRCEA ELIADE[12]

ENDNOTES

1. Don A. Schanache, "Could Oracle of Delphi Have Predicted This?" *Los Angeles Times*, Nov. 11, 1986.
2. Jan Clanton-Collins, "An Interview With Burnam Burnam," *Shaman's Drum* (Fall 1988): pp. 29-33.
3. *Los Angeles Times*, November 11, 1986.
4. *San Francisco Chronicle*, May 27, 1988.
5. Dale Champion, "High Court Won't Halt Road Through Sacred Indian Land," *San Francisco Examiner*, April 18, 1988.
6. Joseph Campbell, *The Mythic Image* (Princeton, NJ: Princeton University Press, 1974), p. 184.
7. These remarks were made during Lester Borley's duties as master of ceremonies for speakers at the First World Congress on Cultural Parks. The research he cites is reported in Max Hanna's "On the Pilgrim Path," *Whitsun* (Spring 1985).
8. Joseph Campbell, *The Mythic Image.*
9. Robert L. Casey, *Journey to the High Southwest* (Chester, CT: Globe Pequot Press, 1983), pp. 354-356.
10. José Lucero, "The Future of the Four Corners Region" (Paper presented at the First Spirit of Place symposium, Sept. 8-11, 1988, Davis, CA).
11. Stanislav Grof, *The Adventure of Self Discovery* (Albany, NY: SUNY Press, 1988).
12. Mircea Eliade, *The Sacred and the Profane* (New York: Harcourt Brace Jovanovich Inc., 1959).

TWO

Varieties of Native American Sacred Places

"Human beings are an expression of their landscape."

LAWRENCE DURRELL[1]

When the temperature rises above 32 degrees on the glaciers of Mount Baker and Mount Shuksan 40 miles east of Bellingham, Washington, glacial melt water starts dripping, forming ever-larger rivulets until the surging gray-green waters of the Nooksack River are born, which race over boulders and fallen tree trunks to join the salty tribe of water people in Puget Sound. Along this journey the turbulent river passes acres and acres of trees of all heights, standing in silent witness to the flow of brother water.

Since early times, Northwest Coast native people have sought out the giant cedar, hemlock, and Douglas fir trees of the cold rainforest, not just for canoes and longhouses, but for spiritual communion. Among the trees themselves of the Pacific Coastal rainforests, the wisest elders are the groves of thousand-year-old red cedars. In the view of the Lummi, Skagit, Nooksack, Duwamish, Snoqualmie, Salish, and other tribes of this area, the presence of these majestic trees creates a precious ambiance which somehow facilitates the human mind slipping into a transcendent state. To the indigenous Indian mind, these groves and certain deep, quiet pools at their feet are sacred ground of the highest order.

With the price of lumber skyrocketing and groves of accessible virgin timber in ever-declining supply, the pressure to log these cedars increases year by year. Seeking regeneration from the stresses of city life, more and more recreationists also flock to the woods, stimulating developmental projects ranging from roads to resorts. In an attempt to satisfy growing demands for lumber and recreation, the U.S. Forest Service recently announced a ten-year-plan to harvest approximately 40 percent of the old-growth cedars of the Mount Baker-Snoqualmie National Forest and to cut new roads for increasing access to the forest's resources.

Led by the coastal Lummis, fourteen tribes of western Washington oppose this plan. Their opposition is supported by some environmental groups as well, but for different reasons. The environmentalists talk about impacts in terms of siltation, erosion, potential negative effects on salmon and steelhead spawning areas, destruction of natural beauty, and disturbing giant trees which are nesting sites for certain woodpeckers and the now infamous spotted owl. According to Kurt Russo of the Lummi Tribal Council, the Indians agree with all these environmental concerns, but they go a step farther. They say that logging these trees will destroy sacred places which collectively contribute to the most precious thing of all—that which in the Salish language is called *skalalitude* or "a sacred state of mind where magic and beauty are everywhere."

Forest managers are not evil people; they are products of an educational system which has never given them the opportunity to fully understand *skalalitude*, why it is important, and how certain places can move the mind toward spiritual consciousness. When they went to school, the creation myth they learned told them about the "big bang." No one ever told them about the age when humans, gods, and animals were interchangeable and the spiritual forces worked more closely with the material ones.

Creation myths help a culture define its norms, laws, and ways of thinking, and provide a root for its cosmology. They provide a starting point from which all life as we know it begins, and they introduce the basic elements which structure the cultural myths. Among the creation myths of the American Indians, one of the most cogent and beautiful is that of the Hopi tribe, which also sheds important light on the identity and value of sacred places.

Photo 5. *Mount Baker is a sacred center of spiritual power for the Lummis and other tribes of the Pacific Northwest. Author photo.*

Photo 6. *Classic Hopi spiral from Mesa Verde National Park, Colorado. Author photo.*

The word "Hopi" means "people of peace," and among the Indian peoples of North America, the Hopi are recognized as experts on prophecy, myth, and spiritual wisdom. While many other tribes have become modern and have lost the old ways, among the Hopi at least nine times every year the streets and squares of their mesa-topped villages in Arizona fill with colorful kachina dancers, conducting rites which move the community and its mind into mythic time, ensuring the continuing connection between this period and contemporary times.

From their underground rooms called "kivas," the Hopi elders speak of earlier times when the people emerged into this world from the Earth. To represent this emergence, they have a simple hole called the "sipapu" in the center of the floor of their traditional pueblo dwellings, which serves as a constant reminder of their origins.

From the wisdom of this lineage comes the tale that in the beginning it was Tiowa, the Great Spirit, who created the Earth. Looking down upon this brown, blue, and white ball circling a golden sun, Tiowa understood in a flash that this should be a place of life. He saw that he would need to have a special guardian to guide this process. Looking among the ranks of the highest angels, he selected a very wise woman, Spider Grandmother, who agreed to accept this assignment.

Descending from the heavens in a spiral, Spider Grandmother set foot on the lifeless Earth and saw that she would need help. She reached down and picked up two handfuls of virgin brown earth. Saying a prayer, she spat into each of them. Instantly two handsome young men sprang from the fertilized soil. The three sat in silent meditation for a time, uniting their minds. Achieving a state of harmony, one man clothed in a silvery white cloak, Poqanghoya, went off to reside at the North Pole. Reaching this crystal apex, he began to work his magic of structure and form, creating the patterns of life which hold things in their shape and keep them together. To the South Pole went a fiery red-cloaked warrior named Palonghoya, a magical musician. Reaching the southern pole, Palonghoya went into a deep trance and searched the universe with his probing mind. Finally he heard a faint rhythm—the heartbeat of Tiowa. He picked up his drum and began to beat out the same steady rhythm, linking himself in harmony with the Great Spirit.

Any engineer will tell you that whenever two objects resonate in a harmonic vibratory state, energy is exchanged. And so, as Palonghoya beat his drum, life-force energy came coursing down into the navel of the Earth at the South Pole, and streamed down into the crystal at the center of the Earth. This magic stone redirected the life-force energy in all directions, like the fluffy seeds on a ripe dandelion head. The energy then rushed upwards, emerging from the Earth's crust. As the energy broke through the surface, the entire planet came to life. At some places the life force was more concentrated, due to the structural magic of Poqanghoya at the North Pole. These special nodes of concentrated vitality are the sacred places, the Hopi elders maintain. They are the "spots on the fawn," places of light, power, creativity, and healing. According to the Hopi, without these places and their powers, the world would fall apart.[2]

Just as Christians devote their churches to certain saints, and Hindus site shrines at special places to honor various deities, and Muslims say that Mecca is the physical center of their faith, Indian people also assert that their sacred places have unique qualities. No two of these places are the same, but they do fall into categories according to the nature of the spirits which prevail there, and their function in Indian reality. The following is a summary of places I have been fortunate enough to be introduced to.

VARIETIES OF SACRED PLACES

Type 1. Graves, Cemeteries & Burial Grounds

The funeral is one of the oldest of all ceremonial forms. Graves of Neanderthal people over 100,000 years old have been found which include simple artifacts lying next to the body. Among Indian tribes the actual treatment of the dead varies considerably, but in 1885 Suquamish Chief Seattle voiced the sentiments toward burial sites when he said, "To us the ashes of our ancestors are sacred, and their resting place is hallowed ground."

While some Plains tribes placed their dead on raised platforms, allowing the elements, birds, and animals to clean away the corpses, most Indian people buried their dead in the ground at special places which showed great respect for the deceased. Often people were buried with artifacts which would assist them in the journey to the next world. In the Indian view, the deceased can return to converse with the living in visions, voices, and dreams. Showing proper respect for the dead then not only acknowledges their contributions while they were alive, but also establishes attitudes which will result in the return of these elders to offer guidance from their new position in the other world, where the conventional boundaries of time and space collapse into one mythic domain.

While working in American Samoa, I became friends with Ma'a Eleasora, a "matai," or chief, who is also the water quality protection officer for this group of seven tiny islands in the South Pacific. One day Ma'a told me that he wanted me to go with him to meet his family in the village where he grew up, which was on the island of Olosega in the Manua group. We flew 64 miles over the open ocean in a small plane to land in a sandy clearing along a sparkling white sand beach. Then, boarding the only transportation a vintage 1950s Ford panel truck belonging to the Samoan Pentecostal Church of Olosega, we bounced along five miles of a two-rut trail through the dense rainforest to arrive in the tiny fishing village of Sili, tucked between the warm blue ocean and steep cliffs rising a quarter mile straight up.

A typhoon had recently swept through, leveling half of the twenty or so *fales*, or homes. As we walked through the rubble, a swarm of children and dogs soon joined us. Lizards skirted back under rocks as we approached, and white sea birds and black, flying-fox fruit bats circled overhead. Ma'a stopped at a bright blue, cement-block house that was still standing, although its windows and doors had been ripped away by the wind and water. "This is where I grew up," Ma'a said, pointing to the house, "sleeping on mats on the floor." He walked around to the side of the house and then stopped. Then Ma'a said simply, "My father," and pointed to a grave which was sited right next to the house. The headstone noted that he had been the high chief of the village and the priest of the village church. Later we walked to an elevated point on the island where Ma'a pointed to pyramid-shaped cairns of stones, "the graves of the high talking chiefs of the island," he said. On the way back down the trail we avoided what looked to be a beautiful beach. I asked Ma'a why, and he replied that a bad *aitu* or ghost lived there, the spirit of an old man who had died unhappily. That night, while sleeping in the house where Ma'a had grown up, a large jolly man in a bright red "lava lava" skirt appeared in my dreams and showed me tracks of giant birds like the moa of New Zealand. The word "Samoa" means "sacred hens." Stories recorded by early missionaries talk about chickens which were saved from a hurricane and became a source of food for the people settling what we now call Samoa. My dream suggested that the now extinct giant birds, like the moa in New Zealand, may be the real sacred hens.

Like the Samoans, some tribes of American Indians build special graves for leaders who have passed on. Early white settlers in the eastern United States came upon strange mounds fifteen to twenty feet high. One of the first to seriously research these mounds was Thomas Jefferson, who reported in his *Notes on the State of Virginia* in 1782 that: "Appearances certainly indicate that [the mound] has derived both origin and growth from the accustomary collection of bones, and the deposition of them together; that the first collection had been deposited on the common surface of the earth, a few stones put over it, and then a covering of earth, that the second had been laid on this, had covered more or less of it in proportion to the number of bones, and then also covered with earth; and so on."

These mounds, which once numbered in the thousands, are thought to have been created during three different periods by several tribal groups. The Adena Indians of the Ohio River valley built numerous burial mounds between 500 BC and 1000 AD, some of the best-known being located close to the Serpent Mound near Locust Grove, Ohio. Another group, the Hopewells, also erected mounds, many of which can be seen in Michigan, Illinois, and Indiana and are thought to have been built during the same time period. Farther south along the Mississippi River and into Florida are many, many mounds created between 700 AD and 1200 AD by Mississippian tribes.

One of the biggest grievances of Indian people today is the manner in which their dead have been treated. From the early 1800s to the 1950s, many archaeologists and anthropologists devoted considerable time to digging up Indian graves for research purposes. Many were sent to the Smithsonian Institution, which today has 18,584 Indian skeletons and 313,096 archaeological artifacts which were shipped to the museum during this period. While steps are being taken to return remains to tribes, many laws still exist which are carry-overs from the past. In Virginia, if human remains are found, there is a determination of their religious lineage. If they are judged to be Christian, they are immediately returned to the local church for reburial. If they are Indian, they are sent via U.P.S. to the Smithsonian for study and storage.[3]

Disruptions of Indian graves are meeting with more and more resistance. Many people heard about the efforts to stop the Tellico Dam because of a tiny endangered fish, the snail darter, but the dam was also opposed by the eastern

Cherokee, as the waters would cover burial grounds. Reburials have helped ease some of these tensions, but all across the United States there are Indian people upset with the treatment of their ancestors' final resting places.

In response, some states have taken steps to afford protection to Indian burial sites. In 1987, following a rash of grave-robberies in which many artifacts were stolen for the purpose of being sold, Kentucky declared grave desecration a felony. The stiffening of the law was prompted by the discovery of over 400 holes dug at an ancient Shawnee burial ground. Ten men were involved who, before they were discovered, had unearthed over 1200 skeletons and removed thousands of objects. The men had said they were going to prospect the area for minerals! Once they had been caught, local Shawnee leader John Thomas and others began reburying the dead and conducting ceremonies every four days to restore peace to the area.[4]

One of the most progressive states in affording protection to Indian graves is California where, since 1976, the Native American Heritage Commission has been charged to "identify and catalog places of special religious and social significance to Native Americans, and known graves and cemeteries of Native Americans on private lands."[5] In 1988, California also made it a felony to remove,

Photo 7. *Aerial view of Serpent Mound, Ohio. Photo courtesy of The Ohio Historical Society.*

obtain, or possess human remains and artifacts from Indian graves. The penalty for desecration was increased after thousands of artifacts were found in the home of a state park employee. The irony is that no charges could be brought against him, for although the police found maps of excavations, no one ever saw the man in the actual act of digging up graves.[6]

Type 2. Purification Places

When people go to health clubs and sit in saunas or steam rooms, the purpose is to relax and/or to lose weight. When Indians conduct sweat-lodge ceremonies, they also enter into a heated, confined space, but while inside, dripping with sweat and inhaling the steam issuing from hot rocks seasoned with herbs like sage, they are also going through a ritual process. The difference in attitude and procedure between a steam room at the YMCA and a sweat lodge sited beside a sacred spring, such as beside Panther Meadows on Mount Shasta, can lead to profoundly different results. As an athlete in college and then later simply to keep in shape, I have been in lots of steam rooms and saunas. I have never seen people burst into tears or have visions or hear voices in these fitness facilities, but in sweat lodges it happens all the time.

"The Mother Earth has special places to cleanse your body, mind, and spirit," asserts Lakota medicine man Wallace Black Elk. At such places the energies and spirit of the place are especially suited for absorbing negative energies, and recharging one's personal life force. The actual purification processes vary considerably. Lummis bathe in icy streams, Chumash elders lead sweat lodges beside the ocean at Malibu, Utes pray and fast on high mountain ridges in the Rockies, Navajo take dust baths after sweat lodges, and Hawaiians bathe in sacred waterfalls.

"When we talk about purification, we mean all of you, not just cleaning your skin," says Bill Fields, retired director of Indian Affairs for the U.S. National Park Service. "Among the Hopi the purpose of ceremony is to drive out the *akina*—disharmony—so we can be in harmony with the Creator. Then we will be healthy and happy and know our purpose in life," Bill relates. In the Indian world, health and wisdom arise from maintaining positive harmonic sympathy with the vital forces which keep life systems moving. Right attitudes and actions help, but only through ceremonial forms can you achieve holistic purity, for it is the primary domain of the ceremonial to access states of being and consciousness which are not ordinarily tapped in daily life. In the Indian cosmology, some geographic places are best for purification, and each of these places is unique in its own right. Cherokee physician Lewis Mehl, M.D., recently told me how extraordinarily different it felt to lead a sweat lodge in France than one in the United States, because the spirits and energies were so distinctly different.

Photo 8. *Esalen Creek as it tumbles onto the beach at Big Sur, California, is the site of a very powerful spirit according to shamans from around the world. Author photo.*

Probably one of the best-known modern purification places is the Esalen Institute in Big Sur, California. The famous warm artesian mineral baths at Esalen, perched on the edge of a cliff overlooking the Pacific Ocean, were once used by the Esselen Indians for similar purposes to those of today.

Type 3. Healing Sites

Modern medicine has until recently given little attention to the power of place in aiding healing. This is somewhat out of keeping with its traditions, as its Greek father, Hippocrates, believed that some places had healing values for certain diseases, while others seemed to make people worse.[7] But thanks to more open-minded researchers, there is more and more support for the position of traditional healers that health is the result of being filled with vital life energy which ignites the flame of the soul and radiates through one's entire being. "People get sick because they lose harmony with the Creator," insists medicine man Rolling Thunder, who has performed profoundly powerful healing rites for medical researchers at such places as the Menninger Foundation and the Association for Research and Enlightenment Clinic.[8] "This harmony starts in the spirit world and works down into the material. When I doctor someone, I must ask the permission of the Creator first. I talk to the spirits of the places too, to ask for help. Each place has powers which can be used and misused, and some are especially good for healing."

In chapter one mention was made of "The Lourdes of America," Chimayó, New Mexico. Another place with a reputation for healing powers is Indian Hot Springs, a group of 22 artesian springs which bubble from the ground near the Rio Grande River in Hudspeth County in West Texas. According to Pat Ellis Taylor, folk healers and physicians on both sides of the border have used the muds, waters, and stones of Indian Hot Springs for hundreds of years, often with dramatic results. Studying the life of the noted healer Jewell Babb, who once operated a small resort at the springs which attracted many celebrities, including Howard Hunt, Taylor reports that each individual spring has its own unique muds, mosses, and waters which can be used to accomplish certain purposes. Those who understand the way the springs work, she says, have developed healing regimens involving treatments with a specific sequence of springs to obtain the desired effects. For example, you might bathe and drink the waters of one spring for general detoxification, sit on a stone beside another to cure menstrual cramps, and rub mud on your body from another to relieve arthritis.[9]

Type 4. Sacred Plant & Animal Sites

If a Haida Indian wants to carve a rattle from a piece of red cedar, he or she approaches the tree with reverence, makes an offering of corn meal, and asks its permission. This invites the tree's spirit to be present as one fashions the rattle. In the Indian world, all things are alive. They have both a material quality of matter, and a spiritual essence which is a connection to another dimension. This dimension is both a channel for life energies and a portal for communication with spiritual beings.

In the animal and plant kingdoms, individual organisms are psychically linked to other members of their species, both in this world and the next. The snow-geese people of my dream would be seen as wise spiritual beings representing that totem animal and all its associated qualities of great strength to fly long distances, sincerity, and sensitivity. Once, while driving down the road with several members of the Klamath tribe of Oregon, we came upon a flock of geese feeding in a field. We pulled over to watch the birds, and elder Marie Norris pointed out to me a small cluster of birds off to one side. "Watch them," she told me, "they are the elders." I took up my binoculars, focusing on the birds. They did seem to be slightly larger, and none of the other birds challenged them for their feeding place. A biologist would call these the dominant birds of the flock, but in the Indian world it is possible to communicate between people and birds. As I sat and watched, it seemed as though a brief sense of rapport developed between myself and the geese. I began to sense the weariness of the birds from their long flight, and their pleasure at being able to feed unmolested in a stubble field of wheat. Then, gently, the feeling washed away, and we drove off down the road.

Plants, too, have tribes. Once Rolling Thunder and I were out walking and he said, "Hey, Jim, let's go over there. There's some plants over there that have something to say." We went over to a thicket of some large horsetails (*Equisetum fluviatile*). Rolling Thunder kneeled down and appeared to be speaking something, softly. Then he sat quietly for a minute or so. Getting to his feet, he reported, "They say you can make a good tea from them, if you need a tonic." He later told me that he learned to talk with plants like this during his teens when his teachers made him live alone in the woods and survive off the land. He said that after he learned how to talk with plants, he could go out and find the ones he needed for a certain medicine even in the wintertime when they were buried under a foot of snow.

When Indian spiritual leaders gather herbs, eagle feathers, bear claws, or deer dewclaws for ceremonial or healing purposes, they want those which have the most power. There are places where the plants and animals are different, they assert, like the deer which live on Mount Taylor in New Mexico, or the sage which comes from Point Conception near Santa Barbara, California. The Huichol Indians of Mexico make an annual pilgrimage from their homes in the coastal mountains of central Mexico to a sacred high plateau, Wirikuta, over 100 miles away, to gather peyote for ceremonies in one of the most public of all Indian sacred rites involving sacred plants. One hundred-year-old-plus Huichol shaman, Don José Matsuwa, says that the peyote buttons collected at Wirikuta have a power found no place else because they are filled with a unique life-force energy called *kupuri,* which is found at Wirikuta. In the Huichol cosmology, the souls

Photo 9. *Sacred palm tree in American Samoa. Author photo.*

of young children fly to Wirikuta during their initiation as adult members of the tribe in the Drum Ceremony.

One of the most important of all the sacred plants is the tree, for it has mythical symbolic value as the axis along which shamans travel to the three worlds: the world above, the middle world where we live, and the world below. Trees are also valued for their offerings of wood, bark, sap, berries and fruit, and leaves. When a member of the Iroquois False Face Society cuts a chunk of wood from a living ash tree to make a mask, the tree is never killed because of the prayers said and rituals used. In the Iroquois region, the ash is the "tree of life," just as the cottonwood is to the Plains tribes, the maple is to northeastern tribes, the cypress is to the Seminoles, the oak is to California Indians, and the red and yellow cedars are to Northwest Coast tribes. In Europe, the Druids honor the oak tree, the Sami respect the birch, and the tribes of Siberia worship the larch in a similar fashion. Contrary to what former U.S. president Ronald Reagan may have said, one tree is not like every other one.

Type 5. Quarries

Stones and minerals are also alive in the Indian mind, and each has its own special quality and uses, as well as its spiritual values. Turquoise is associated with purity and protection, while obsidian from certain veins is supposed to have special potency for making weapons and knives. Indians of the northern Great Lakes and the Pacific Northwest place great importance on pure copper, which once was found at certain sacred places. Copper plates are associated with wealth by some tribes, and copper is used for jewelry and to decorate boxes, rattles, and other shamanic power objects.

There is not universal agreement among Indian people about the respective uses and values of each kind of stone, but most tribes share the view that certain stones have powers, and that the most potent stones come from special places. One system which reflects the potential complexity of assigning values to stones is that of Chippewa medicine man Sun Bear. In his "medicine wheel" system, which is an astrological formulation related to his medicine-wheel ceremony, each month of the year corresponds to a member of the mineral kingdom which manifests a certain power. For example, quartz, for December 22 through January 19, helps with rain-making and seeing into the future; silver, for January 20 through February 18, increases intuitive perception; turquoise, for February 19 through March 20, creates protection; and opal, for March 21 through April 19, produces the power to make people invisible.[10]

Crystals have special medicine value, according to Dr. Leslie Gray, a San Francisco psychotherapist of Oneida, Powhattan, and Seminole ancestry who combines traditional shamanic techniques with modern counseling methods in her practice. Dr. Gray believes that the "bones of our ancestors," as she calls crystals, can remove negative intrusions in a person's mind field with the same kind of power as tobacco because they are absorbers of energies. Having studied the use of crystals among more than 450 tribes in North America, she concludes that all tribes agree on crystals having special powers. They also agree that crystals should be cleaned with pure water and charged with energies in a ritual process to maximize their ultimate value for serving as conduits of spiritual energies to aid healing and stimulate intuitive perception. Also, crystals vary in their powers, depending upon where they come from.[11]

Perhaps the most famous quarry for stones of power in North America is the sacred Pipestone Quarry in Minnesota, which is a religious site of great importance to tribes within a thousand-mile radius or more, and is protected by the Yankton Sioux. A mile-long vein of soft red catlinite stone is found here, lying between layers of harder quartzite. The stone is easily carved, and its most popular use is for making long-stemmed medicine pipes which are smoked on ceremonial occasions.

The myth of the origin of this sacred quarry was recorded by George Catlin in 1836:

> Many ages after the red men were made, when all the different tribes were at war, the Great Spirit sent runners and called them all together at the 'Red Pipe.' He stood on the top of the rocks, and the red people were assembled in infinite numbers on the plains below. He took out a piece of red stone, and made a large pipe; he smoked it over them all; told them that it was a part of their flesh; that though they were at war, they must meet at this place as friends; that it belonged to them all; that they must make their calumets from it and smoke them to him whenever they wished to appease him or get his goodwill—the smoke from his big pipe rolled over them all, and he disappeared in its cloud; at the last whiff of his pipe a blaze of fire rolled over the rocks, and melted their surface— at that moment two squaws went into a blaze of fire under two medicine rocks, where they remain to this day, and must be consulted and propitiated whenever the pipe stone is taken away.[12]

The two rocks described remain today near the site as its "guardians."

The value of this quarry is therefore not just that the stone is easy to carve, but that it has a spiritual power which is invoked through proper use. Legends about the origin of this quarry vary from tribe to tribe, but all share respect for its sacred value. Surveying the northern plains in 1898, explorer John Wesley Powell, then director of the Bureau of American Ethnology, said, "The site of the quarries was a sacred place, known to the tribesmen of a large part of the continent. . . . It is not too much to say that the great Pipestone Quarry was the most important single location in aboriginal geography and lore."[13]

In view of Powell's report, it is sobering to note that Jennings C. Wise, an attorney for the Yankton Sioux, has gathered evidence which shows that in 1891 a railroad was constructed which did considerable harm to the quarry, and the siting of the railroad was purposefully instigated by federal officals to destroy the sacred quarry. According to Wise, sacred ledges of Pipestone Quarry were deliberately blasted to make it impossible to use them for ceremonial purposes.[14]

Type 6. Astronomical Observatories

Before the invention of the clock, time was marked by the movements of the stars, which were frequently studied from special ritual spaces. This combination of mathematics and the sacred was purposeful, for in the Indian cosmology, like that of many peoples around the world, stars are also associated with myths, stories, and images. In such cosmologies, astronomy and astrology blend into one.

Figure 2. *Early Sketches of Pipestone, Minnesota, Sacred Quarry. Reprinted courtesy of the U.S. National Park Service, Pipestone National Monument.*

Pencil sketch showing geologic cross section of quarry; pipestone is stratum B. National Archives.

Pencil sketch of the quarry made in 1836 by George Catlin. National Archives.

Sited at an elevation of 9,640 feet on the shoulder of Medicine Mountain between Lovell and Sheridan, Wyoming, the Big Horn Medicine Wheel is clearly an American Stonehenge. From a central stone cairn, 28 spokes of stones radiate outward, reflecting the 28 days of the lunar month and creating a symbolic statement of the power of the moon. These spokes are enclosed within a circle which seems related to the sun and certain stars.

Photo 10. *Bighorn Medicine Wheel near Sheridan, Wyoming. Photo courtesy of U.S. Forest Service.*

On June 21, the Summer Solstice, two of the six peripheral stones on the western side of the circle mark the positions on the horizon of the sunrise and sunset. Other positions around this medicine wheel give accurate readings on the star Aldebaran in the constellation of Taurus, the star Rigel in the constellation of Orion, and the star Sirius. All of these readings fall within one month of the Summer Solstice. Those who planned this circle understood the seasons well, for the site is normally free of snow for only about two months during the year.[15]

Throughout the Plains region, the building of such wheels is an ancient tradition, although many of the wheels are not as elaborate as the Big Horn Medicine Wheel. According to Professor R.G. Forbis of the University of Calgary, there are more than half a million stone rings scattered through the Great Plains. Dr. John Eddy of Boulder, Colorado, believes there are even more, perhaps as many as five to six million, many of which may be as much as 10,000 years old.[16]

In 1988, stone circles believed to date back as far as 3000 BC were found on Beaver Island in Lake Michigan. The primary circle was discovered by Terri Bussey, a Chippewa and a member of the Grand Rapids Inter-Tribal Council. It is 397 feet in diameter and made of boulders from two to ten feet tall. At the center is a large rock containing a basketball-sized hole that archaeologists believe may have been a sundial marker. These finds are unique in that such elaborate stone circles are not usually associated with eastern woodland tribes.[17]

Another dramatic ancient American Indian astronomical observatory was discovered by artist Anna Sofaer, accidentally, in mid-June of 1977 at Chaco Canyon National Monument in New Mexico. Sofaer was with a class studying rock art. Her assignment was to investigate Fajada Butte, a pillar of rock which stands like a guardian to Chaco Canyon, which was once the home of an Anasazi pueblo settlement. She scrambled up the monolith and was recording petroglyphs when she happened to look behind three large boulders and noticed a bright sliver of light shining on a rock face with several large, spiral pictographs. She felt drawn to the markings, and then suddenly realized that it was almost Summer Solstice and that the ''dagger'' of light was almost perfectly bisecting the largest spiral. Subsequent investigations revealed that this slender shaft of light only came through the crack between the stones for a short time—precisely eighteen minutes on the Summer Solstice. Additional work revealed that the other remaining spiral petroglyphs were related to other solar and lunar cycles, including the nineteen-year lunar cycle.[18]

No one really knows if the three giant boulders on Fajada Butte had fallen into place naturally, or were put there by Anasazi priests, but for an agricultural culture, marking the seasons has important survival value. Bill Fields notes that while the observatory is obviously important, the entire butte is a sacred place to the Hopi and is guarded by rattlesnakes. Hopi come here to gather rattlesnakes for the Snake Dance ceremony, Tuuatikibi, which takes places every other August. Fields says, ''People think this is a rain dance, but that is not so. The Snake Dance drives away the *akina* or disharmony, and when all things are in harmony then it rains.'' After the dance is over, the snakes are returned to their homes.

Type 7. Shrines, Temples & Effigies

When one thinks of monuments or shrines at sacred places, one usually thinks of far-off places like shrines in India, temples in the Orient, or pyramids to honor the sun in Central America. But five miles north of the tiny town of Locust Grove, Ohio, lies one of the most spectacular shrines to the Earth god/goddess in the world: the Serpent Mound. Somewhere between 1000 BC and 1000 AD, the Adena Indians began carrying stones from nearby river bottoms to place on top of a dome-shaped hill rising from a lowland ringed by higher hills. Following a design which must have come from inspired minds, they built a serpentine form five feet high and 50 feet wide. The form begins with an open mouth and, after going through seven major curves, ends 1300 feet later with a tightly coiled tail. The Adena tribe topped off the effigy with hand-packed clay. Exactly how the Serpent Mound was originally used is unknown. More mystery is added to this sculpture—the largest Earth sculpture in North America, and the largest serpent-shaped Earth sculpture in the world—if one talks with a member of the Hopi

Snake Clan, for they say their ancestors built it. What is much clearer to understand are the nearby smaller domes, which are more recent burial mounds of tribes with certain identity.

Visitors today can gain a better perspective of the Serpent Mound form from a three-story-high observation tower nearby. Yet, even from this height, the overall scene looks more like a fairway on a golf course, for the form of the serpent cannot be fully viewed from the ground. One can only truly appreciate the spectacular design of the mound from the air, which has inspired more than one mind to speculate that the snake's purpose is to communicate with space beings or gods from the sky. A more apparent purpose for the mound is to honor the Earth force, which all around the world is commonly depicted as a dragon or snake.

The Serpent Mound may be the largest Earth effigy in the United States, but it is hardly the only one. Along the Colorado River, in a desert land as large as New Hampshire that lies between Needles, California and Yuma, Arizona, and stretches into the mountains of New Mexico, lies a mammoth mural of forms called ''geoglyphs.'' Seen from a plane flying overhead, the desert floor is dotted with pumas, horses, lizards, quail, snakes, and more abstract forms, some nearly 200 feet long. From an inspection on ground level, it can be determined that the patterns were formed by someone digging down into the earth to reveal a lighter subsoil, as well as placing rocks around dugout patterns. According to archaeologist Jay Van Werlhof of Imperial Valley College, these Earth artworks range in age from 150 to 10,000 years. Evidence of dance circles is visible nearby, suggesting that the sculptures were created as an act of spiritual communication. Living Indians do not know much about the origins or use of the geoglyphs; nonetheless, they assert that these forms are of great spiritual value. According to Bureau of Land Management archaeologist Pat Welch: ''They [Indians today] claim that if you are in tune, you will feel the essence of the old ones when you go into the area.''[19]

The desert markings of the Southwest bear resemblance to the famous Nazca Markings located in the arid Pampa de Ingenio Desert of Peru. These were made famous by author Erich von Daniken, who has championed the view that such forms are an attempt to communicate with beings from outer space.[20] Such a thesis is not impossible. Some tribes of North American Indians have creation myths about coming from distant stars, such as the Cherokee myth which traces their tribal origin to the Pleiades. No one really knows what did happen in the distant time. My guess, however, is that these forms were etched in deserts as part of rain-making rituals, calling upon sky gods to invoke their powers and bring rains to drought-stricken areas in much the same fashion that Hopi Indians continue to use ceremonies to invite the kachinas to help set all things in harmony and bring the rain.

Just across the Mississippi River from St. Louis, Missouri, lies a fascinating complex of Earth mounds, Cahokia, which were created sometime between 900 AD and 1200 AD by the Mississippian Indians. One of the most impressive of the group is Monk's Mound, which covers about fourteen acres and is approximately 1,000 feet long, 700 feet wide, and 100 feet high at its maximum elevation. Nearby are the remains of a circle of eighteen-inch-diameter cedar poles, called Woodenhenge, which is a well-documented astronomical observatory oriented to the sun.[21]

Throughout the Midwest and South there are many lesser-sized mounds, temples, effigies, and shrines, all built from rocks and earth without the elaborate stonework found in other parts of the world. (The only pure stone shrines of any size in the United States are the stone ceremonial platforms of Hawaii, which are called *heiau*.) The origin and purpose of many earth mounds are not entirely clear, which seems to give freer rein to the minds of those who interpret them. Barry Fell has written a fascinating book about how he feels some of the stone and earth works of New England were created by white people of European origins who came to this country long before Columbus.[22] Many Indians and archaeologists scoff at this thesis, but according to Kayendres, a Mohawk Clan Mother, there is a story in her tribe about the "early white people." Rolling Thunder has also told me that one reason so many Cherokees have lighter skin

Photo 11. *Buddhist temple located at the Valley of the Gods on Oahu, Hawaii. Author photo.*

is that some of their early people came from the Mediterranean regions.

This same theme is found as a primary inspiration for another researcher of the mound builders, Joseph Smith, founder of the Mormon religion. One night, in 1823, Smith said he was visited by an angel named Moroni, who told him about a book written on golden pages which he could find buried at a place near Palmyra, New York. By 1830, with the aid of divine inspiration, Smith had produced the *Book of Mormon*, the core of the teachings more than two million active Mormons today. Smith's story tells of a tribe of Israelites who fled from Jerusalem about 600 BC to eventually land in what today is America, where they were guided to build earth forms, including great mounds.[23] In the late 1800s and early 1900s, a number of anthropologists and archaeologists also believed that at least some of the mounds and effigies of the East and Midwest were the works of "a race of Mound Builders, distinct from American Indians," to use the words of U.S. Bureau of Ethnology researcher Cyrus Thomas. While the actual origins of the mounds remain uncertain, most scientists today believe that the era of mound building was due to an influx of Indians from Mexico and South America into North America. This influx resulted in the Adena, the Hopewells, and the Mississippian tribes who left us remnants of the fascinating Temple Mound culture which still can be seen today at Cahokia in Illinois, Grave Creek in West Virginia, Serpent Mound in Ohio, Etowah Mounds in Georgia, Moundville in Alabama, and elsewhere.[24]

Type 8. Historical Sites

Graves mark the final resting places of those who have passed on to the next plane, and to many American Indian people certain places where the old ones once lived also have significant spiritual value, for one can feel the old ones' presence and commune with their spirits in some of these places. Sioux author/attorney Vine Deloria, Jr., speaks of "a place on the Santee reservation in Nebraska where a group of Sioux warriors died fighting the Pawnees almost 200 years ago. People say that on a warm summer night when the wind is just right that you can hear the warriors singing their death songs and smell the Indian tobacco on the evening breeze."[25]

The value of such places to Indian people was demonstrated in the fall of 1988 when actor John Voight acted as a messenger from the Hopi tribal elders, carrying a request for Lucasfilm Ltd. not to shoot planned chase scenes from a forthcoming *Indiana Jones* movie in the Long House Ruin at Mesa Verde. Learning of these wishes, the filmmakers quickly changed the setting for the shoot, honoring the elders' feelings about the sacred values of these ancestral ruins.[26]

Sometime between 1200 AD and 1300 AD, the Anasazi Indians living in cliffside pueblos on the summit of the 8,000-foot raised plateau we call Mesa Verde reached a population of about 5,000. Then, for some mysterious reason, they left, abandoning this verdant mesa. Today nearly 3,900 ancient sites have been found within Mesa Verde National Park, some 600 of them cliff dwellings. The most obvious sacred structure is the Sun Temple, an oval foundation of stones perched on a south-facing cliff which has a 50-mile view of the land 2,500 feet below. In the mind of the Indian peoples, however, other less dramatic places at Mesa Verde also have spiritual value. Tucked away in some of the sheltered ravines one can find ample evidence of much earlier habitation. There are circular areas where the earth has been packed down by bare feet, with a hole in the middle of the floor, which is the sipapu, a reminder of where we came from. At other ruins you will find spirals and other petroglyphs, expressing prayers, recording travels, and marking the presence of various shamans. It is little wonder that in 1906 Mesa Verde became a U.S. National Park, and then was selected by the World Heritage Convention of UNESCO to be among the first seven places in the world to be recognized as a World Cultural Heritage site.

Today there are 23 archaeological national monuments, three archaeological national historic parks, and only one archaeological national park in the United States. Two-thirds of these lie in the Southwest, one-third of which lie in Arizona. People flock to these places and say they do so to study history, but deep down inside there is another calling to which modern society does not readily admit. Part of knowing who we are and what it is to be human involves understanding the procession of human history. Adaptability is a primary trait of the human species, and in the fast-paced modern world it's all too easy to forget our kinship with our past and the animal allies which live within each of us. When visiting ancestral sites like Mesa Verde, Hovenweep, Chaco Canyon, Wupatki, and the Grand Canyon, as well as some of the more than 34,000 places which are listed on the National Register of Historic places, we too may be blessed by dreams and visions of times past. The value of such experiences to modern life was stated beautifully by Carl Jung when he said:

> Every forward step in culture is psychologically an extension of consciousness that can take place only through discrimination. An advance, therefore, always begins with individuation, that is to say, through the fact that an individual, conscious of his uniqueness, cuts a new way through hitherto untrodden country. To do this he must first return to the fundamental facts of his own being, quite irrespective of all authority and tradition, and allow himself to become conscious of his own distinctiveness.[27]

Type 9. Places of Spiritual Renewal

Indians and Eskimos do not have a concept in their language for what we call a "park." Rangers in northern Canada have told me that the Eskimos' words for parks, roughly translated, mean "places where white people play."

Some of the places which we call parks, however, have sacred value to Indians, one of which is Mount Rainier in Washington state, which is known as "Tahoma" to the Cowlitz, Puyallup, and other tribes of the southern Puget Sound area. In 1980 I met Don Clouette, Chairman of the Cowlitz tribe, who told me:

> For as long as we know, Mount Tahoma has been a sacred place where my people have come to pray. We come and climb up her slopes to reach certain special places where we make medicine. Some are just special stones. Others are caves and springs. We pray to the Creator and leave offerings, for the spirit of the mountain is very strong. You can see what happens when a mountain gets angry, look at her sister, Mount Saint Helens. She blows her stack, and it's because of the pollution and the radiation being made near her. You talk about geological forces, but we say that Tahoma and her sisters and brothers are alive, and there to help if we respect their power.

Not all places of renewal are mountains. For the Taos Pueblo people, Blue Lake in the nearby Sangre de Cristo Mountains is the place where their creation myth says they came from. Every year the tribe journeys to Blue Lake from the pueblo to conduct a ceremony for keeping this memory alive, in much the same fashion that pilgrims go to Mecca, Mount Omei, Jerusalem, or Mount Fuji.

In the rugged Siskiyou Mountains along the California-Oregon border, there are renewal places too. Up on some of the rocky ledges in the "high country" there are depressions in the rocks, worn by centuries of Karok, Tolowa, and Hoopa people coming to sit and pray to the Creator. These people assert that the sacred songs which they use in ceremonies like the White Deer Dance came to them when they were sitting in prayer on these ledges. They say that if the peace, quiet, and isolation of these places is destroyed, the memory of the places will suffer and it will not be possible for people to go into the mountains and learn these songs from their source.

Type 10. Mythic & Legendary Sites

North of Honolulu on the New Pali Road, the turn-out at the summit for the Nuuanu Pali Lookout offers a spectacular view of the north shore of Oahu. Looking *makai*, which means "seaward" (Hawaiians traditionally do not talk about the four directions, but instead refer to things as *makai*, "toward the sea," or *maulea*, "toward the mountains"), there is a large bright-green spot dotted with open water ponds. This is the Kaiwainui Marsh, the largest freshwater marsh in Hawaii, home of the endangered Hawaiian coot and the Hawaiian gallinule, the two birds which brought fire to the islands. In the Hawaiian traditional mind, this marsh is a very sacred place. One indication of its traditional value are the

Photo 12. *Mount Rainier in the Cascades, Washington. Photo © 1990 by Michael Powers.*

three large stone-platform *heiaus* which are still found along its banks. According to legend, these black volcanic stoneworks were laid by the *menehune*, the little people—the Hawaiian elves. Near the town of Kailua, you could once find the Makalei tree, a stick from which supposedly had the power to attract and bewilder the fat mullet fish in the marsh. Once a giant named Olomana lived here, but he was killed by the heroic Mahi-nui. The slain giant's body can be seen today as the nearby Mount Olomana. Guarding the marsh are the *mo'o*, two women who can change into the shape of lizards at will. They are the daughters of Haumea, the Earth goddess and mother of fertility who also resides here.

When one reads about mythic tales like these, they seem like great fantasies, perhaps inspired by unusual landforms. In the traditional mind, however, myths are forces and intelligences which live in the other world, and which can visit people in dreams and visions, or seep into their minds and move them to do certain things at various places. If one walks out onto Krider's rock, a house-sized boulder on the west shore of Kaiwainui, and someone mentions Haumea, people fall silent and some begin to cry. *Kapunas* (elders) like Auntie Thelma Bugbee say this is because Haumea's spirit is strong there.

The mythic identification of place, which Ananda Coomaraswamy called *landa-nama*, has tremendous importance to primal-minded people. Places like

Goberner's Nob in New Mexico, where the Navajo say Changing Woman lives, or Mount Olympus in Greece, are the physical locations where spiritual beings manifest most readily. When the Cherokees say that Jommeoki, a spirit guide, lives at Pilot Mountain, North Carolina, or the Penobscots say that Pomola, a powerful spirit creature with the wings of an eagle, the body of a man, and the head of a moose, presides over Maine's Mount Katahdin, or the Zoque Indians in Mexico say that a huge seven-headed serpent, Tsahuatsan, lives in the sacred Chimalpas Mountains, they mean that these entities actually make their residences at these hallowed places. To invoke their power in one's life, one performs special ritual acts to honor their presence, much as a Navajo medicine person creates a sand painting to invoke the powers of the four sacred mountains and their spirits, using sympathetic magic to restore harmony and balance. According to indigenous people around the world, the living landscape is filled with mythic beings who live at various places, and even when ceremonies are not conducted to propitiate the deities, seeing, thinking, and talking about these places keep their values in mind, which aids cultural stability. In Polynesia, you can tell if traditional people like you according to which places they mention in their conversation, for to say the name of a sacred place is to call up its sentiments, which is like a gentle blessing.

People scoff about living myths, but those people who live around the Kaiwainui Marsh are not so skeptical. It seems that every so often the local police get a call from some worried person who has seen two women wearing white robes walking around out in the marsh, near the dangerous muds which could swallow them up. The police can never find these adventuresome women, but the calls keep coming in. Some say that this is to remind the people that the mo'o still live and want their marsh to stay protected.

Type 11. Vision Questing & Dreaming Places

All over the world, one of the special powers of sacred places is their mysterious ability to open the portals of the mind to waking visions and vivid dreams. Before he became the pharaoh, Thotmes IV slept near the Great Sphinx and had a dream instructing him to clear the sand from that monument. Jacob slept with his head on a stone and had a dream of a great ladder ascending to heaven: this moved him to set up a temple there called Bethel. Moses and Saint Catherine both had visions of God on Mount Sinai. More recently, three young children reported visions of the Madonna in Portugal, leading to the erection of the popular shrine for Our Lady of Fatima.

In the northwest corner of the Black Hills of South Dakota there is one of these places which people who live close to the earth say is a powerful stimulator of dreams and visions: Bear Butte, or Nohawus to the Cheyenne and Pahan Wakan or Mato Paha to the Lakota. "Seven spiritual people in the Beginning came to the Black Hills and they chose Bear Butte as the altar, the heart of the center of the Black Hills," declares Oglala Lakota medicine man Pete Catches. Charles Under Baggage, an Oglala elder, agrees, and says that he believes Bear Butte is "a thundering mound butte of the Black Hills . . . a spiritual power dream place."[28]

Just as Jerusalem is a place of power to Jews, Christians and Moslems, so is Bear Butte a sacred place to the Cheyenne and Lakota tribes. Every year, some 4,000 Indians come to pray in silence on this very sacred land. Unfortunately for them, it is also a South Dakota State Park, which draws over 100,000 tourists a year. One result is an ongoing court battle. Other incidents provoked by this spiritual-land conflict have nearly escalated into armed conflict, especially in the early 1980s when the State Parks Department wrote a letter to 50 medicine men saying that Bear Butte would be closed to them from June through September, and that access to the butte for religious purposes would require a fee and a use permit.[29]

Until very recently, modern people who have had vivid dreams, seen waking visions, or heard voices have been automatically labeled schizophrenic and recommended for psychiatric care. A much earlier way of thinking says if people do *not* have vivid dreams, see visions, and hear voices, they are referred to the medicine people for treatment, for they have lost close touch with the Creator. Medicine people, like good psychotherapists, hope to evoke dreams from their clients to enable healing to occur. But they do not wait for people to get stuck before they work on their dreaming: they purposefully stimulate dreaming and visioning through rituals conducted at special places.

Type 12. Rock Art Places

Troubled Bear Butte is clearly a dreamtime therapeutic center, as are the many caves tucked away in the coastal mountains between Santa Barbara and Los Angeles, California, which have been colorfully decorated by the Chumash tribe. According to Campbell Grant, there are thousands of caves carved by wind and water in the windswept Santa Ynez, San Rafael, and Sierra Madre mountains, many of which bear colorful pictographs painted in up to six colors. It seems likely that many of these paintings depict dream images from Chumash who sought guidance in these caves, possibly while under the influence of Jimson weed (*Datura stramonia*).[30]

Rock carvings—petroglyphs—are also found in many parts of the United States, one of the most famous sites being Newspaper Rock State Historical Monument in Utah. This site contains hundreds of etchings by prehistoric Anasazi peoples of the Archaic, Basketmaker, and Pueblo historical periods and the Fremont Culture, as well as markings of modern Utes and Navajo.

Photo 13. *Petroglyphs in Dinosaur National Monument depict shamans with horned figures and hands radiating power. Author photo.*

It is important to preserve the art of the past to keep alive the spirit of our ancestors, and it is just as important to remember that rock art has many meanings. At Grimes Point in western Nevada, there are animal forms etched on black stones which crop up from the sagebrush desert around a depression which once was a lake. Researchers now believe that these markings were used in ritual hunting rites, as were those in the famous caves at Lascaux in France. Newspaper Rock appears to mark the passage of people and tribes, and to record events, serving as a stone tabloid of the history of that place. The vision caves of the Chumash, like those found along the Columbia River in Washington and Idaho, seem to record spiritual experiences. In Hawaii, rock carvings often mark the boundaries of land use, or indicate the prevailing spirits associated with various places. Another series of stone carvings in Arizona appears to be associated with Navajo puberty rites.

In the United States, rock art dates back at least 15,000 years, with most of it being found west of the Mississippi. Unfortunately, this art is often difficult to protect from the elements, as well as from vandalism. Roman soldiers carved their names on Egyptian ruins, and the modern urge to carve on soft rocks seems not to have diminished. However, carving the names of two lovers in stone is not the same thing as purposefully defacing rock art of earlier people. The first is hard to find fault with if the location is appropriate, but the second is most likely a racially or religiously motivated crime.

Critical to the understanding of ancient rock art is the fact that the location of the work is its foundation. Rock art can mark a place as being spiritual, but the recognition of the power of the place came first. In modern religious art, it seems more often that the work creates the sacredness of the place, rather than the Earth manifesting something special to be honored by the art.

Type 13. Fertility Sites

Thanks to the Nature Conservancy, Ring Mountain in Tiburon, California, is preserved forever as a nature sanctuary. Aside from being a high point for observing the San Francisco Bay area, Ring Mountain was purchased because of its unique serpentine rock outcroppings which offer a microhabitat for rare plants, including the Tiburon mariposa lily (*Calochortus tiburonensis*). Also on Ring Mountain is an unusual display of rock art of the coastal Miwok tribe. On a garage-sized serpentine boulder on the southern face of the mountain, just below its 602-foot crest, there is a series of raised forms which are either full circles or paired semicircles. According to John Littleton, who has been studying this area for some time, the markings represent female genitalia. When a Miwok woman wanted to ensure having a child, she and her lover would climb the hill and rub tiny particles from this soft green rock on her body. This supposedly ensured

Photo 14. *The Miwok fertility stone on Ring Mountain in Tiburon, California. Photo © 1990 by Cindy A. Pavlinac.*

Photo 15. *Miwok Indian couples once carved these petroglyphs in the shape of the vagina and then rubbed the powdered serpentine rock on the woman's body to increase fertility and ease labor. Photo © 1990 by Cindy A. Pavlinac.*

her fertility and made childbirth easier. Tragically, while the preserve seems to have saved the Tiburon lily from extinction, vandals have nearly destroyed these markings. Sigmund Freud would have had some interesting things to say about someone who hacks at a fertility stone rather than recognizing its value and seeing if it might help love blossom.

This rock outcropping is the only American Indian fertility spot I have visited, but my understanding is that there are others found throughout the United States, often associated with special stones, caves, springs, or herbs. It seems possible that their location has been carefully guarded to avoid destruction by missionaries and zealots.

In Europe, fertility sites are more well known. Some standing stone dolmens have the shape of phalluses, while others resemble female genitals, such as England's Men-an-thol, which is a stone with a hole large enough for people to crawl through.

Type 14. Sunrise Ceremonial Sites

As the sun rises above the rugged mountains of southeastern Utah on the morning of June 21, there is a magical place on the west bank of the Colorado River in Canyonlands National Park where the first rays of the morning sun strike

Photo 16. *Sunrise rock altar in the Sierra Nevada mountains near Graeagle, California. Author photo.*

a flat ledge. Traveling through the area, I first became aware of this site through a dream. In the dream I watched the sun rise, heard people singing, and then perceived a voice which simply said, "This is a sacred place, too." I have since been able to verify that this place does exist and has been used for special sunrise ceremonies.

A similar sunrise site is located in the Sierras near the town of Graeagle, California. At this location, which has no name, a large boulder some 50 yards long emerges from the ground near a place which once was a summer hunting camp for Maidu Indians. At the very top of the boulder, a chunk of rock three feet deep, fifteen to twenty feet wide and thirty feet long was removed many years ago to leave a flat, table-like altar. The altar area is marked by numerous petroglyphs which appear to be the markings of clans which once came to this place. My sense is that the clans recorded their visits at this altar, during which they conducted ceremonies of peaceful coexistence and offered prayers for bountiful hunting and food gathering. This natural altar is situated so as to receive the first rays of the morning sun in the summer months.

§

"Emotions are automatic psychological responses, involving both mental and physiological features, to our subconscious appraisal of what we perceive as the beneficial or harmful relationship to some aspect of reality or to ourselves,'' according to psychologist Nathaniel Brandon.[31] Looking at the variety of American Indian sacred places reveals that there is considerable diversity in their natures. Yet the common quality which they possess, according to Indian people, is the ability to evoke a special mental-emotional state of mind, which the Salish Indians call *skalalitude* and which modern people call ''spiritual consciousness.''

Modern people still do value the sacred in their lives, as evidenced by the abundance of churches, synagogues, and mosques of the world, but modern society seems to disavow the potential of natural places as being capable of arousing sacred feelings in us. In the Indian mind, sacred places in nature not only represent physical touchstones for evoking sacred values, but they also hold an important key to personal power. This power is called *wakonda* by the Lakota, *orenda* by the Iroquois, *pokunt* by the Shoshone, *manitou* by the Algonquins, *yek* by the Tlingit, *naula* by the Kwakiutl, *sgana* by the Haida, and *mana* among the Hawaiians.

''Wherever I found the living, there I found the will to power,'' reported the gloomy Nietzsche, who himself felt that he spent most of his life living in the wrong place.[32] In Funk and Wagnall's standard two-volume dictionary there are thirteen different definitions of ''power,'' but none of them translate in terms of the power of sacred places. ''Power'' in modern language has come to mean gaining control over something, and then using that force to change the world. By contrast, in the Native American mind, power is a personal empowerment arising from a surrendering of personal ego consciousness to become aligned with a spiritual world beyond this one. ''I have no power,'' says medicine man Rolling Thunder. ''When I heal someone or make it rain, it's because I'm working as the agent for the Great Spirit.''

Symbols, forms, and conditions in the world can move people, which is how the advertising industry works its magic. If a place has historical significance or natural scenic beauty, it is understandable how it can stimulate one's sentiments. It is something very different, however, to understand how a place can create the emotion of ''sacred.'' ''Man becomes aware of the sacred because it manifests itself, shows itself, as something wholly different from the profane,'' observes Mircea Eliade.[33] To be *sacred* is something beyond being religious, Rudolph Otto pointed out in his 1917 classic work on spiritual psychology, *Das Heilige*. Religion today has become associated with morality, Otto said, thus equating it with goodness, whereas true spiritual power includes both the light and the dark. He suggested that for truly sacred things the term ''numinous'' be used, which arises from the Latin words ''numen'' and ''omen''—implying a power of raw natural origins which contains both good and bad elements.[34] In the face of true spirit we are awed, and contained in that potent emotion are fear, wonder, and sacredness all rolled into one.

Nature is numinous. A majestic mountain may enthrall the viewer with its snow-capped peak, but that same snow pack can rumble down with the speed of a runaway freight train and can kill someone in an avalanche. A surging river may captivate the imagination, but if someone falls in and drowns, the same river becomes a killer. A thunderstorm can be romantic, but it can also fry someone if they are struck by lightning. The Koyukon Indians of central Alaska say that at certain places there is a threatening spirit, *huyeega hoolaanh*, which makes these places dangerous to people who visit them.[35]

It is clear that, in Native American culture, nature is a numinous force. The Native American belief system arises in direct psycho-emotional contact with the trees, clouds, mountains, rivers, deserts, birds and animals. The result is an experience which we who live in modern society have difficulty fathoming, but which others with a similar lifestyle all around the world understand. Describing the mindset of the Saami reindeer herder, Jorgen Eriksson reports: "A reindeer herder easily goes into an altered state of consciousness when he is in the fells (the high hills) alone and perhaps without food or sleep for several days. Then you will get all sorts of visions and you will become more wild. . . . It is a kind of a wild state in which the reindeer herder "joiks" (sings) much and comes to strange places where he might have spiritual experiences which are difficult to explain."[36]

In this chapter I have attempted to give insights into the Native American reality and to assign categories to sacred places, both of which are difficult tasks to accomplish. For one thing, more often than not a place may have more than one sacred aspect, which compounds its presence. The rugged Purgatoire River region of southern Colorado, for example, holds burials, springs, sacred plant sites, rock art, ceremonial sites, and ancestral sacred sites.[37] The area is also the U.S. Army's Fort Carson-Pinon Canyon Maneuver Area, used for testing tanks. This is perhaps another example of how the raw power of a place can attract energies of many kinds. The same could be said about the combination of sacredness and conflict in the holy lands of the Middle East.

At the 1984 World Congress on Cultural Parks at Mesa Verde, I presented these categories of sacred places to representatives of indigenous tribes from all around the world. While there were tribal variations—Glen Morris, an Australian Aborigine, noted that his people have "Dream Trek" trails as well as caves— there was agreement among all present that this system represented a working language for describing the nature of sacred places around the world. I have since shared this classification in popular and professional articles and presented it to a wide variety of people and audiences. While respondents may debate details, in general these categories seem to describe sacred places all around the globe.

In this chapter I have given a brief overview of the nature of sacred places for many native peoples. Hopefully this will enable non-Indians to better understand sacred places and how they work in the Native American culture and mind. Just as modern people entrust scientists with microscopes to tell them about strange worlds most people seldom give much thought to, so Native Americans can help them better understand nature, because for centuries they have been doing a better job of living in harmony with nature than modern society has.

The United States, however, is no longer occupied only by red-skinned people. In other parts of the world also, the voices of the indigenous peoples represent tenuous minorities. It is strange how quickly people seem to forget that everyone is descended from people who worship sacred places in nature. If modern people are going to appreciate sacred places as being of value to modern society, then we must also try to understand the value these places have to all people.

> *"Our Sacred Spirit put us on these Six Sacred Mountains [the sacred mountains of the Four Corners Area of the American Southwest]. And the Six Sacred Mountains are not outside us—they are inside."*
> KATHERINE SMITH YINISHYE, BIG MOUNTAIN NAVAJO[38]

ENDNOTES

1. Lawrence Durrell, "Landscape and Character," *New York Times* Magazine, June 12, 1960.

2. Frank Waters, *The Book of the Hopi* (New York: Viking Press, 1965).

3. Rick Hill, "Mining the Dead: Even in Death American Indians Are Threatened," *Daybreak* (Seattle: Daybreak Star Center, Summer 1988).

4. *Los Angeles Times*, Feb. 11, 1988. News release, Dennis Bean, c/o Spirit of the Land, 1746 Belmar Drive, Louisville, KY, 40213.

5. *Marin Independent Journal* Dec. 30, 1987.

6. *Earth Island Journal* (San Francisco: Earth Island Institute, Summer 1988).

7. Hippocrates, *Airs, Waters, Places.*

8. Stanley Krippner and Alberto Villoldo, *The Realms of Healing* (Albany, CA: Celestial Arts, 1976).

9. Pat E. Taylor, *Border Healing Woman: The Story of Jewell Babb* (Austin, TX: University of Texas Press, 1981).

10. Sun Bear and Wabun, *The Medicine Wheel: Earth Astrology* (Englewood Cliffs, NJ: Prentice-Hall, Inc., 1980).

11. LESLIE GRAY, "CRYSTALS: BONES OF OUR ANCESTORS," *The Crystal Congress Quarterly*, (Palo Alto, CA: Spring 1988).

12. George Catlin, "Account of a journey to the Coteau des Prairies, with a description of the Red Pipe Stone quarry and granite boulders found there," *The American Journal of Science and the Arts*, 38 (1839), 1:138-146.

13. John Wesley Powell, 1898 (quoted in brochure of Pipestone National Monument, Pipestone, MN 56164).

14. American Indian Religious Freedom Act Report, P.L. 95-341. Federal Agencies Task Force, U.S. Department of Interior, Washington, DC, August 1979.

15. Joseph Campbell, *The Way of Animal Powers*, vol. 1, *Historical Atlas of World Mythology* (San Francisco: Harper and Row, Inc., 1983), pp. 222-223.

16. John Eddy, "Medicine Wheels and Plains Indian Astronomy" in Anthony E. Aveni, ed., *Native American Astronomy* (Austin, TX: University of Texas Press, 1977).

17. *Detroit News*, June 18, 1988.

18. A. Sofaer, V. Zinser, and R. Sinclair, "A Unique Solar Marking Construct," *Science* 206, no. 4416, Oct. 19, 1979, pp. 283-92.

19. Robert Locke, "Message to the gods: California's desert geoglyphs," *San Francisco Examiner/Chronicle*, May 8, 1983, pp. A4-A5.

20. Erich Von Daniken, *The Gold of the Gods* (New York: G.P. Putnam and Sons, Inc., 1973).

21. Joseph Campbell, *The Way of Animal Powers*.

22. Barry Fell, *America B.C.* (New York: Quadrangle New York Times Books, 1977).

23. Robert Silverburg, " . . . and the Mound Builders Vanished from the Earth" in *A Sense of History: The Best Writings from the Pages of American Heritage* (New York: American Heritage Press, 1985).

24. Ibid.

25. Vine Deloria, Jr., "How We Come to Ourselves: Land, Places, and Knowing" (Paper presented at the 1989 Spirit of Place symposium, "Sacred Places and Spaces," Grace Cathedral, San Francisco, CA, August 18, 1989).

26. *Marin Independent Journal*, August 24, 1988.

27. Carl G. Jung, *Psychological Reflections: An Anthology of the Writings of Carl Jung*, ed. J. Jacobi (New York: Pantheon Books, 1953), p. 30.

28. Anita Parlow, *A Song from Sacred Mountain* (Pine Ridge, SD: Oglala Legal Rights Fund, 1983).

29. Ibid.

30. Campbell Grant, *The Rock Paintings of the Chumash* (Berkeley: University of California Press, 1965).

31. Nathaniel Brandon, *The Psychology of Romantic Love* (Los Angeles: J.P. Tarcher, 1980).

32. F. Nietzsche, *Thus Spake Zarathustra* (London: tr. Thomas Common, 1932).

33. Mircea Eliade, *The Sacred and the Profane* (New York: Harcourt Brace Jovanovich Inc., 1959).

34. Rudolph Otto, *The Idea of the Holy* (New York: Oxford University Press, 1923).

35. Richard K. Nelson, *Make Prayers to the Raven: A Koyukon View of the Northern Forest* (Chicago: University of Chicago Press, 1983), p. 35.

36. Jorgen I. Eriksson, "Saami Shamanism: The Noajdie Today," *Newsletter of the Foundation for Shamanic Studies*, vol. 1, no. 3 (Winter 1988-89): p. 4.

37. Kate Kellogg, "The Ecology of Indian Religion," *Michigan Today*, October 1986, pp. 6-7.

38. Anita Parlow, *Cry Sacred Ground: Big Mountain U.S.A.* (Washington, DC: Christic Institute, 1988), p. 8.

THREE

The Right Place
at the Right Time

"The observer of nature sees, with admiration, that the world is full of the glory of God." CARL LINNAEUS, TOUR OF LAPLAND, 1732.

Spirits of place, healing waters, enchanted valleys, talking stones, homes of the "tribal chiefs" of the plants and crystals, continuing relationships with the dead, fertility enhancers, and portals to the gods: the living landscape in the Earth wisdom of traditional American Indian culture is a rich tapestry of powers, intelligence, and awe. Preserving this wealth of cultural heritage has not been easy, considering the trail of broken treaties, massacres, relocations, thefts of Indian children, and the establishment of Indian schools where traditional language and the transmission of cultural values and knowledge were forbidden. As humanity rushes into an age of ever-increasing technological sophistication, and at the same time becomes more aware that technology unconnected to nature's laws is suicidal, it becomes apparent that traditional wisdom holds keys to restoring sanity and balance in our lives. Sadly, in some cases, we cannot turn to Indians for guidance, for they have been swept away like tumbleweed in a dust storm. Of this predicament, award-winning poet Gary Snyder writes:

> I live on land in the Sierra Nevada of Alta, California, continent of Turtle Island, which is sometimes wild and not terribly good. The indigenous people there, the Nisenan or Southern Maidu, were almost entirely displaced or destroyed during the first decade of the Gold Rush. Consequently we have no one to teach us which parts of the landscape were once thought to be sacred, but with time and attention, I think we will be able to identify such sites again. Wild land, sacred land, good land.[1]

Carl Jung once wrote that people cannot conquer a new land until they have made peace with its spirits and their minds have sunk to the level of its indigenous inhabitants. The Indian cosmology skimmed through in chapter 2 represents over 10,000 years of intimate association with nature. Even if they wanted to, no more than a handful of people could return to living like the Indians did a hundred years ago. There are new cultures, new languages, and new technologies, as well as new land-use patterns. What is needed is a new legitimate paradigm to "mind the Earth," as Joseph Meeker calls human-nature harmony. New words and concepts must be conceived and integrated into a new Earth language which can articulate a consciousness rooted in an honest experiencing of place.

With or without Indian guides, there are certain places which draw us to them, and we need to pay attention to these feelings. For some people, a mountain is enchanting because of the steepness of its slopes, or the lure of a river arises from the difficulty of navigating its churning rapids. Challenges are good for motivation, but if that is the only reason for venturing to wild places, then why not try climbing the Empire State Building? Its slopes are less crowded than Yosemite's these days. The pull of sacred places is something more than just the challenge of performing a physical feat.

There are many different breeds of people who love nature. Some find their greatest pleasure in hunting or fishing. Others enjoy sailing or canoeing. For some, the world of nature is an ever-changing mixture of new species to see and understand. Still others wish only to surrender to the silence and engage in a mystical blissful rapport with flowers, bird songs, and billowing clouds. Many, many people of all persuasions feel the power of places but are afraid to admit it. Peter Matthiessen tells of a visit to the "High Country" of the Lower Klamath River—the sacred lands of the Yurok, Tolowa, Hoopa, and Karok tribes. He and two companions came upon a certain place which took away their breath with its ambiance. After a few uneasy minutes of sitting there in the silence, finally one man could no longer remain quiet:

> John Trull frowned and cleared his throat, "You're very close to heaven up here," he muttered. He glared at us, as if daring us to laugh, then he spoke about a time up in the mountains, when he had found himself suddenly in a beautiful, strange place where he had never been before and yet which seemed somehow familiar, as if remembered from another life. He had walked along as if entranced, weeping and laughing simultaneously, as if on the point of remembering something that would bring him instantly forever a profound understanding of the world, of life and death. Now, bewildered and uncomfortable, he stopped speaking, and for a little while we sat in silence on the mountainside.
>
> But I had been to this place, too, and so had Dick. We were silent, not because we were embarrassed, as John thought, but because we were awed by John's precise description.[2]

In the late 1970s a nationwide Gallup poll of 1,533 adults found that one-third of those interviewed said they had had a religious experience of some type, such as "other-worldly feelings of union with a divine being."[3] The experiences reported by Peter Matthiessen and his friends, as well as those documented by the Gallup poll, are called transcendental or mystical experiences. According to William James, who pioneered the modern psychological study of the sacred, mystical experiences begin with a sense of ego surrender to a higher force, and then unfold for usually no more than one-half hour.[4] During this magical period, according to Walter Stace, seven common qualities of feeling tend to occur: (1) a sense of unity or a feeling of identity with all things; (2) a sensation of timelessness and spacelessness; (3) a sense of being in touch with some sort of objectivity or ultimate reality; (4) a feeling of blessedness or joy; (5) a sense of the divine presence or sacredness; (6) a feeling that the experience is unutterable or not capable of being related in words; and (7) a sense of paradox or understanding the polarity of opposites at the same time, like the "teeming desert," the "dark lightness," or the "chilling heat."[5]

While doing research for *The Ultimate Athlete*, his popular book on expression of the human potential through sports, author George Leonard went on

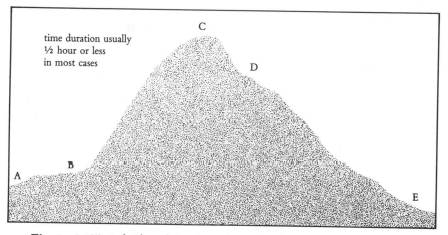

time duration usually
½ hour or less
in most cases

Figure 3. *Typical Chronology of a Transcendental Experience.*

A = Emotional arousal and a sense of being guided by a higher force.

B = Encounter with a trigger in the environment which causes ego destabilization and begins a rapid shift in the state of consciousness, leading to a peak experience.

C = A peak experience, with feelings of energy, bliss, wonder, joy, awe, and love; intense excitement and relaxation at the same time.

D = Manifestations of power such as visions, prophecies, interspecies communications, the hearing of music, etc.

E = A return to normal reality, feeling inspired and deeply touched; a beginning of integrating the experience.

a lecture tour. Every place he went, he would read off a list of qualities of mystical experiences like Stace's, and ask the audience how many of them had ever had such experiences. Commonly he would find that 10 to 30 percent of the audience had had at least one such experience. Many people also said that in raising their hands, they were sharing this in public for the first time. In Eugene, Oregon, Leonard appeared as part of a 1974 symposium on sports and consciousness, "Exploring the Human Potential Through Physical Activity: Body, Mind and Spirit," which I organized with marathon runner Mike Spino. Addressing a capacity crowd of some 500 people, Leonard asked the audience of marathon runners, mountaineers, white water enthusiasts, and hippies how many had ever had such an experience. Over three-quarters of them raised their hands. Most said they had talked about their experiences before, but not outside their immediate community of friends.

"The greatest religious leaders of the West all had mystical experiences on mountains," reports Marghanita Laski in her classical study of transcendence, *Ecstasy: A Study of Some Secular and Religious Experiences.*[6] Down through the ages, the historical record reports that visions and mystical reveries are the realm of saints, Indians, yogis, lovers, poets, and madmen. In most psychology and psychiatry textbooks, the feelings of spiritual wonder that Walter Stace describes, along with seeing visions, hearing voices, and feeling rushes of "extra energy," are considered symptoms of acute schizophrenic episodes. The definition of "normality" implied here is one of the reasons why people are reluctant to talk about their moments of ecstasy. No one who is sane wants to be regarded as insane, and few sane people would claim sainthood in their own lifetime. Hence we live with a taboo on the open discussion of transcendental experience, unless we are willing to be considered "abnormal," which for some is the equivalent of being declared mentally ill.

Since the late 1960s, the barriers to open discussion and study of mystical experiences have dissipated, thanks to the consciousness revolution started by the hippies and related tribes. The data which have accumulated since then show that many people can and do have transcendental experiences, with the critical factors for their occurrence including the people's mental state and their environmental setting.

It can now be said with some certainty that these extraordinary experiences follow a pattern. They begin with an emotional arousal, then build with a loosening of ego boundaries. When the experience is not induced by an ingested psychoactive like LSD, some type of environmental condition becomes a "trigger" for sending the participants into the overdrive of ecstasy. Mystics and saints undergo long ordeals of prayer and fasting, usually in isolation, to achieve communion with God or holy persons such as Jesus, Mohammed, Buddha, or the

Virgin Mary. Shamans journey through the three worlds in spirit flight stimulated by drumming, dancing, singing and/or ingesting peyote, magic mushrooms, or some other hallucinogen. In insanity, whether during a brief psychotic episodes or life-long bouts with schizophrenia, troubled people also report rapture, conversations with divine beings, and feelings of extra energy. A major difference between people who are mentally disturbed and those who are spiritually adept appears to be the ability of the latter to gain mastery over a transcendent state of consciousness without losing touch with reality.

Statistically, saints, shamans, and schizophrenics represent a small portion of the total population. Research now shows, however, that the rest of us can also have mystical experiences, and that in fact many of us do.

One of the most important breakthroughs in our understanding of the psychology of transcendence comes from Abraham Maslow's investigations of the lives of people who achieve more of their personal potential than normal, who he called "self-actualizers." Reviewing the biographies of the Lincolns, Gandhis, Martin Luther Kings, Margaret Meads, and Benjamin Franklins of the world, Maslow found that as these people tapped more and more of their personal potential, "peak experiences" of transcendence became increasingly commonplace. Extreme psychological health and mystical experiences go together, Maslow concluded.[7]

People tend to associate the "new mysticism" with the increased use of psychedelic drugs popularized by the "flower children," and clearly a lot of people have "tuned in" and "turned on" this way. But in reviewing the lives of hundreds of world-class athletes, Michael Murphy and Rhea White found that a common quality of peak athletic performance was a state in which things seemed to slow down, life took on a magical surreal quality, deep feelings mixed with awe and merged into a state of grace, and extraordinary mental and physical powers occurred.[8] World-class distance runner Ken Foreman talked about losing himself in a strange fluid oneness with nature when he ran a record-breaking distance race. Former all-pro San Francisco 49ers quarterback John Brodie talked about how he would sometimes slip into an unusual state of mental clarity at the height of peak performance in a big game. One woman parachutist described how she "talked with angels" during a freefall descent through a thunderstorm. Once athletes started talking about unusual things that happened to them at the height of competition, mystical experiences became very commonplace.

Additional support for the thesis that transcendence is much more common than we might suppose comes from the work of psychiatrist Stanislav Grof. Grof began research on altered states of consciousness with studies of the therapeutic uses of LSD in Europe and then the United States in the 1960s, recording the nature of the experiences which his subjects reported during psychedelic sessions.

What he found was a rich diversity of experiences which bore resemblance to those reported by mystics and shamans from other cultures. Because of governmental restrictions on psychedelics, however, he began experimenting with other mind-altering techniques, especially hyperventilation accompanied by evocative music, which he terms "holotropic therapy."[9] To his surprise, he found he could obtain the same results in the proper settings from breathing as he could from LSD. Additional studies have found that transcendental states can be brought on by a wide variety of techniques and experiences including sleep deprivation, fasting, repetitive prayer, ritual, sensory deprivation, dancing, drumming, singing, intense athletic activity, sexual love, near-death experiences, yoga and martial arts, and meditation, as well as various psychotic states.

The works of Grof, Ralph Metzner, Charles Tart, and others suggest that modern people have the capacity for the same kinds of experiences which have deeply inspired people of all faiths and creeds down through the ages. But in contrast to our ancestors, modern people don't have a cultural context in which to see transcendence as normal or desirable. The bulk of today's knowledge about altered states of awareness comes from research in laboratory settings or from therapy sessions. Historically, in contrast, spiritual excursions into other realms have resulted primarily from either rituals at sacred shrines or from isolation in wilderness settings. In these historical cases, the physical places which have triggered the experiences have been of far more importance than for the vast majority of inner-space travelers studied today. Thus, the relationship between sacred places in nature and transcendental experiencing is not at all understood in modern psychology, in striking contrast to the understanding of this relationship in other cultures and earlier times. The effect of this modern void was pointed out to me at a hearing to save a sacred mountain, when an irate developer asked the perfect koan. He said, "If getting high is so important, can you you prove to me that there is any difference between dropping acid in a penthouse apartment while watching a slide show of beautiful art or nature photos and listening to music, and being on the slopes of this mountain? Can't you do it better in the city than where I want to build my ski resort?"

THE SACRED PLACE AS A TRIGGER

An altered state of consciousness, or ASC, is defined by Charles Tart as "a qualitative alteration in the overall pattern of mental functioning, such that the experiencer feels his consciousness is radically different from the way it functions ordinarily."[10]

Shifting mental gears is the result of an interplay between a person and the surrounding environment. If one drinks a glass of wine or two at a candlelit dinner with a lover, talk and feelings seem to flow more easily. However, if one lives at sea level, then hops on an airplane and flies to a mountainous area with an elevation a mile or more high, like Denver, the same pleasant drinking can lead to dizziness and vomiting due to the altitude. In either elevation, if one continues drinking, speech begins to be slurred and coordination declines, until one drops over in a coma.

For the Tarajumara Indians of the rugged mountains of central Mexico, distance running is a necessity. In the process of traveling to other villages and working in the fields of corn and beans, it is normal for them to put in ten to twenty miles a day on foot. At certain times of the year the Tarajumaras hold a special festival called a *rarapira*. The celebrations begin with people drinking large quantities of corn liquor for several days. Then, just when most people would be under the table, the Tarajumaras assemble into teams to race cross-country ten to fifty miles nonstop. To spice up the contest, they run barefoot, kicking between them a wooden ball made from the root of a sacred tree.

In the American Southwest, similar distance running is also a tradition for the Hopi and other Pueblo tribes. As with the Tarajumaras, the races are run as part of rituals, with the boundaries of the courses being associated with sacred places and the passage of the sun in the sky. For the marathons of both cultures, the mindset of the participants is an ecstatic one, with the ritual and the culture from which it arises contributing to the performance. This is why modern distance runners fare poorly when attempting the *rarapira* and why Tarajumaras are not the world's reigning Olympic champions. Modern people run against the clock with the setting being of little importance. The Indians run with the spirit, inspired by beliefs rooted in the natural world which surrounds them, rather than against linear time.

After reviewing data on hundreds of accounts of mystical states experienced by people in ancient and modern times, Marghanita Laski concludes, "Ecstasy almost always takes place after contact with something regarded as beautiful or valuable or both."[11] Typical triggers for transcendence include stately groves of trees, carpets of beautiful flowers, strong aromas, sunsets and sunrises, water of all kinds, and clouds.

Most of us certainly don't fall into a swoon every time a beautiful landscape appears, but contact with nature's primal vitality stirs deep waters inside us. While living in cement, steel, glass, and plastic cities, we buy nature books, hang photos of animals and sunsets on our walls, keep goldfish in tanks, and care for houseplants to keep alive at least a glimmer of the fire of the spirit that wilderness can kindle into full force.

According to traditional culture wisdom, sacred places in nature are unique because they have a power which can more readily move us into spiritual consciousness. We can quickly grasp how picturesque places like Mount Fuji, Mount

Kilimanjaro, Mount McKinley (Denali), and Niagara Falls can trigger ecstasies. They are profoundly beautiful. There is more to the sacredness of place than meets the eyes, however, in traditional consciousness.

Over a period of seven years, Jake Page and his wife, Susanne, became *ikwat-si*, or "close friends," with the Hopi Indians. One reward for this trust was being allowed to journey with elders to all eight of the principle sacred places of the Hopi which ring their pueblos. The pilgrimage covered 1,100 miles, and the Pages report, "The sacred sites themselves are unnoticeable, merely locations near rocks or bushes where generations of Hopi have made offerings."[12] One was a ledge in the Grand Canyon. Another was in a marsh. Still others were located in canyons, and on mountains and hills, many of which do not even have names on regular maps.

The Pages report that only a handful of Hopi are alive who know all of these places. Like their brothers and sisters around the world who still feel and sense the power of place, these wise minds say that the power of sacred places lies in more than visible beauty. They acknowledge that history is important, but of much greater importance, they insist, is spirit. This spirit can work with people of all races, but only if one's mind is clear and one's heart is pure.

The wisdom of the elders stimulates a hypothesis: that certain special places in nature have the capacity to facilitate people entering altered states of awareness which are called "spiritual" as a result of direct mental and/or physical contact with them. This is a hypothesis which would be nice to accept without questioning, but in all cultures where shamanism is the core religious system, the shaman has two faces. One face speaks the truth, and the other is a trickster —the clever coyote, the wily rabbit, or the sharp-witted hare—who never says anything in a straightforward manner. Spiritual lying, one of the primary tools of the trickster, is used when one cannot grasp the truth of a situation directly. Recognition can only occur when one is tricked in stumbling onto the truth or into achieving the proper state of consciousness to perceive the situation at hand with true clarity.

When visiting the Huichol Indians of Mexico, many people report feeling confused and frustrated if they meet several members of the tribe together. It seems as though assembled Huichol engage in a rapid, babbling conversation in which several people talk at the same time about almost anything. To the rational mind, this kind of behavior is maddening. So, after trying to keep up with them, the visitor's mind becomes totally scrambled, and, in frustration, they simply have to let go. In that moment, as the pilgrim's ego consciousness loosens, the Huichol suddenly change their conversational pattern, sensing that the visitor has now shifted to non-rational perception—the domain where they live—and harmony in the mind-field of the group has been established.

The Huichol coyote conversations serve the purpose of cognitive destabilization, one of the prerequisites of attaining intuitive consciousness. For similar purposes, Eskimos always apologize profusely when they come together; Samoans and Hawaiians weave long stories about magical places into everyday chatter; and Yanomamo Indians of the Brazilian rainforest shout at each other upon meeting. The process also facilitates telepathy, which is a primary perceptual mode of traditional cultures where tribal consciousness is fundamental to daily existence.

Understanding the spiritual con-artist/trickster role in traditional societies helps one appreciate their behavior, but one can't just blindly accept whatever these tricksters have to say. To know the truth, one must learn to sense it intuitively—know it in your bones.

Another approach to the search for truth calls for the use of an objective system based on external measurements—science—but it is not always easy to apply external yardsticks to the study of human consciousness. Conducting research on transpersonal states with psychedelic chemicals typically involves administering specific doses under safe environmental conditions, and then recording what the subjects report. These studies show that when subjects are given enough LSD or mescaline, they almost always report unusual things happening. Exactly what happens is not predictable, although the use of ritual forms increases the chances for certain specific experiences to occur. Under the right conditions, it is relatively easy to move people into altered states using chemicals, hyperventilation, hypnosis, or various emotional-release techniques used in some New Age psychology seminars. A problem with these methods is that, although people's consciousness can be shifted into unusual states through such manipulations, these states may not be in the best interest of the people having them, especially for those who come from a culture which is emotionally and spiritually suppressed and has no context to understand or accept transpersonal states and the potential psycho-emotional turmoil they may stir up.[13] In the final analysis, improved perception of reality should be the goal of consciousness exploration. Ecstatic states by themselves are seductive, but filled with dead ends, pits, quagmires, and dangerous places for the unprepared spiritual seeker. In terms of overall personal growth, the question "what did you learn?" is far more important than "what did you feel?"

When studying place as a factor in transpersonal experiencing, controlling the design of the study is very difficult, especially when no chemicals are taken prior to the encounter with the sacred site and no ritual process is involved in the pilgrimage. Results seem to manifest best when the visitor blends into the totality of the experience at the right time for them, but predicting the timing of this with certainty is in the domain of the skilled shaman, with a good deal of luck thrown in. Approaching Mecca, Muslim seekers are counseled to prepare themselves carefully, for the wisdom of the ages says that a pilgrimage may make a good person better, and it may also make a bad person better or worse.[14]

Using a controlled experimental design, probably the most reliable way to study how a place affects someone would be to hook the person up to various sensitive and sophisticated electrical instruments, like an electroencephalogram, and then expose them to the place and see what changes occur. In a later chapter, the existing state of the art of studying subtle scientific fields and how they influence people will be described in more detail.

Another approach to studying how people react to certain environmental conditions is to gather personal accounts of what occurs at a certain place after they have been there, which in psychology is called "phenomenology." Since the early 1970s, I have been gathering data on the phenomenology of personal experiences associated with certain places, which nearly twenty years later has resulted in the accumulation of several hundred accounts gathered first-hand, as well as others gleaned from the literature.

I began this process at the University of Oregon, where I was then teaching, by asking students in my classes about unusual experiences they had had. At first my questions were met by silence. I later discovered that this was because they were afraid I was an undercover agent checking for drug users. But, in time, they began to open up, moving me to continue and expand my search. The case histories included in this chapter have come from several primary sources: clients I have seen as a spiritual therapist; people who have responded in person to me at lectures, in workshops, or through media appearances; and those who have shared their experiences with me in writing as a result of articles I have published in magazines or media appearances I have made.[15] In analyzing the data, I have created categories with the hope of developing a taxonomy of potentiality of human experiences arising from visiting sacred places. Significantly, none of the experiences reported here involved either the ingestion of psychoactive chemicals or the purposeful conduction of rituals with the intent to have sacred experiences. Instead, the common element in all cases was a feeling of being drawn to a certain place by a pull which seemed to arise from a source beyond normal rational consciousness. Then, upon reaching the destination, an experience unfolded which was out of the ordinary in terms of inner experience. For many people there was also a simultaneous environmental happening of an unusual nature. If being at the right place at the right time is the mark of correctness of action, as many mystical schools teach, then all the following experiences seemed to arise more from this format than from anything else.

Photo 17. *In the hills above Point Conception, California, there are many caves where the Chumash once sought visions, sometimes using Jimson Weed (Datura stramonicum) to aid in the vision seeking. Author photo.*

VARIETIES OF SACRED EXPERIENCES ASSOCIATED WITH SACRED PLACES

1. Ecstasies

Back in 1954 I spent a day driving through the Black Hills [of South Dakota]. I remember writing in my journal that being in the Black Hills was like being recollected at a deep and high level of prayer and contemplation. Each leaf and blade of grass seemed to shine with a light not only of this world. It was a spiritually invigorating experience. I did not then know it was a place of power.   (Rhea White, personal correspondence)

An ecstasy, according to Laski, is a personal experience of great intensity which involves an inward turning stimulated by contact with some environmental condition which seems to trigger the onset of transcendence.[16] Laski describes three types of ecstasies, and the above quotation by writer Rhea White is a classic example of a "union ecstasy." Typically, such moments of ecstasy involve deep feelings emerging from the unconscious followed by insights which reveal new levels of meaning and higher truths. As the ecstatic experience runs its course, the world around seems to take on a new freshness and clarity as all the senses perceive new, more refined levels of beauty and truth.

Carl Jung reported a memorable union ecstasy he experienced while standing on the slopes of Mount Kilimanjaro in Africa:

Standing on a hill in the East Africa plains, I saw herds of thousands of wild beasts, grazing in soundless peace, beneath the primeval world, as they had done for unimaginable ages of time. And I had the feeling of being the first man, the first being to know all this is. The whole world around me was still in the primitive silence and knew not that it was. In this very moment in which I knew it, the world came into existence, and without this moment it would never have been.[17]

When such experiences occur, they tend to change one's life, often providing new clarity on life's meaning and increased love for nature. As a freshman in college, William Stapp went on a biology-class field trip to explore some rich tide pools along the California coast. He had lived near the sea most of his life, but somehow had never taken the time to really explore the ocean ecosystem closely. As he peered into a shallow pool, a myriad of tiny creatures of all sizes, shapes, and colors seemed to work a spell on him. A sense of deep appreciation for living things came over him, and in this moment of wonder, the realization that everything is connected to everything else popped into his mind. He was so overcome with the rapture of being in that place that he almost drowned with the incoming tide. Within a year afterwards he had changed his major to biology and switched colleges. He has since gone on to become one of the leading figures in environmental education in the world today, founding UNESCO's environmental education program.

A second type of ecstasy, the "adamic ecstasy," involves plunging into negative emotions like fear, guilt, and depression and then bottoming out in a moment of pure ecstatic clarity of joy and realization of truth. An undergraduate student in one of my classes at Western Washington State University in Bellingham, Washington, several years ago failed his law school admission test. When the results came back, he was despondent and went on a binge of drinking and smoking marijuana. After a couple of days he saw that this was self-defeating, and so he stopped. He felt himself drawn toward nearby Mount Baker, a snow-capped volcanic cone 10,778 feet in elevation that is sacred to the Lummi Indians. He drove to the mountain and walked out to the edge of giant glacier. Standing beside the slow-moving ice wall, his spirits were very low. Somehow the ambiance of the glacier spoke to him, reminding him of how slowly time passes and the power of persistence. A nearby tree stump caught his attention. It was old and dead, and he said that it made him think of himself, which made him start to cry. Then a strange thing happened. He looked at the stump again, and it seemed to have a face on it, at least in his mind's eye. Wood carving had always been a pleasant hobby for him, and he found himself wondering if he could carve on something as large as that stump, reproducing the face he saw on it. He came back down off the mountain, went to the ocean beach and collected a van full of driftwood and began carving. He has since become a skilled wood carver, specializing in creating warm, friendly elfish faces on old pieces of wood.[18]

The third variety of ecstasy is the "knowledge ecstasy," in which a person has a deep and profound insight into the nature of truth and reality that is not personal, such as the "aha!" of the scientist realizing a new principle after a considerable period of difficult searching. Michael Cohen, founder of the National Audubon Society Expedition Institute, tells of a time when he was at the bottom of the Grand Canyon. The surrounding red walls seemed to reach out and stir him as he sat at the bottom of this very sacred ancient portal into the Earth. He began to think about his relationship with the planet. He had read many books about ecology and about how people should feel about nature, but somehow there had always been a split between his intellect and his experience: the words were someone else's, not his own original thoughts. As the power of the place entrained his mind, the concept of homeostasis—the self-regulating property of all living things—popped into his consciousness. In that moment he felt a mental doorway open, and the theory of Earth being a living organism came into his mind with a surge of power and certainty. A year and a half later, he sponsored the world's first scientific symposium to consider the Gaia Hypothesis—the idea that the Earth itself is a living organism.

2. Visions of Mythical Beings

"The first function of a mythology is to reconcile waking consciousness to the 'mysterium tremendum et fascinatus' of this universe as it is; the second is to render an interpretive total image of the same, as known to contemporary consciousness," Joseph Campbell observed.[19] At the root of a mythology are the numinous symbols which come to our minds in such twilight zones of consciousness as dreams, reveries, and visions. Since the earliest times, sacred places in nature have been generative sources for many of the world's greatest religions and mythologies, as when Moses saw the burning bush at Mount Sinai, or when visions of the Virgin Mary were seen at Our Lady of Fatima and Our Lady of Guadalupe, or when White Buffalo Calf Woman appeared among the American Indians.

Among many shamanic cultures, people seek visions through planned rituals, like the Plains Indians at Bear Butte. There are also a growing number of non-Indians leading successful vision quest experiences.[20] In addition, many people experience visions without any ritual preparations. One college-age man reported to me that he felt drawn one day to a quiet wooded area along the Huron River in Michigan. He sat down against a tree, noticing that things had taken on a special clarity. Then, like a wind, a rush of energy filled him. In that moment, the ground in front of him appeared to open up, he said, and suddenly it seemed like he was living in a fantasy movie of extraordinary clarity. From the doorway in the ground emerged a giant woodchuck. The man was scared stiff, but he could not move. After a short time, the scene evaporated. He reported that he had experimented with marijuana, but not immediately before this occurrence. If anything had been a trigger for the experience, he speculated, it had been reading one of Carlos Castaneda's books on sorcery shortly before going out into the woods.

A similar experience was reported by Sig Longren, an officer of the American Dowsers Society. He was with a group of people on a field trip studying some of the stone monuments in New England, which some people feel were erected by early Norsemen or Druidic explorers long before Columbus. It was Summer Solstice, and everyone was scurrying around taking measurements of shadows with the rising sun. Despite his interest in this research, he felt compelled to go into one of the stone chambers and sit down quietly. A peaceful, energizing ambiance seemed to fill the stone-walled room. Then, as if they had been beamed down in a Star Trek movie, a group of twenty some people materialized around him. Many were bearded and wore long white robes. They assumed positions all around the room. Longren then saw that a woman was lying in a grave in the middle of the floor. The people proceeded to conduct a ceremony, and then they all faded away. Longren reports that it felt like he was being given some kind of initiation.[21]

Another somewhat similar experience befell psychologist Alberto Villoldo when he and six friends visited an ancient Inca initiation cave high in the Andes Mountains of South America. Entering the cave, their guide, a Peruvian healer named Fausto Valle, told them to extinguish their candles and stand quietly in the silent blackness. In a few moments, Villoldo reported, he felt "an intense warmth in my belly, radiating into my chest, followed by a trembling in my arms." As this state occurred, the ceiling around him disappeared, and a sky filled with twinkling stars came into view. Before him he saw an altar, and standing beside it was a bearded, white-robed man, eight or nine feet tall, radiating streams of light. The man vacillated between being a ball of light and a human form, and a great sense of peace filled Villoldo. The man spoke and said, "Welcome my sons; welcome to the land of your ancestry. We are the children of the Sun. We are your ancestors. . . ."[22] The speech went on for several minutes, and then the image vanished. Of the seven people present in Villoldo's group, four later reported seeing and hearing a "luminous being." The other three did not see or hear anything, but reported feeling a deep sense of reverence and awe in the sacred cave.

If only one person had reported something unusual, this account might have been dismissed as fantasy. But since four people independently reported a similar vision, the chances of this having been a common fantasy with no relationship to any external event seems very remote. The ability to see with the mind's eye varies from person to person, and may account for individual differences in perception. Placed in the same environmental setting, people may variously feel things, hear voices, hear music, sense presences, find their minds filled with creative reveries, or see visions. The fact that all seven people in Villoldo's group experienced something unusual, even if their perceptions were not all the same, speaks for the power of that cave.

3. Unification with an Aspect of Nature

If one sees an animal, plant, stone, or some other aspect of nature change into human form in a dream or vision, then that transforming piece of nature is an object of great power, says medicine man Wallace Black Elk. As if honoring this belief, Hawaiian *kahunas* (shamans), when they want to judge the truth, recite long poetic divining verses. These chants typically begin by invoking the spiritual powers, followed by a string of truisms about nature and life, and ending with a statement of which they want to test the truthfulness. An example of such a closing might be "the sky is blue, the ocean has waves, the clouds are white, the palms are swaying in the breeze, and Auntie Jennie took my book." If, after striking harmonic notes of natural and mythic truth in the first phrase, the final phrase does not feel right, then the final phrase is suspected to be false, for it breaks the harmonics of the mood set by the litany. Using a similar pattern of harmonics, shamans all around the world make things happen through the power of songs and chants.

Shamans feel that the potency of incantations arises from the origins of their words. That is, if someone utters the name ''Jesus'' in a prayer, it will have more power if that person has previously experienced Jesus, as in a dream or vision. In a similar fashion, when Huichol Indians chant, ''We are one with the infinite sun, forever, and ever and ever,'' this has considerable meaning and power to them, for they often say they see the sun and merge with it while eating peyote, especially that which comes from the sacred plateau of Wirikuta.

A number of people interviewed described automatic unions they experienced with parts of nature while visiting sacred places. Having gone to a sacred waterfall on Oahu, a young man felt sleepy and lay down in the shade to rest. Suddenly he felt as if he were leaving his body. He surrendered to the pull and found himself drawn up into space until he merged with the sun. During this brief moment of union, he felt oneness with the fiery sun and experienced heat, warmth, and peace.

While traveling in England, another man reported feeling drawn to Stonehenge. Giving in to his intuition, he went there. He was captivated by the place and, after wandering around, finally decided to sit still and relax. While lying on the ground, he felt a wave of energy come up from the ground and fill his body. When it seemed as though a oneness had been achieved, he experienced an emotion of ''deep and profound love,'' as if the place loved him.

An even more startling experience was reported by a college professor who went camping on the Olympic Peninsula in Washington State for some relaxation. His campsite was near an old Indian village, and he spent an entire day poking around for artifacts. That night he had dreams of Indians and artifacts. The next day, when he got up, he felt magnetically drawn toward a point of land jutting out into the ocean. Arriving there, he felt a rush of energy like an invisible tornado pulling him upward. He began shaking and shivering, and then felt a lightning bolt of energy shoot through him. At that precise moment, it began to snow. I later shared this incident with Rolling Thunder, who simply said that this person had a calling to become a rainmaker and that this was the Great Spirit's way of letting him know it.

These unification experiences sound a good deal like the shamanic journeys for power objects which anthropologist Michael Harner leads. In Harner's seminars, which use a background of drumming or chanting, people see themselves traveling down long tubes into one of the three worlds, where they search for power animals. When they find one, they take it with them. Upon returning to everyday reality, they dance as if they are the power animal to integrate it into their minds and bodies. The result is an increased sense of personal power and health.[23]

4. Vivid Dreams

"The dream is a little hidden door in the innermost and most secret recesses of the soul, opening into that cosmic night which was psyche long before there was any ego-consciousness, and which will remain psyche no matter how far our ego-consciousness extends," Carl Jung once wrote.[24] According to medicine man Rolling Thunder, there are two kinds of dreams. "Dreams of the body" concern personal matters like health, repressed emotions, relationships, and situations. They are the kinds of dreams which Freud liked to analyze. "Dreams of the spirit," Rolling Thunder believes, are vivid and mythical, and arise in the spirit world, where all things begin. My dreams of the snow goose people and of finding the location for the first Medicine Wheel Gathering fall within this latter category.

In ancient Greece, temples were built at special places as dream incubation chambers. No doubt some of the caves of the Chumash and those along the Columbia River gorge in Washington have a similar potency. According to Jaime T. Licauco, Mount Banahaw in the Philippines has a number of dreaming caves which are heavily used today, nurturing powerful dreams among their users. The local shamans say of these dreams, "When the mountain calls you, you cannot refuse."[25]

The dream world is extremely creative. It is clear that one can do certain things to stir up the unconscious to increase dreaming, such as being in psychotherapy or getting acupuncture treatments. My personal experience has been that each type of therapeutic style stimulates different dreams. The dreams of Freudian analysis are often complex, containing many elements and considerable sexual symbolism. When in Gestalt Therapy, people seem to have dreams about "unfinished business" concerning emotional relationships and neurotic patterns of avoidance. The dreams of people in somatic therapies like Rolfing or Reichian vegetotherapy are often vivid and have obvious meanings. While each of these therapies seems to be able to encourage a certain style of dreaming, however, the content of these dreams still cannot be predicted by the therapy mode. In contrast, there is evidence that people visiting certain geographical places without prior expectations not only have lucid dreams, but often have dreams which contain consistently similar symbols. These symbols are not suggested by any obvious imagery at the places. This would suggest that these places not only have the ability to ease people's access to the dreamtime, but that they actually play an active role in forming the content of the dreams.

One such place which seems to have such a power of triggering dreams is Indian Hot Springs in West Texas. While doing research on the life of folk healer Jewell Babb, who once ran the resort at the springs, Pat Ellis Taylor found that many people not only had vivid dreams while using the springs, but that their dreams characteristically contained tall, dark-skinned, nearly naked Indians and bands of wild horses. Mrs. Babb said that on many occasions the dreams were "as real as life" and that people would wake up in the middle of night feeling like they were being attacked by the Indians.[26]

In another area of Texas near the town of Alpine, a woman reported that, upon arriving in town, she felt drawn to a certain place called Ranger Canyon. She went along with her feelings, and discovered that the canyon was a beautiful place to walk. Then, one night after exploring the canyon, she had a dream. It was dark and the wind was howling. She was in the canyon in a cabin. Suddenly the door opened and a shining silver wolf was standing there. She woke up frightened. Several days later, she started reading a book on the folklore of the area. A chill went down her spine when she discovered that Indian legends said the canyon was the home of a silver spirit wolf.

Sometimes it seems like the spirits of places in dreams want to lend us a hand in dreams. While doing research on goddesses, psychologist Elinor Gadon of Harvard University visited New Mexico near Santa Clara pueblo. Exploring the nearby mountains, she came upon a cave which contained a number of vivid pictographs. She studied them seriously for some time, trying to decipher their meaning, but without much success. That night she had a vivid dream in which an Indian princess came and told her what the symbols meant.

5. Interspecies Communication

"In the beginning God . . . did not speak directly to man," Pawnee chief Letakots-Lesa told Natalie Curtis, "but sent certain animals to tell man that he showed himself through the beasts, and that from them, and from the stars and the sun and the moon, man should learn."[27]

Traditional wise people say that if you want to know the truth you should go talk to the animals, for they are the cleanest source of knowledge. Indians say that among the tribes of the four-leggeds and flying ones (the animals who walk and fly), those who live at special places are especially good sources of wisdom. This wisdom is not just the knowledge of the animals, but of the Creator. When an animal acts in the role of agent for the Creator, one feels an extra energy, and senses that something important is taking place. It may seem as if the animal is communicating a message through its behavior, or even telepathically.

In American Samoa there is a special black volcanic rock along the ocean shore in the village of Vaitongi on the island of Tutuila: Shark and Turtle Rock. This rock is situated near blow holes where, at high tide, the pounding surf sends billows of salt water high into the air like a whale spouting. According to ancient Samoan legend, if the children of the village come together and sing a special chant at this stone, a shark and a sea turtle will emerge from the blue tropical ocean just offshore, swimming together in a circle for several minutes as an affirmation of kinship. The shark and the turtle supposedly are two women who once jumped into the sea during a famine, sacrificing themselves so the children could have their portions of food.

I visited this rock one day when there were no children in sight, so I had no hopes of seeing the myth come to life. To show respect for this sacred site, I made an offering of food, said a prayer, and sang a sacred song. No sooner had I finished when, just offshore, a giant whale breeched! Speechless, I stood there watching, and for the next five minutes the whale frolicked on the surface, then slipped under water and disappeared.

One of the most moving accounts of interspecies communication is told by conservationist Bert Schwarzschild of Berkeley, California. On a trip to Europe, Schwarzschild visited Mount Subasio in Italy, where Saint Francis preached his famous sermon to the birds. Pope John XXIII is said to have once described this holy place as, "this enchantment of nature, this artistic splendor, this charm of holiness which appears in the air."

As he began to ascend the slopes of the mountain, Schwarzschild was shocked when he heard shotguns blasting away nearby. He walked along the trail and found the ground littered with red and blue shotgun casings left by songbird hunters. In Italy, many songbirds are fair game. He reached the summit and felt great remorse as he spread out his sleeping bag to spend the night on top of the mountain. Although he was cold, tired, and depressed, he could not sleep. The presence of the mountain seemed so strong. Lying there in his sleeping bag, he heard a faint rustling in a nearby bush. Then there were fluttering sounds followed by the beautiful melody of a bird's song. In the darkness he could not see the bird, but he judged it to be about fifteen to twenty-five feet away, and by the song it could only have been a nightingale.

Schwarzschild then relates that "it was the first bird I had heard on the mountain all day, and it seemed to be asking for help, almost as a spokesperson for the birds of Assisi. Then, the bird flew away, and in that moment, I was deeply touched and knew that I should do something to help bring the birds back to Saint Francis' mountain."[28]

Moved so deeply by this encounter, Schwarzschild came down off the mountain and began talking to people about saving the birds of Assisi. He persisted, and ultimately spearheaded an international campaign which resulted in the establishment of a regional nature preserve at Mount Subasio, where no hunting is allowed. Inspired by this success, he has continued to champion nature preservation and education in the spirit of Saint Francis by founding an international conservation organization: the Assisi Nature Council.

A woman psychotherapist told me how a long bout with depression had moved her to go camping alone to work through her heaviness. She felt drawn to a certain Oregon forest campground, which was otherwise unoccupied. No sooner had she stopped her car and gotten out to look around than a blue jay flew down, as if to greet her. She did not feel very comfortable being alone in this place, but the bird skipped up to her, made contact, and then began hopping down a trail. The bird did this several times until finally the woman came to the realization that the bird wanted her to follow it. She did, and for 50 yards or so the woman followed the blue jay. The bird led her to a spectacular overview of Mount Hood. Then, the jay flew up into a nearby pine tree. As the woman stood in that place, a sudden surge of energy passed through her like a bolt of gentle lightning. The world around her suddenly felt more beautiful than she could ever recall feeling before. Deeply moved by what she saw, she began to cry, and in her tears she came to an awareness of the beauty in all life. For the next few minutes, emotions and feelings from her past bubbled up as she passed through an adamic ecstasy. Her depression evaporated much like the dew on the leaves around her was evaporating in the morning sunshine. As soon as she felt cheerful and positive again, the jay hopped back down to the ground and led her back along the trail to her car.

Approaching an Anasazi ruin at Mesa Verde National Park, a professor of theology reported feeling a heavy ambiance which pulled down his spirits. Standing amidst the crumbled walls of this archaeological treasure, a flock of buzzards alighted in a nearby tree, and his mood became even more somber. He left and went back to his hotel room, where he found a message that a close relative had just died.

6. Sightings of Monsters & UFOs

Wild places are often seen as the homes of strange beasts like dragons, basilisks, unicorns, half-human and half-animal creatures, dwarfs, gnomes, elves, giants, jinns, brownies, and sprites, as well as creatures from outer space. One interpretation of these entities is that they are mythic beings, and that people who see them are having visions. This could account for some of the sightings, but there are many sane, reputable people who describe encounters with monsters at wild places as if they were contacting actual life forms.

One of the most common monsters appears in the form of large, hairy, apelike creature. In the Himalayas this monster is called *yeti*, or the "abominable snowman." In the United States it is referred to as Bigfoot or, in the Pacific Northwest, Sasquatch. It seems likely that the Green Man of Europe is a relative.

The Freudian interpretation of Bigfoot sightings is that they are projections of the human "id," as the hairy ape represents an archetype of people's lower animal self. No doubt some sightings are precisely this, but, in general, medicine people I have discussed this with feel differently. Rolling Thunder says that the Bigfoots are a relic species of humans left over from an earlier era, the "old ones" that Indians sometimes talk about. He says they have learned the ability to materialize or dematerialize, which is why one has never been caught. Many Indian stories associate these creatures with being the guardians of certain places, especially some sacred mountains and swamps.

I have interviewed a number of very sane people who have seen a Bigfoot, including a whole busload of college students who witnessed one cross the road in front of their bus one night while driving through the Sierras. Typically, witnesses say that their first awareness of Bigfoot was a stange sense of hyperactive energy, like a strong charge of static electricity on a cold winter day. "The air feels real tense, they smell like hell, and scream like a wounded person," a professional guide told me one afternoon in a bar in the North Cascades of Washington. He then proceeded to show me a series of photos of giant footprints in the snow which he had taken. The tracks were similar to huge human feet, twenty inches long, and could not have been made by any ordinary bear. When the guide had made this find, he had reported it to the local media. Within hours, people had come from all across the country to see the tracks. "One guy came up to me and quietly said, 'I'll give you one million dollars dead and two million alive for one of those things, no questions asked,' " the guide told me. In Washington it's against the law to shoot a Bigfoot, "but I'd never kill one, cause they've got a right to live like us," he replied very seriously.

Nearly everyone I have interviewed agrees that people tend to first sense the Bigfoots' presence, and then smell them as a musky odor. If you hear them cry, you will never forget it, they say. I must admit that I was a skeptic until I was taken on a Bigfoot expedition by some friends. We packed into a rugged mountain region in the North Cascades near the Canadian border, fording a rushing river because the only bridge into the valley had been washed out by a spring flood just a few weeks before. The snow had just melted off the lower areas, and the ground was soft. It appeared that we were the first people to visit the area that spring. About 100 yards beyond the river we came to an old cabin which had been ransacked; it looked like the work of a bear. Then one person in the group let out a whoop, and we all ran over to look at what he had found. There in the sand was a fourteen-inch foot print, with clearly discernible toes, the longest of which was the big toe (supposedly a characteristic of the Bigfoot). I had studied wildlife management in college, and had spent years in the woods, but I had never seen anything like this. It was too narrow for a bear, and too fresh to be a human footprint enlarged by water, or freezing and thawing. I later had the chance to measure the mammoth feet of six-foot-ten-inch-tall professional basketball player Jack Sikma, and they were about the same size. Jack swears he wasn't running around in the woods barefoot right before we went out.

The tracks could have been faked by someone. However, an amazing collection of Bigfoot-track plaster casts like those of anthropologist Dr. Grover Krantz of Washington State University seem to prove that something is going on here beyond a joke. After seeing the tracks in the stream bed, I had a series of dreams about the Bigfoot, which agreed with what Rolling Thunder had told me about them.

The scientific study of Bigfoot, the Loch Ness monster, giant bats, living dinosaurs, dragons, and other monsters is called cryptozoology, a field which is delightfully described in Ivan Sanderson's book *Investigating the Unexplained*.[29] The difference between cryptozoology and the hunting of mythic beasts is that the cryptozoologist is looking for physical evidence. A Bigfoot may never be captured, but there is the case of the Stone Age Indian Ishi, who was found in California near Mount Lassen in the early 1900s. There is also the coelacanth,

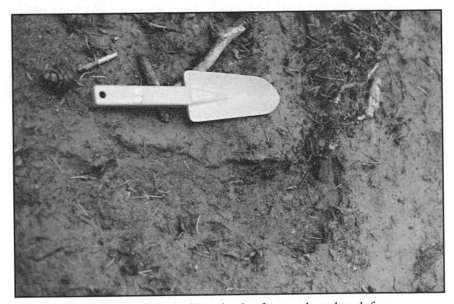

Photo 18. *A twelve-inch trowel lying beside a fourteen-plus-inch track from a very large foot of some kind. Note the distinct toe markings, suggesting the track was not made by a foot wearing a boot. Author photo, 1981.*

a fish supposedly extinct for millions of years that was caught alive off east Africa in 1938. If Bigfoot does exist as a being that can do what the medicine people say it can do, then humans could have a lot to learn from it.

Carl Jung suggested that flying saucer sightings are projections of the unconscious reflecting a difficulty in dealing with ordinary life. They may also be perceptions of spiritual intelligences in the upper world, interpreted through modern minds. When there is no physical evidence of an extraordinary entity, its existence is more strongly validated if people from several different cultures report independent sightings of a UFO. I often wonder, for example, if when looking at the same energetic manifestation an Indian might see a spirit while a person from modern society might see a spaceship.

Regardless what UFOs are, people report seeing them in great numbers, especially at and around sacred places. "They come and sit down in the upper pasture sometimes," a farmer and his wife from Mount Shasta told me. "We drive up there to get a better look, but it gets feelin' weird if you get too close, so we just keep our distance," he told me seriously.

In Steven Spielberg's epic film *Close Encounters of the Third Kind*, people have a first-hand meeting with creatures from outer space at Devil's Tower in Wyoming. Devil's Tower is a very sacred place to the Lakota, who traditionally conducted the Sun Dance at its base around the time of the Summer Solstice, while honoring a stellar constellation they call Mato Tipila, "The Bear's Lodge."[30] Sightings of UFOs near or at sacred mountains are common around the world, from the Andes to the Orient and the sun pyramids of Mexico. One wonders if Spielberg's use of Devil's Tower as the site for the movie was not just by chance.

Recently, psychologist Michael Persinger at Laurentian University in Ontario and ley-lines expert Paul Devereux of Great Britain have published theories which suggest a relationship between UFO sightings and electrical energy discharges in the ground. They feel that sightings of UFOs occur most commonly along earthquake fault lines and during magnetic storms, when people's minds entrain with stronger than normal electromagnetic fields, resulting in the stimulation of creative imagery.[31] Another way to look at this, however, is that the amplified energetic fields in these situations allow people to experience other dimensions more easily.

Sightings of Bigfoot, the Loch Ness monster, *yeti*, and UFOs continue. Physical evidence is the acid test of whether or not these phenomena exist as material objects in the physical dimension. However, even if these sightings are all products of the fertile creative mind, that does not mean they are worthless. It is the twilight zone between the worlds, where myths and visions dwell, which has often been the fertile seedbed of cultural creativity. Physical evidence simply proves in which dimension the objects you perceive exist.

7. Unusual Odors, Sounds & Ambiances

Writer/editor Patricia Kollings tells of driving her car up to the snow line on Mount Shasta, pulling over, and going for a hike. The silence, the snow, and clear blue sky were breathtaking. Then she began to hear tiny tinkling bells, which seemed to be playing music. The sound did not seem to be coming from below, but from all around her. Returning to her car, she described her experience to a friend who lived in the area. Her friend just smiled and said that many people hear "bells" on Mount Shasta because it is a holy place.

That night Kollings had a powerful and vivid dream. In it, she was looking down into the depths of the slumbering volcano at Mt. Shasta's base—into the heat, the molten rocks, the flowing magma. It was like looking down to the core of the Earth, she says. Afterward, she woke up and wrote: "Unexplained phenomena—miracles—are craters in the rational crust of the earth, where the deeper, molten energy is formed, occasionally bubbles up in a state that is fluid, not yet rigidified into forms that reason can grasp."

A husband and wife told me about a time they were climbing in the Himalayas, walking along a narrow trail beside a steep drop of thousands of feet. At one point the excitement of this precarious walk, they began to smell pungent incense, like they were inside a Buddhist monastery. Half an hour later they rounded a bend and found an actual monastery. When they went inside, the odor was identical to that which they had smelled on their trail. The monks said they pray for the safety of people walking the trail. They also said that the monastery is sited on a very sacred place. The wind had not been blowing in any way which would have brought this odor to them beforehand, they said.

"Sometimes, like in the Shenandoah Valley, or at Carmel down at Big Sur, I hear 'music' in the sunset or in the woods," relates keyboard artist Steven Halpern. One of the pioneers of modern spiritual music, Halpern says that each geographical place has its own special melody, which is more easily heard at some places than others.

Polynesia is a sensuous land, but a woman who went to Hawaii for her vacation found more sensation than she bargained for at a quiet beach. The beach felt special to her, she said, and so she chose a place to sit in some rocks there which afforded privacy. As she relaxed, the warm sunlight and water drained away her tensions. Then she began to hear distant chanting and drumming. It grew louder, and she smelled what she thought was roast pork cooking over an open pit. She got up to look for the luau, but could not find it. Later she discovered that the beach she had been visiting was an ancient ritual site where pigs were commonly roasted and dancing and singing were common.

A similar tale comes from the magical British island of Iona, said to have once been a focal point for Druidism and then later for Christian spiritualism. Approaching the island monastery, a couple on vacation simultaneously smelled the beautiful pungent odor of flowers. They assumed the odor was from a special garden, but found to their dismay that there were only grass lawns in the area. Studying the guidebook for the island, they came upon a passage describing a spiritual fragrance which sometimes permeates the place, supposedly associated with the spirit of Saint Columba coming to comfort weary farmers returning from the harvest.[32]

Visiting the ruins of Rome, well-known sensitive Anne Armstrong recounts how she had feelings in her body of past orgiastic rites which had taken place there.

A radio announcer told me between breaks interviewing me on his talk show that he had felt something similar while hiking on Mount Olympus. The feeling had moved him to do a wild ''Zorba the Greek'' dance there for nearly an hour. As soon we came back on the air, he refused to say anything about the incident.

P.L. Travers, the creator of the popular Mary Poppins character, writes about a time when she was visiting Chartres Cathedral: ''Once, at Chartres, left alone by a party of friends who wanted to look at the crypt, I just sat there in the great silence feeling something—I still can't give it a name—gathering about me and the top of my head slowly rising. Something is going to be told me, I thought.'' The group came back shortly and she left, but later shared this experience with an archaeologist. He told her that she had been sitting in an area where the old Neolithic stone circle that predated Chartres had been located.[33]

8. Hearing Voices

While traveling among the Igulik Eskimos in the early 1920s, the Danish explorer Knud Rasmussen came upon a wise old shaman who told him that ''the best magic words are those which come to one when one is alone out among the mountains. These are always the most powerful in their effects. The power of the solitude is great beyond understanding.''[34]

The prophet Mohammed received his communications from the Lord on Mount Arafat, a very sacred place. Not far away in the Sinai desert, Moses spoke with God on Mount Horeb and later received the Ten Commandments on the same mountain. Elijah also spoke with God on Mount Horeb. The rest of us may hear spoken words at special places, too. Lummi Indian Kenneth Cooper says the wisest words he knows come to him when he is alone on Mount Baker.

Hot Sulfur Springs in the Middle Park of Colorado was used by the Ute tribe for healing people and horses long before contemporary health spas came into being. Several people have told me that they have been to Hot Sulfur Springs and, while meditating, could distinctly "hear" Indian chanting and drumming.

Another woman spoke with great feeling about visiting Lourdes in France. The sight of the many pilgrims approaching the shrine in hopes of healing touched her deeply, and she sat down to watch. In her silence, she heard a voice talking to her. She looked around but could find no person. The voice then calmly told her that she had healing powers and should develop them. Within a few months after returning home, she dropped her clerical job and began to study massage.

In Western society, if one talks to God, it is called prayer, but if God talks back to someone, it is symptomatic of psychosis. In contrast, among the Eskimos and other shamanic cultures, if spiritual voices do not come to one's mental ears then one is considered mentally ill. The failure of modern psychology to appreciate the potential value of such common perceptions as hearing voices is a serious limitation of the existing Western belief system. Skin color has absolutely nothing to do with the psychological merits of hearing voices. The real issue is not whether one hears voices, but what the voices say, and how one reacts.

In 1967, Guenn Nimue was living in Richland, Washington, with her husband, a scientist, and her family. She had been an artist and mother for nineteen years. Quite suddenly her mother, who had been a powerful influence in her life, passed away. Within four days after her mother's death, Nimue's consciousness was flooded with strange voices, "like all the circuits of a telephone operator's switchboard opened at once." The voices were overwhelming, and she sat in a confused catatonic trance, unable to stop the chatter. Because she could not cope with this state, she was hospitalized, which the voices agreed was a good idea.

While in the hospital, Nimue learned to listen to the voices, which guided her through simple exercises, such as walking to certain places, saying certain things, dancing particular steps, and so on. This behavior seemed crazy, but as she followed the voices guidance, she felt better and better. Finally, after a couple of weeks, she was released from the hospital.

At home, the voices continued, leading to her family's rejection of her transformed state. She left her family and moved in with a friend in Seattle. At this point she was receiving compensation from the state, for her voices could not be controlled.

For the next several years Nimue spent her time quietly, discovering that if she wrote down the voices, she felt better. The more she let go and opened up to their energy, the more her handwriting of the voices became like old English script. Then one day, in a flash, she wondered if she could draw who was talking to her. To her delight, the pages of her sketchbooks soon became filled with enchanting pictures of gnomes, fairies, elves, and sprites, which subsequently were turned into full-color portraits.

Figure 4. *The Spirit of the Milky Way Galaxy, Hamallodkheannh. Painting appears courtesy of the artist, Guenn E. C. Nimue.*

About the time that the portraits were beginning, Nimue was visited by her aunt. Seeing the pictures, her mother's sister looked at Nimue and asked her if her mother had ever told her about her grandmother. Nimue replied that she had not. Her aunt then told Nimue that her grandmother had been the Grande

Dame of the Druids of Brittany. In a flash of revelation, they realized that, with her mother's death, Nimue had received her own spiritual heritage, and that her mind had been catching up with what would have been normal shamanic development in a culture which recognized the validity of such things.

For the last decade Nimue has been painting her voices and the scenes which have come with them. In her own evolutionary process, she first came to acknowledge guides from the various earth, air, water, fire, plant, and animal kingdoms. Then, as she became grounded in her new cosmology, she began to have lucid dreams of various places with humanoid forms arising from them. She drew portraits of these spirits of places, each of which then spoke to her about that place and its subtle qualities.[35]

Guenn Nimue's story is more profound than that of most of the people I have interviewed, for her journey is classically one of the shaman, in the true sense of that term. However, many people I interviewed reported hearing, at certain locations, voices of various origins, ranging from "talking stones" to Indian chants to the chattering of tiny people. Many of these people claimed to have no faith in psychic phenomena or channeling, so they suppressed these experiences rather than taking them seriously and studying them to find out what they really were, which would have been a more appropriate holistic, scientific approach.

9. Death & Rebirth

At the crux of every transcendental experience is a process of surrendering the ego, resulting in a psychic death and rebirth. For some people, an encounter with the sacred at a special place involves an actual feeling or experience of dying and being reborn.

One college student told me that he had been feeling very frustrated with himself and his life, so he went for a solo backpacking trip in a wilderness area. He camped beside a hot springs and, bathing in them, felt invigorated. That night in a dream he saw himself in a coffin, which terrified him so that he woke up. Upon going back to sleep he dreamed of himself as a little child. Returning home, this student changed his major in school, dropped his girl friend, and got a job instead of taking money from his parents for his education.

A woman told me that she had felt moved to go a certain beach along the Maine coast. It was vacant and she decided to dig a hole in the sand. She dug for awhile and then came to the realization that she was digging a grave for herself. Not knowing why, she lay down in it and even tossed some sand on herself. A sense of deep peace came upon her, and she slipped into an altered state in which she journeyed down a long tunnel into the Earth. In her mind's eye, she then popped through into another world where she encountered several animals, one of which merged with her body as in one of Michael Harner's

Figure 5. *The Spirit of Mount Tamalpais in Marin County, California. Drawing appears courtesy of the artist, Guenn E. C. Nimue.*

shamanic journeys.[36] Returning to her own body, she felt like she had both lost something and gained a new, fresh approach to life. She had also obtained a deeper admiration for nature, she said.

Spiritual initiation often arrives with a flood of extra energy which can result in shaking and trembling of the physical body. I personally experienced this in the early 1970s on the slopes of Mount McKinley in Alaska, shortly after attending some Eskimo ceremonies in Anchorage. As the trembling came on, I recall looking up at the mountain and saying to myself that if I was about to die, this was at least a beautiful place to go. After that experience I began a new career direction, studying to become a psychotherapist.

SYNTHESIS

Reviewing his years of research on "peak experiences," Abraham Maslow made the following observation:

> We have made studies of peak experiences by asking groups of people and individuals such questions as "What was the most ecstatic moment of your life?" . . . One might think that in the general population, such questions might get blank stares, but there were many answers. Apparently the transcendent ecstasies had all been kept private because there was no way of speaking about them in public. They are sort of embarassing, shameful, not "scientific"—which for many people is the ultimate sin.[37]

In reviewing the variety of unusual experiences reported in this chapter, which are meant to be descriptive and not inclusive of everything which can occur in the human psyche at a place of power, a common pattern emerges. Initially the people about to have the experience feel drawn to the place by a source beyond normal consciousness, as if they were being guided to be at that particular place at a certain time. Surrendering to this magnetic pull, they travel to the place. As they reach their destination, a sense of emotional arousal and extra energy are present. Then something happens which seems to "trigger" their mental process, shifting their mindset into some new dimensions of consciousness. In this transcendent state, unusual events take place in which the normal time-space frame of reference is non-existent, and the personal experience is intense and engages mind, body, and spirit. While in this state of expanded mindfulness, an extraordinary feeling of unity with reality occurs, and unusual events happen in the surrounding world. As Stanislav Grof observes, "Transpersonal experiences seem to be inextricably interwoven with the fabric of events in the material world."[38] Finally, when consciousness returns to normal, the participants integrate their lives at a new and more meaningful level, often resulting in changes in their careers and personal lives. As a result of this experience, feelings of love for nature deepen. In other words, "for those who have a religious experience all nature is capable of revealing itself as cosmic sacrality,'' as Mircea Eliade concludes.[39]

This pattern is clearly shown in the Bible by the story of Jacob's dream (Genesis 28:10-14, 18-19, King James Version), which portrays the potential for transcendental experiences to move people to action. Leaving Beer-sheba hurriedly for Harran at sunset, Jacob stopped to rest at a certain place and fashioned a pillow from stones. Slipping off into welcome sleep, he dreamed of a ladder ascending to heaven, and saw the Lord descending on this ladder rooted to Earth. The Lord then said to Jacob:

> ''I am the Lord God of Abraham thy father, and the God of Isaac; the land whereupon thou liest, to thee I will give it and thy seed; and thy seed shall be as the dust of the earth, and thou shalt spread abroad to the west, and to the east, and to the north and south; and in thee and in thy seed shall all the families of earth be blessed. . . . ''
>
> Jacob then awakened from his sleep and said, ''Surely the Lord is in this place.'' And he was afraid, and said, ''How dreadful is this place! This is none other than the house of God, and this is the Gate of Heaven.'' And Jacob . . . took the stone he had put out for his pillow, set it up for his pillar, and poured oil on top of it. And he called that place Bethel, the House of God.

Jacob's experience and his reaction to it are characteristic of many people's encounters with the sacred. University of Miami Professor of Psychiatry Stanley Dean concludes, after reviewing hundreds of case histories of such transcendental episodes, historical as well as modern, that higher states of consciousness may be a natural and very important aspect of human life. He found that among the benefits resulting from transpersonal states are mental and physical health; a deepening of the potential to feel love for self and nature; an increased commitment to social causes; a gain of important insights into problems and truth; and accurate glimpses of the future and a better understanding of the past. Such benefits, Dr. Dean concludes, ''may ultimately prove as essential as technology in saving our planet from ecological and military ruin.''[39]

In *Sand County Almanac*, which many environmentalists consider their bible, wildlife biologist/philosopher Aldo Leopold points out that much of our environmental management seems to forever involve fighting brushfires rather than being a comprehensive approach to creating harmony with nature. Leopold calls for the creation of an ''ecological conscience'' as the only way to ever prevent environmental catastrophes.[40] In searching for what this consciousness should be like, many people turn to the writings of Ralph Waldo Emerson, Henry David Thoreau, and John Muir. ''In the woods is perpetual youth,'' Emerson declared in his essay *Nature*, and when we go there ''we return to reason and faith.''[41]

In a July 16, 1851, passage from his *Journal*, Thoreau says: "The earth was the most glorious musical instrument, and I was the audience to its strains. To have such sweet impressions made on us, such ecstasies begotten of the breezes! . . . With all your science can you tell how it is, and whence it is, that light comes into the soul?"[42]

Thoreau's references to the "divine," the "infinite," and "light" coming into the soul clearly mark him as a mystic, but among modern nature mystics none can surpass John Muir, who once climbed to the top of a swaying pine tree in the middle of a thunderstorm to be closer to the wildness of the storm. "All the wilderness seems to be full of tricks and plans to drive and draw us up into God's light!" Muir declared in pages filled with descriptions of ecstasies he had experienced alone at Yosemite and other special places.[43]

These writings seem to originate from a well of inspiration which, when translated into words, makes the reader's spirit soar. They are a touchstone of consciousness arising from conservationists who link their commitment to nature to their mystical experiences at wild places. Aldo Leopold himself confessed that his sense of compassion for wild things deepened when he looked into the eyes of a timber wolf caught in a trap, which he had to kill. U.S. Supreme Court Chief Justice William O. Douglas linked his lifelong work as a conservationist to a mystical bonding with Mount Adams which he felt during his youth while standing beside the grave of his father. Douglas admitted in later life that the mountain had become his second father, and he often spoke of the "spiritual values" of the mountains. Rachel Carson is remembered for her warnings about the dangers of pesticides in *Silent Spring*. She was moved to write with a passion both in this book and in the *The Sea Around Us* by her deep feelings about the regenerative powers of the ocean, where she would retreat to write in mystical reverie.

Native Americans plan for people to have mystical bonding experiences through ceremonies and rituals. They also give people names with mythic sentiments to help keep these bonds intact. More and more, modern people are educated about loving nature through being showered with facts about ecology and pollution, rather than through being helped to establish deep psychological bonding experiences with the natural world. As environmental educator Thomas Tanner has pointed out, the whole field of environmental education has shied away from trying to develop a psychologically based approach to teaching ecology, despite the fact that research clearly indicates this is what is needed.[44] People know more about ecology than ever before, but for many this knowledge is second-hand, based on words and media, which are never as deep and meaningful as direct experience. The greatest risk to forming an ecological conscience may be well-informed futility, a fairly common affliction in our information age.

The origin of the word "conservation" is an example of the power of transcendental states to shape human affairs. Gifford Pinchot, chief forester in the administration of President Teddy Roosevelt, went for a ride on his horse "Jim" through Rock Creek Park near Washington, D.C., on a foggy February morning in 1905. Roosevelt had told him to come up with a unified policy to use in managing all the many, varied resource issues of the day—oil, wildlife, forests, water, soil erosion, and minerals. Each seemed to have its own unique management problems. Pinchot was a trained forester and the complexity of the problem boggled his mind. He relates in his autobiography how, in a deep depression, he thought of the tracts of land in India called "conservancies," which were managed for the greater good of all. Pinchot then said that "suddenly the idea flashed through my head that there was a unity in this complication . . . here was one single question with many parts . . . the one great central problem of the use of earth for the good of man." He rode off hurriedly, arrived at the White House on the run, and rushed in to share what had happened with Roosevelt. That night, at a special cabinet meeting, Secretary McGee coined the word "conservation," defining it as "the use of the natural resources for the greatest good of the greatest number for the longest time." Thus the conservation movement was born in an adamic ecstasy at a special place, and the resulting policy went on to become, in Pinchot's view, "the single most significant achievement of the T.R. Administration."[45]

This review of transpersonal occurrences suggests that regardless of culture, and without planning, many people can and do have profound transcendental experiences while visiting certain places. These experiences, which come without expectation, can be unsettling and transformative in people's lives, but I have yet to find a person who has approached a sacred place with an attitude of humility and has had a "bad trip." In contrast to psychedelic drugs and sensationalist human-potential seminars, both of which are "non-specific amplifers" of consciousness and therefore a little like playing Russian roulette with the psyche, sacred places seem to know what is best for people. The only people I interviewed who had negative experiences at such places were those who went to a place and did not respect its power or the indigenous peoples who had considered that place sacred for centuries.

Not everyone who goes to a special place has a wild experience, of course. For many people, perhaps most, the experience is simply invigorating and inspiring, which in itself seems important, since so many places in the modern urban environment are energy drains. Not long before he passed away, I had dinner with Joseph Campbell and asked him about sacred places, which occupied the pages of so many of his books. Campbell thought for a minute and said simply that there were three places which were especially powerful for him: Delphi, Palenque, and Lascaux. I then asked him if he had ever had any profound mystical experiences at these locations. He said, "No," and then took a drink of French wine and stared off into space. After nearly a minute, he looked me straight in the eye and said, "These places are important to me because I, Joe Campbell, felt more powerful there, and I damn well don't know why."

TOWARD A PSYCHOLOGY OF SACRED PLACES

Some 300 kilometers from Caracas, Venezuela, is Sorté Mountain, a Venezuelan national park. Should one make the drive through the dense tropical jungles laced with intermittent cascading mountain streams and arrive at the mountain on a weekend, one will likely hear the sounds of drums beating and voices chanting. Sorté is a sacred mountain, and today it is a healing retreat center for members of the Maria Lionza religion. This modern shamanistic spiritual group blends Christian, Haitian Voodoo, African Yoruba, and ancient Jaguar religions of central and south America in a potent formula. The practice of such cross-cultural blending is called "syncretism."

Imagine for a moment that a man in Caracas stops at a streetside counseling shrine and complains of depression. The oracles are consulted and the prescription is a trip to Sorté, guided by one or two shamans. Along the trip route, they stop at special places to make offerings and consult the spirits. Typically their offerings are anything from chocolate to chicken sacrifices.

Arriving at Sorté, the man is led to a circle of mediums sitting cross-legged on the ground while they chant deep guttural sounds. In the background, the voices of drums, rattles, and sticks clacking against each other set the tone for a harmonizing of minds. Approaching the circle, the client is directed to several people smoking large black cigars, who blow smoke onto him to cleanse his energy field.

Having been purified, he is led into the middle of the circle by a *santero*, a shaman who specializes in entering an ecstatic state with his client to seek healing. The drums intensify, and the patient looks around at the faces of the mediums locked into rapture as they chant. He smells the acrid cigar smoke and incense vapors, and sees the lush green vegetation and tropical flowers. Sweat beads up all over his body. His heartbeat quickens. The *santero* has now clearly moved into another world, judging by his facial expression, and he looks into the eyes of the patient, speaks words of an ancient tongue from the days when the jaguar was Christ to people of the area.

A rush of energy pours through the patient. It is as if a struggle has been going on within him. Feeling the conflict, he falls to his knees and begins to sob. Deep groans and growls come from him, almost as if the jaguar is inside him. Then he vomits and begins to cry like a baby. As his emotions subside, he is led out of the circle to a quiet place nearby, where he is told to lie on the ground. Another shaman now takes out white powder and sprinkles it around the man to protect him from negative influences. Then the shaman says prayers. Using powder, he draws some lines radiating from the four directions toward the prone man, which bring in new positive energies. Glasses of water are placed near the man's head, and some fresh flowers are sprinkled beside him, their aroma swelling up like perfume. He is told to lie in this place for a while so it can cleanse his old negative energies and recharge him with new ones.

This type of ritual process is performed regularly at Sorté. To the members of the Maria Lionza religion, it is simply spiritual healing according to their tradition. Psychologically, Christie Kiefer and Ken Cowan call it "context-dependent retrieval." Using Jung's metaphor of the mind being like an apartment building, Kiefer and Cowan have been studying healing rituals for years. They conclude that trained ritual masters get results and never harm people because the masters know how to alter their consciousness to gain access to the "floor" of the patient's mind where the problem is. Then, because they have already been there themselves and they understand the mental maps involved, they work with the appropriate symbols, sounds, and energies to drive out the patient's conflict. In this way, natural harmony and balance can return and health can be restored.[46]

In Western psychology, the importance of destabilizing ego-consciousness to facilitate access to altered states is well understood. There is ample evidence to show that yoga, tai chi, meditation, various psychoactive drugs, fasting, repetitive prayer, and breathing exercises all shift the mind into new states. But psychology has not yet developed its own road maps of the mind, in part because it has no good paradigm to account for the multidimensional mind and how it works. In need of a guidance system, Western psychology must therefore turn to other cultures and older traditions which have more holistic views.

In India it is said that the body is in the mind, but the mind can and does go beyond the body. Hindu wisdom speaks of subtle centers of consciousness called "chakras" which reside in special regions of the body. The seat of power and pleasure lies at the base of the spine. Love and compassion are focalized in the chest. Spiritual intelligence rides on top of the skull in the area of the fontanel, or soft spot, of new babies. While modern science has yet to confirm the physicality of life energies and the chakras, it seems significant that nearly all traditional societies believe in the existence of subtle centers in the body. The Sufis of the Middle East refer to "latifae"; the Chinese see various "cauldrons" and "gates" in the body; the Hopi Indians talk about five centers of the mind-body; and the Jewish mystics who study the Kabbalah speak of many subtle qualities of consciousness located throughout the body.

Modern society lives primarily on one floor of the apartment house of

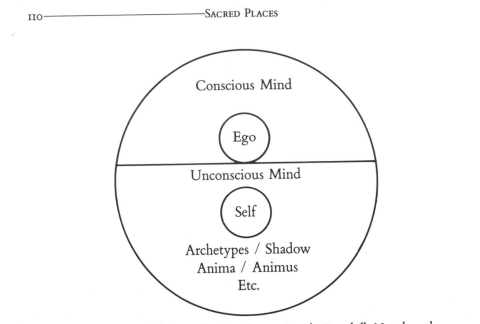

Figure 6. *Model of the Psyche According to Joseph Campbell. Note how the self lies below consciousness, which is the realm where the primal energies and symbols that are harmonic with nature also reside. From "Visionary Journey," a lecture delivered in Seattle, Washington, June 13, 1982.*

consciousness—the head. Many of the primal qualities of the lower chakras lie in the unconscious mind, and in the map of the psyche developed by Joseph Campbell to describe Carl Jung's model of the mind, the self also resides in the unconscious. This is why troubled people in modern society enter therapies to uncover the misconceptions which cloud access to their true selves. They dive down into the waters of the unconscious to discover who they really are.

In figure 6, the region below the line demarking consciousness may be equated to most of the human body other than the head. To simplify discussion and illustrate how consciousness is focused in various realms, I will use the Hindu tantric system of seven energy centers, or chakras, lying along the spine. Other cultures share the notion of decentralization of consciousness but differ in their beliefs of how many centers exist and just where they are. The first or basal chakra lies at the base of the spine and is concerned with control, power, and pleasure. The second chakra is located just below the navel and deals with emotions and sexuality. The third is at the solar plexus and deals with ordering worldly activities, a sense of community, and the will to power. The fourth is centered in the chest, and its attributes include love, compassion, and the desire for truth. The fifth chakra is located at the throat and deals with creative expression and the will. The sixth is the mystical "third eye" at the center of the forehead, and concerns thinking. The seventh, or crown, chakra sits on top of the head, and centers on spirituality and higher intuition.

Studying the world's mythologies and their impact on human life, Joseph Campbell linked various mythic themes and symbols to each of the chakras. Bears, apes, elephants, dragons, monsters like King Kong and Godzilla, jungles, caves, and snakes symbolize the world of the first chakra. Rabbits, lovers, the moon, sea shells, fish, and water resonate with the second chakra. Rams, sharks, and political leaders are linked to the third chakra. Mothers, children, young animals, and love are associated with the heart center. Animals like the mountain goat with its great endurance, or talkative birds like parrots and ravens are associated with the throat chakra. The owl, philosopher's stones, crystals, and eagles are activators of the sixth, mental chakra. The spiritual center on the top of the head is the domain of angels, mountain tops, tree tops, geese, and cathedrals.[47]

Theories like the chakra theory leave some scientists cold, because no one has found a way to measure the existence of a chakra, let alone the life energy which activates it. This may be more of a problem with the scientific paradigm than anything else, however. Where the chakra system becomes convincingly evident is in deep therapies, such as Reichian vegetotherapy, Stanislav Grof's holotrophic breathing, Rolfing, or Gestalt therapy. When various segments of the body are opened with such methods, the symbols which Campbell talked about appear consistently in client's dreams and creative visualizations, affirming the power of the shamanic mind to see into places which science has yet to understand.[48]

Additional support for the imagery of the chakra system comes from the use of musical notes to activate various chakras, such as musician/researcher Steven Halpern has described. Not content to just play music, Halpern has created a popular sound which is based on a worldwide study of healing music. He asserts that special notes activate each of the centers. The base of the spine chakra is associated with the key of middle C. The second chakra is activated by D, the "key of the devil." The third chakra is an E, which perhaps is why many popular rock-and-roll and rhythm-and-blues tunes are played in E. The note of the heart is F: Gordon Lightfoot lovers. The throat chakra, the center of the hero, is G, one of John Denver's favorite keys. The sixth chakra, for the thinker, is activated by A. And the seventh, spiritual chakra resonates with a high B.[49] When Halpern's system is used with people in meditation, and the people are directed to explore those symbolic realms through hearing the correct key chords, time and time again the mythic symbols of Campbell's theory appear to them. (To explore this system in the detail it deserves, see Joseph Campbell's classic work *The Mythic Image.*)

My purpose in describing the chakra system is to provide a more sensitive and comprehensive model of the mind which can help shed light on the many aspects of consciousness. If one looks at a Northwest Coast Indian painting which portrays eyes coming out all over the body of an animal or the trunk of a tree, one can now see that this represents how the mind lives in the entire body, and how each chakra has its own unique aspect of reality with which it deals. Sufi mystics insist that each chakra has special organs of perception, and Northwest Coast art indicates how American Indian culture agrees that the world works that way.

Many insist that modern people do not live with their consciousness attuned to all their chakras. Actually, the problem is more that modern society does not help us become consciously aware of perceptual abilities of each chakra. Anyone who is good at their work, whatever it is, is intuitive. Intuition is the sensing of totality, and if the entire body is in the mind, then the whole body must be a sense organ for intuition.

Although consciousness is multifaceted, people can achieve a single focus with their mind, eliminating all other factors except the one central point of concentration. For example, as a test of their warriors' readiness for war, one Indian tribe had a provocative ritual trial. They chose a beautiful young woman and had her strip naked in front of the equally naked warriors. She then engaged in her most seductive overtures. The men were supposed to be able to keep their minds honed to combat. If any man got an erection during this test, he was disqualified from going on the war party because he had not yet learned to control his mind properly.

Environmental factors, such as the sight of a naked body, influence human realms of consciousness. Our feelings are different when we walk into a place which has been burned by a forest fire than if we venture into a lush forest. In addition to these visible conditions, sounds and odors and a myriad of other invisible waves of energy constantly pour through us, for in between our atoms and molecules there is still open space. As these energies travel through our bodies, our tiniest particles vibrate. In a sense, we are all musical notes being played by nature all the time. Think of all the love music of the world, and how frequently it refers to the moon, a symbol of the second chakra, the seat of Eros. In his hauntingly beautiful book *The Sensitive Chaos*, Theodor Schwenk describes our love affair with the moon in the following terms:

> As the moon wanders over the different waters of the earth, they respond to a greater or lesser degree with their "note" according to how closely their natural period of vibration is tuned to the rhythm of the moon. All together they are like a great musical instrument, spread out over the earth, on which the moon plays an inaudible melody, which wanders with it round the earth.[50]

Chakra	Associative Organ	Musical Note	Cycles/ Second	Consciousness	Mythic Images
top of head	pineal gland	B	493	spirituality, integration	crystal, star, mountain peak, angel
brow	pituitary gland	A	440	thinking, decision-making	scholar, skull wise people, owl, eagle
throat	thyroid	G	392	will, expression, communication	hero or heroine, mountain goat, explorer
heart	thymus gland	F	349.2	love, compassion, great virtues	mother & child love, alchemist's gold
solar plexus	pancreas	E	329.1	assertion, community	ram, shark, will to power
chi	spleen	D	292.1	creativity, sex, emotions	eros, lovers, water, rabbit moon, art
base of spine, kundalini	sexual glands	C	261.1	power & pleasure	dragon, ape, bear, bull, business, elephant, whale

Figure 7. *The Seven Spinal Chakras, Their Attributes & Influence on Con sciousness. Chart by James A. Swan after information in Joseph Campbell's* The Mythic Image; *the original source is Sanskrit.*

Just as the moon plays the bodies of water on Earth, so does it play our human bodies, for we are more than half water. All geographic places have their own "notes," arising from their unique interplay of countless harmonic associations between rocks, trees, mountains, lakes, streams, valleys, and waterfalls. In some places, the amplitude of this note seems much higher. This causes different people to resonate more powerfully with different places, according to who they are as well as the specific power of a place. When someone feels pulled to a certain place by a higher force, they are getting a message about their need to be activated in a certain way. If they surrender to the call of intuition, they are renewed, perhaps transformed.

Once a person heeds the call of place and allows the process to simply unfold, magic happens. Poet Michelle Berditschevsky felt compelled to take a walk on Mount Shasta one day, not far from Panther Meadows. This place has been used for Indian ceremonials for centuries. Out of the blue a voice said to her, "I need protection." Shortly thereafter, she discovered that a large ski area was planned for that exact place. She then realized that the voice had been the mountain asking for help. Having had no experience with organizing, she dove into environmental politics and organized the Save Mount Shasta group to protest the developmental plan. She reported that once she surrendered to the process, she needed only three to four hours of sleep per night, and that suddenly her dreams became filled with scenes and symbols of the mountain. This spurred her to collect over 700 signatures on a petition to stop the proposed ski development.

University of California at Davis psychologist Robert Sommer reports a similar experience in his life. One day while driving home from vacation, he felt drawn to drive through the canyon of California's Stanislaus River. The beauty of the river valley captivated him and his wife. On that drive, however, he discovered that the river was to be dammed and that the particular stretch he was enjoying so much was going to be flooded. As a psychologist, he began to look at how others saw the slow death of the canyon. The language of protest which seemed to work best for many people, he found, was graffiti on the rocks and bridges to be flooded. This was especially significant, considering that ancient Indian rock art would be covered as the river rose. Sommer went on to write a book about this, and at the first Spirit of Place symposium, held September 8-11, 1988, at the University of California at Davis, he spoke with great emotion about watching the canyon sink under water.[51] When someone asked him why he thought he had been drawn to this place, Sommer reflected for a moment and simply said, "Like others at this conference, I am a spokesperson for a place. I cannot say how or why I was chosen for this role, but I have accepted it and it has changed my life."[52]

For anyone who has ever had a spiritual experience at a sacred place, the value of special places is forever understood. It cannot be known, however, which people really do have transpersonal experiences in nature, except by what they say. People can and do lie about visions and mystical encounters. Also, not everyone has had a sacred experience at a place of power, nor can they appreciate that this can even happen and why it is important. As a result, all around the world, bulldozers, earth movers, and chain saws stand waiting to transform sacred places into mines, mills, parking lots, factories, and shopping malls. What can we say in defense of these sacred places?

ENDNOTES

1. Gary Snyder, *Good, Wild, Sacred* (Madley, Hereford, U.K.: Five Seasons Press, 1984).

2. Peter Matthiessen, "Stop the Go Road," *Audubon*, January 1979, pp. 46-64.

3. Reported in *Brain-Mind Bulletin* 2, no. 9, March 21, 1977.

4. William James, *Varieties of Religious Experiences* (New York: Modern Library, 1902).

5. W.T. Stace, *Mysticism and Philosophy* (New York: Lippincott, 1960).

6. M. Laski, *Ecstasy: A Study of Some Secular and Religious Experiences* (Bloomington, Indiana: Indiana University Press, 1962).

7. A.H. Maslow, *The Farther Reaches of Human Nature* (New York: Viking Esalen Press, 1971).

8. Michael Murphy and Rhea White, *The Psychic Side of Sports* (Reading, MA: Addison-Wesley, 1978).

9. Stanislav Grof, *The Adventure of Self Discovery* (Albany, NY: SUNY Press, 1988).

10. Charles Tart, "States of Consciousness and State-Specific Sciences" *Science* 176, June 16, 1972, pp. 1203-1210.

11. Laski, *Ecstasy.*

12. Jake Page, "Inside the Sacred Hopi Homeland," *National Geographic* 162, no. 5, November 1982, pp. 607-629.

13. Richard Adams and Janice Haaken, "Pathology as 'Personal Growth': A Participant-Observation Study of Lifespring Training," *Psychiatry* 46, Aug. 1983, pp. 270-280; and Richard Adams and Janice Haaken, "Anticultural Culture: Lifespring's Ideology and Its Roots in Humanistic Psychology," *Journal of Humanistic Psychology* 27, no. 4, (Fall 1987): pp. 501-517.

14. Idries Shah, *The Way of the Sufi* (New York: E.P. Dutton, 1970).

15. James A. Swan, "Sacred Places in Nature and Transpersonal Experiences" *ReVision* 10, no. 3 (1988): pp. 21-26.

16. Laski. *Ecstasy.*

17. C.G. Jung, "On a Higher State of Consciousness," *Eranos Jarhbuch* (1938).

18. James A. Swan, *Returning to Our Roots: Organic Education and Social Transformation* (Beverly Hills, CA: Sage Public., Sage Research Papers in the Social Sciences, vol. 3, 1975).

19. Joseph Campbell, *The Masks of God: Creative Mythology* (New York: Penguin Edit., 1976), pp. 4-5.

20. NatureQuest, Drawer CZ, Bisbee, AZ 85603.

21. Sig Longren, "Sacred Space" (master's thesis, Goddard College, 1979), pp. 64-65.

22. Stanley Krippner and Alberto Villoldo, *The Realms of Healing* (Berkeley: Celestial Arts, 1976).

23. Michael Harner, *The Way of the Shaman* (New York: Bantam, 1982).

24. C.G. Jung, *Civilization in Transition*, vol. 10 of *The Collected Works of Carl Jung* (New York: Pantheon, Bollingen Series 20, 1964), p. 144.

25. Jaime Licauo, *True Encounters With the Unknown* (Manila: National Book Store, 1986).

26. Pat Ellis Taylor, *Border Healing Woman* (Austin, TX: University of Texas Press, 1981). pp. 63-64.

27. N. Curtis. *The Indians Book* (New York: Harper and Bros., 1907), p. 96.

28. Bert Schwarzschild, "Earthwatch: No Birds Sing on Saint Francis' Mountain," *Audubon* 85, no. 2, March 1983.

29. Ivan Sanderson, *Investigating the Unexplained* (Englewood Cliffs, NJ: Prentice-Hall, Inc., 1972).

30. Ronald Goodman and Stanley Red Bird, "Lakota Star Knowledge and the Black Hills" (Paper presented at the First International Ethnohistory Conference, Smithsonian Institution, Sept. 1983, Washington, DC)

31. Michael Persinger, "Geophysical Variables and Behavior: IX Expected Clinical Consequences of Close Proximity to UFO-related Numinosities," *Perceptual and Motor Skills* 56 (1983): pp. 259-265. Also, see P. Devereux, *Earth Lights* (London: Turnstone Press, 1982).

32. E.M. Case, "The Odor of Sanctity" (privately printed, no date).

33. P.L. Travers, "If She's Not Gone, She Lives There Still," *Parabola* 3, issue 1, 1978, p. 79.

34. K. Rasmussen, *Intellectual Culture of the Igulik Eskimos*: Report of the Fifth Thule Expedition, 1921-1924, vol. 7, no. 1. (Copenhagen: Gyldendalske Boghandel, Nordisk, Forlog, 1925).

35. Stanislav Grof, *The Adventure of Self-Discovery.*

36. Michael Harner, *The Way of the Shaman.*

37. Abraham Maslow, *The Farther Reaches of Human Nature.*

38. Stanislav Grof, *Beyond the Brain* (Albany, NY: SUNY Press, 1985).

39. Stanley Dean, "Metapsychiatry and Psychosocial Futurology" (3d Distinguished Lecture Series of the Institute of Psychiatry, Northwestern Memorial Hospital, and Dept. of Psychiatry, Northwestern University Medical School, May 18, 1977).

40. Aldo Leopold, *Sand County Almanac* (New York: Oxford University Press, 1966).

41. See L. Lutwack, *The Role of Place in Literature* (Syracuse, NY: Syracuse University Press, 1984).

42. Henry David Thoreau, *The Journal of Henry D. Thoreau*, 2 vols., eds. Bradford Torrey and Francis Allen (New York: Dover, 1962).

43. John Muir, *My First Summer in the Sierras* (New York: Houghton-Mifflin, 1916).

44. Thomas Tanner, "Significant Life Experiences: A New Research Area in Environmental Education," *Journal of Environmental Education* 11, no. 4, (Summer 1980): pp. 20-24.

45. Gifford Pinchot, *Breaking New Ground* (New York: Harcourt, Brace and World, Inc., 1947), p. 40.

46. Christie Kiefer and K. Cowan, "State/Context Dependence and Theories of Ritual" (Paper delivered at Faculty Seminar, University of California, San Francisco, 1978).

47. Joseph Campbell, *The Mythic Image* (Princeton, NJ: Princeton University Press, 1974).

48. Stanislav Grof, *Realms of the Human Unconscious* (New York: E.P. Dutton, 1976).

49. Steven Halpern, *Tuning the Human Instrument* (Belmont, CA: Spectrum Research Institute, 1978).

50. Theodor Schwenk, *The Sensitive Chaos* (New York: Schocken Books, paperback ed., 1978), p. 30.

51. Robert Sommer, *Scenic Drowning* (Davis, CA: Gray Cats Press, 1984).

52. Robert Sommer, "Stanislaus River Canyon" (Paper presented at the 1988 Spirit of Place Symposium, University of California at Davis, Davis, CA).

Photo 19. *A recent U.S. Supreme Court decision permits a logging road to be built near very sacred places of the Indians of northern California. This decision illustrates how difficult it can be to prove that a place may be sacred, and makes it easier to log or mine places which cannot be verified as being sacred and critical to the preservation of the practice of an ongoing religion. Photo of logging site by author.*

FOUR

Sacred Places
on Trial

"There are spiritual values in mountains."

CHIEF JUSTICE WILLIAM O. DOUGLAS

O n Sunday afternoon, March 8, 1964, Allen Cottier, a member of the Sioux nation and then the director of the Bay Area branch of the American Indian Council, accompanied by four other Native Americans dressed in traditional tribal costume, landed on the rocky shores of Alcatraz Island in the middle of San Francisco Bay. The infamous escape-proof federal penitentiary had been vacated that year. Cottier and his friends planted an American flag on the hillside and performed a ceremony. Then they held a press conference and declared "the Rock" to be Indian land under the 1868 Fort Laramie Treaty. A good ceremony brings about harmony and balance, driving out negative forces as well as drawing in desirable ones. As smoke from their medicine pipe rose upward, an irate National Park Service caretaker appeared and ordered the Indians to leave. They climbed into their boats and pushed off from shore, saying they would return. Then, as an eagle flew overhead, they quietly rowed away.

"Indian time" operates according to a clock located somewhere other than a wall or a bell tower. It wasn't until November 20, 1969, that a party of Indians returned to Alcatraz Island with the intent of staking their claim. Led by Mohawk organizer Richard Oakes, over 80 Indians came ashore. Grandfather Semu Huate, a Chumash medicine man, conducted a ceremony, and a two-year occupation of Alcatraz by Indians began.

From 1969 to 1971, this core group of Indians was visited by thousands of sympathizers of many heritages from all around the world. Among the visitors was a Sioux medicine man named Eagle Feather. One morning during his stay on Alcatraz, Eagle Feather called people together to tell them about a vision which he'd had in a dream the previous night. In his vision he had seen that there would come a time in the future when many dark forces would surface and seek to destroy the continuing heritage of Native American people. To call attention to this shroud of oppression, Eagle Feather's vision had instructed him that a march should be held, beginning on the West Coast and ending on the Eastern Shore. Eagle Feather had also seen that his pipe should go along on the march, to carry the medicine of the vision to Washington, D.C.

The Indians proposed transforming Alcatraz into a spiritual center, where the sacred plants of all Indian peoples would be grown and a special Indian university would be created. They said this center would be a balance to Ellis Island on the East Coast, welcoming all those who entered San Francisco Bay with an Indian sacred place. The Department of Interior disagreed. One summer morning in 1971, after numerous diplomatic attempts to get the Indians to leave Alcatraz, fifteen armed U.S. Marshalls came ashore on Alcatraz. The Indian occupation force left quietly, without bloodshed.

Years slipped away, and Eagle Feather's prophecy began to come true. In 1977, several bills were introduced into the U.S. Congress which, in the opinion of many wise observers, would strip the Native American tribes of power and set the stage for the destruction of an Indian nation with an intact traditional cultural heritage. Around the country, as lobbists pushed for the speedy passage of these bills in Congress, many council fires were held and medicine pipes smoked. Heeding Eagle Feather's vision, the word was passed along that a nationwide march was about to start.

On February 11, 1978, with almost no recognition from local or national media, the Longest Walk left San Francisco, headed eastward to where the sun rises, with Washington, D.C. as its goal.

Five months later, on July 15, 1978, the marchers reached the nation's capital, some of them having walked the entire route. They were then joined by 1500 people led by medicine man Ernie Peters. The march flowed peacefully to the Mall, where the participants erected a teepee village with the permission of the National Park Service—the first such encampment permitted since Resurrection City sprang up on the Mall in 1968. Eagle Feather's pipe came along with throng, carried in a beaded deerskin pouch, preserving the invisible thread of connection to Alcatraz and the vision.

During the next few weeks the Indian camp was visited by many people, including Dick Gregory, Max Gail, Marlon Brando, and California Congressman Ron Dellums. While ceremonial fires burned on the Mall, sparks flew inside Congress as the slate of anti-Indian bills was being scalped. In their place, a new law entitled the American Indian Religious Freedom Act of 1978, P.L. 95-341, was passed. As President Jimmy Carter put pen to paper to make the bill become law on August 11, 1978, outside on the Mall, Eagle Feather's pipe sent plumes of white smoke into the air, celebrating victory.

The American Indian Religious Freedom Act takes up only one page of the Congressional Record, and reads as follows:

PUBLIC LAW 95-341 [S.J. Res. 102]; Aug. 11, 1978
AMERICAN INDIAN RELIGIOUS FREEDOM

For Legislative History of Act, see p. 1262
Joint Resolution American Indian Religious Freedom.

Whereas the freedom of religion for all people is an inherent right, fundamental to the democratic structure of the United States and is guaranteed by the First Amendment of the United States Constitution:

Whereas the United States has traditionally rejected the concept of a government denying individuals the right to practice their religion and, as a result, has benefited from a rich variety of religious heritage in this country;

Whereas the religious practices of the American Indian (as well as Native Alaskan and Hawaiian) are an integral part of their culture, tradition and heritage, such practices forming the basis of Indian identity and value systems;

Whereas the traditional American Indian religions, as an integral part of Indian life, are indispensable and irreplaceable;

Whereas the lack of a clear, comprehensive, and consistent Federal policy has often resulted in the abridgment of religious freedom for traditional American Indians;

Whereas such religious infringements result from the lack of knowledge or the insensitive and inflexible enforcement of Federal policies and regulations premised on a variety of laws;

Whereas such laws were designed for such worthwhile purposes as conservation and preservation of natural species and resources but were never intended to relate to Indian religious practices and, therefore, were passed without consideration of their effect on traditional American Indian religions;

Whereas such laws and policies often deny American Indians access to sacred sites required in their religions, including cemeteries;

Whereas such laws at times prohibit the use and possession of sacred objects necessary to the exercise of religious rites and ceremonies;

Whereas traditional American Indian ceremonies have been intruded upon, interfered with, and in a few instances banned: Now, therefore, be it

Resolved by the Senate and House of Representatives of the United States of America in Congress assembled, That henceforth it shall be the policy of the United States to protect and preserve for American Indians their inherent right of freedom to believe, express, and exercise the traditional religions of the American Indian, Eskimo, Aleut, and Native Hawaiians, including but not limited to access to sites, use and possession of sacred objects, and the freedom to worship through ceremonials and traditional rites.

American Indian Religious Freedom. 42 USC 1996.

42 USC 1996
NOTE.

Presidential
report to
Congress.

SEC. 2. The President shall direct the various Federal departments, agencies, and other instrumentalities responsible for administering relevant laws to evaluate their policies and procedures in consultation with native traditional religious leaders in order to determine appropriate religious cultural rights and practices. Twelve months after approval of this resolution, the President shall report back to the Congress the results of his evaluation, including any changes which were made in administrative policies and procedures, and any recommendations he may have for legislative action.

Approved August 11, 1978.

LEGISLATIVE HISTORY:

HOUSE REPORT No. 95-1308 accompanying H.J. Res. 738
    (Comm. on Interior and Indian Affairs).
SENATE REPORT No. 95-709 (Comm. on Indian Affairs).
CONGRESSIONAL RECORD, Vol. 124 (1978)
    Apr. 3, considered and passed Senate.
    July 18, H.J. Res. 738 considered and passed House;
        proceedings vacated and S.J. Res. 102, amended, passed in lieu.
    July 27, Senate concurred in House amendment.

With respect to sacred sites, there are two key phrases in this act. At the end of the first section, the law expresses a desire to "protect and preserve" the American Indian religion, "including but not limited to access to sacred sites, [and] use and possession of sacred objects." This wording gives birth to a new land-use category—the sacred place in nature—at least according to American Indian spiritual traditions.

The second key phrasing is in section 2, in which all federal departments and agencies are charged with consulting "native traditional religious leaders" to determine how their policies and procedures need to be changed to preserve and protect the American Indian religion, including determining which places are supposed to be sacred. They were to have done this in one year's time and reported back to the president, who in turn was to tell Congress the results of the evaluations. True to its intent, in August 1979, the Federal Agencies Task Force, led by Cecil D. Andrus, then secretary of the Interior, released its report in a ⅝-inch-thick paperback volume with a bright red cover titled *American Indian Religious Freedom Act Report, P.L. 95-341.*[1]

Contained within this report are copies of letters from all the agencies surveyed, and some summaries showing conclusions. In spirit, this is a monumental document, but a close reading of the report and its conclusions is troubling. For example, on page 89 the report states: "The major sites of Native American religious ceremonials are well known, and any future controversy must revolve around known sites, not any additional sites that might come into being. . . . The known shrines and sites originate in creation and migration traditions, which by their very nature are foreclosed for the remainder of the world.'' The implication of this statement is that all the major sites are already known, presumably as a result of the survey conducted for this report, because clearly they were not known beforehand. Also, the definition of a ''major site'' versus a ''minor site'' remains an issue of great debate and potential danger. Someone might claim, for example, that such and such a place is not a major site, and therefore is not of any significant value, so it can be strip-mined.

The report goes on to worry about any commercialism which could result from the publicizing of these sites, which is a legitimate concern. The American mind seems to have a knack for commercializing almost anything, from Christianity to abortion and when Humphrey the whale was stranded in San Francisco Bay. The possibilities of tourist attractions to go see Chief So and So's grave or to climb an Indian sacred mountain are very real, not to forget the lucrative black market for Indian artifacts illegally taken from old graves.

The report then calls for non-Natives to take responsibility to ''help Natives prevent non-Natives from exploiting Native culture.'' Here again, the intent seems commendable. Indians get rightfully angry if non-Indians without tribal recognition say they are practitioners of Native American religion. This is like someone saying they are a Christian priest without ever having gone to Bible college and having been ordained. Some Indians call non-Indians who try to copy their religion and culture ''Wannabees.'' The Wannabees want to be Indians, but are another color, according to those who feel this way.

As with the Civil Rights Movement of the 1950s and 1960s, the report supports non-Indians who are working to prevent exploitation of Indian culture. If this means exposing ''Indian jewelry'' made in China or Japan for what it is, then the proposal is right on target. But the call for protection and confidentiality has in many ways weakened the power of this law as much as it has helped to keep Indian knowledge intact.

The cover of the American Indian Religious Freedom Act report depicts the U.S. Department of Interior logo, a western scene showing the sun rising over some mountains and a buffalo standing in the foreground. This scene looks remarkably like the Black Hills or even Bear Butte. The choice of such a design demonstrates the power of places to move people and the desire to use them in developing mythic standards. Passing a law like this one should give places like Point Conception or Bear Butte more protection, but reviewing the consequences of the passage of P.L. 95-341 shows that this has generally not been the case.

''The law [P.L. 95-341] is unusually general and cryptic,'' observes attorney Ellen M.W. Sewell of the American Indian Religious Freedom Act after four years of studying its implementation.[2] The federal government did carry out the law's directives to survey its policies and practices concerning American Indian religious freedom. The resulting report finds that U.S. history shows a long history of both the church and the state seeking to destroy the practice of the American Indian traditional religion. It was not until the passage of the 1934 Indian Reorganization Act that the practice of the Indian religion was recognized as being legitimate and not a crime. The report also recognizes that the core belief of the Indian religion is that everything is alive, and that spirituality is sought through intimate communion with the natural world. In addition, the report also acknowledges that

> the Native peoples of this country believe that certain areas of land are holy. These lands may be sacred, for example, because of religious events which occurred there, because they contain specific natural products, because they are the dwelling place or embodiment of spiritual beings, because they surround or contain burial grounds, or because they are sites conducive to communicating with spiritual beings.[3]

It's heartwarming to hear a U.S. government report say things like this, but translating such philosophic law into action involves several steps. There is the level of words—making sure that things say on paper what they should say. Then there is the level of relationships, which involves human personalities. Finally, there is the level of implementation, which includes such things as where the fences and roads go, what the law-enforcement officers enforce, and, most important of all, when there are several different views about a single piece of land's value, choosing among these views.

At the level of paperwork, the American Indian Religious Freedom Act has forced all government agencies to review their land holdings and practices in relation to the Indian religion. Anyone who has ever sat at a desk in Washington, D.C., pushing a pen and shuffling papers, like I did one summer for the Bureau of Land Management, will know that trying to keep close tabs on what the government is doing as a whole is a little like trying to keep track of all the members of a giant ant colony. People might ask each other questions, write letters, and check files to be sure their act is covered, but to thoroughly review the entire government's actions and holdings in a year is impossible.

The law specifically calls for "the various Federal departments, agencies, and other instrumentalities responsible for administering relevant laws to evaluate their policies and procedures in consultation with native traditional religious leaders." This means that agencies cannot just compile the records they have on file and come up with a legal report. They have to talk with Indians as well. This ensures at least some personal Indian input into the implementation, but the crucial question is who they actually talk to.

The problem is that American Indians do not have a system like modern religions such as Judaism, Christianity, or the Muslim faith which clearly spells out who is a legitimate spiritual leader. Among the more than 300 Native American tribal groups which are recognized as having existed (some are considered extinct, although Indians debate this), there is considerable variation in their exact practices of religion and in what they require for someone to be a legitimate spiritual practitioner. In many tribes, for example, a medicine person is not paid for his or her services, except perhaps for a token gift of tobacco. To offer anything else would be an insult. Among some Pacific Northwest tribes, on the other hand, piles of blankets, copper tablets, and smoked salmon are traditionally heaped at the feet of the shaman just to see if he or she will even consider the case.

For the Pueblo tribes, which have well-defined clans and systems for attaining priesthood, it's much easier to determine who is a legitimate spiritual leader than among traditionally nomadic peoples with many bands and a more shamanic path to becoming a spiritual leader, like the Lakotas or the Eskimos. Yet even among the Pueblos there is dissension. For example, the traditional Hopi support allowing the Navajo to remain at Big Mountain, while the progressive Hopi want the Big Mountain Navajo relocated so that the Hopi nation can claim the mountain.

Among tribes in which the medicine person is more an individuated shaman than a ritual priest, becoming established as a medicine person has many paths. Sometimes becoming a medicine person is largely a matter of clans and family traditions. Other times it is the result of a schooling process which is well known and accredited by the tribe and involves apprenticeships and ceremonies to mark the passage through the stages of becoming a medicine person.

This problem of determining legitimate spiritual leadership is further compounded by divisiveness within the Indian community over legitimate tribal political leadership. Some Indians assert that many of the "official" tribal councils are puppet governments created by the U.S. Bureau of Indian Affairs. When I was working with the Klamaths and Modocs in southern Oregon, there were at least five different people and/or groups who insisted that they alone were the real spiritual leaders and that all the others were phony. On some reservations, regardless of the spiritual powers of the respective holy people, there are no real practitioners of the traditional religion left. One example is tribes of the Northwest on whose reservations there are now Shaker churches—which can have plenty of spirit—but this is not the traditional religion. Does this mean, given the wording of the American Indian Religious Freedom Act, that these tribes can't stake claims to any sacred places? Only the courts can decide such issues.

The point is simply that, considering the way the law reads, it is all too easy for a government agency to find the ''spiritual leaders'' it *wants* to talk with, interview them in private, and keep the reports confidential, with no way to document the validity of what they've been told. Then, if this government agency announces plans to go out and cut a grove of trees or mine a mountain and Indians suddenly object because these are sacred places, the agency can pull its confidential files out of the drawer and use them to justify its actions.

The problem is further compounded by trying to determine who is a ''legal Indian.'' Few full-blooded Indians remain, and, even if someone is 100 percent Indian blood, this doesn't mean they are the automatic experts on Indian religion. Many, many Indian children were taken away from their homes in the 1800s and early 1900s, and led to believe that their old ways were evil. Floyd Westerman, a Sisseton-Wapeton Lakota, talks about how, when he was growing up in a white school, he was told that if he got caught speaking Lakota his head would be cut off. For many tribes, keeping their traditions alive was for years a clandestine matter. Thus, the individuals who today appear to be the spiritual leaders may actually be only those who are recognized by the federal government and who may or may not be real shamans. Many of the most powerful Indian shamans I have met aren't registered with the Bureau of Indian Affairs (BIA) as Indians, because they protest such a practice. This leads to their being challenged as phony by other Indians and the BIA. Real shamans are determined by a force far more powerful than a federal government agency.

Being a ''legal Indian'' in most places is either a matter of tribal membership or of proving that a person is a certain percentage of Indian blood. Tribal membership sometimes requires a person to be born on a reservation, which could mean that full-bloods born elsewhere are not tribal members. Some federal programs require proof of one-quarter Indian blood to be a legitimate Indian. Other programs may only require one-eighth. In Texas, you only have to prove 5 percent Indian heritage to legally possess peyote to use in ceremonies of the Native American Church, which some Indians say isn't a legitimate Indian religion at all.

The consequences of the confusion over who is a legitimate Indian spiritual leader become apparent when someone wants to develop an area which particular Indians say is sacred. At Craven Canyon in the Black Hills of South Dakota, there are rock petroglyphs so old that no one knows who put them there. No one has been using Craven Canyon for specific religious rites, so 22 or more uranium-mining companies want to mine there. They say that since no present-day, official tribal spiritual leaders use this place for ceremonies, it is instead only an archaeological site, and therefore can be adequately protected by putting chain link fences around the rock art while the drilling rigs and giant cranes sink their shafts into the ground just a few feet away. Even if medicine people of the Lakotas or other tribes used Craven Canyon for rites, their use of the canyon still would not sanctify it as a sacred place according to the American Indian Religious Freedom Act, because these tribes didn't traditionally live in the Black Hills.

Proof of the sacredness of a place is virtually impossible, according to P.L. 95-341, if the indigenous tribe of the area no longer exists. My neighbor, Mount Tamalpais in Marin County, California, is a sacred place according to the Coastal Miwoks, who supposedly no longer exist as a distinct tribe. Fortunately, however, the mountain is a California state park, and Muir Woods National Monument is on its west flank, so it is protected from development. Shamans from all over the world who visit the mountain declare Tamalpais, supposedly a resting maiden in the Miwok cosmology, a very sacred place.

One of the most popular ceremonies on Mount Tamalpais is conducted each Easter by dancer-choreographer Anna Halprin, who brings together spiritually minded people from all faiths to honor the living myth of the mountain. I have a photo I took one spring of the heart of the ceremony, showing Floyd Westerman singing a spiritual song at sunrise, and Anna kneeling beside him holding a staff with an eagle feather dangling from its shaft. When I show this slide to groups of people, their breathing softens in response to the obvious sacredness of the event. Technically, however, since Floyd is a Lakota and this is a Miwok sacred place, Floyd's actions do nothing to lend official credence to the idea that Mount Tamalpais is an Indian sacred place. This would only be true if he were someplace in South Dakota, home of the Lakota. Anna is Jewish. She is holding the eagle feather, and since she is white, she can't legally own an eagle feather because eagles are an endangered species. Therefore, one analysis of the picture is that it shows an Indian man and a white woman committing an illegal act on top of a mountain in front of an audience. (The feather, incidentally, belongs to Anna's son-in-law, Jasper, who is an Indian.)

If you think this is a deplorable situation, consider the plight of the Klamath and Modoc tribes near Klamath Falls, Oregon. In the early 1970s, timber companies offered these tribes considerable money for reservation land holdings. "Progressive" tribal members wanted to sell, while traditionals opposed the sale. An election was held to determine what to do. The progressives, who many say were a small minority of the tribe, got all their friends out to vote. The traditionals sent their representatives to cast their ballots, which was customary in that culture. It was a white man's popular election, and so the progressives won. Now the Indians of Klamath Falls no longer have any land, except for perhaps Chief Eddie Chiloquin, who never cashed his settlement check.

Reviewing the history of court actions concerning the protection of American Indian sacred places is a depressing experience. Judges tend to think of religion as being "faith-centered" and capable of being expressed anyplace, rather than being linked to specific natural places. Modern religions build buildings to mark where spirit is, implying that it is the building which makes a place spiritual and not the place's natural essence—just the opposite of the Indian worldview. Native traditions feel that the place itself is of paramount importance.

For example, in 1981 the Navajo Medicine Men's Association went to court to say that tourism should be restricted at Rainbow Bridge in Rainbow Bridge National Monument because this is a sacred shrine where a spirit lives. The Navajo wanted to restrict tour boats on Lake Powell from sailing too close to Rainbow Bridge. In the district court hearing on this case, *Bandoni* v. *Higginson*, the court ruled that the Navajo had no legitimate claim under the First Amendment because they had no property rights at the monument. An appellate court review of the case then decided that a group does not have to own land to claim that the land has religious value to them; however, the court also decided that the real issue was one of highest use. It said that the creation of the dam which formed Lake Powell had implications for flood control, irrigation, electrical power generation, and recreation, all of which were linked to national security. Placed on a scale against Navajo religious values, the court said the dam and the resulting tourism program, including excursion boats bringing visitors to Rainbow Bridge, represented a use of higher value to the country.[4]

This shows how fragile the Indian religion can be in a court of law when it is viewed by nonmembers of the religion. The Navajo talked about how the spirit at Rainbow Bridge was well known to their medicine people, as it had appeared in their dreams. Dreams, the judge said, are not legitimate proof in a court of law. To make his point, the judge cited a case where a man had claimed that he had had a dream of the Lincoln Memorial which told him that it was a sacred place, and he had asked to hold ceremonies on its steps. The judge then asked how one man's dream could be better than another's, and dismissed the case.

Similarly, in 1988 the United States Supreme Court ruled that the U.S. Forest Service could not be prevented from building a logging road—the infamous G-O Road—through the Six Rivers National Forest in northern California. Writing for the majority, Justice Sandra Day O'Conner said, "However much we might wish it were otherwise, government simply could not operate if it were required to satisfy every citizen's religious needs and desires."

In a related case, *Wilson* v. *Block* (1983), the Navajo and Hopi medicine people both opposed the expansion of the Arizona Snow Bowl Ski Area, which lies in the San Francisco Peaks of Arizona. The court did not challenge the sacredness of this well-known home of the kachinas (spirits), but said simply that just because some people say a place is holy, it does not mean the place can be protected from development of all kinds. The court further said that because the San Francisco Peaks were not used directly for ceremonies, but were instead honored from a distance, that preventing development of ski runs would be an "unconstitutional establishment of religion."[5]

The First Amendment guarantees protection of religious freedom, but it cannot be used to aid the establishment of a religion, which could be a prejudicial act. Therefore, if an Indian tribe can prove that it is presently using a site as an integral part of its religious practice, and that it has been using this site for decades (or better, centuries) in the same fashion, then the site's legitimacy as a sacred place is affirmed. However, if a tribe is no longer recognized as existing, then none of the sacred places in its ancestral homeland can be protected under existing laws, unless the sites contain archaeological artifacts. Also, proof of continued use of sacred sites by existing tribes is made further difficult if the religion is practiced in private, without leaving any physical traces.

The easiest sacred places to validate and protect are those which have obvious historical value. The Antiquities Act of 1906 gave the president the power to set aside national monuments like Pipestone National Monument, Canyon de Chelly National Monument, and Effigy Mounds National Monument, because they possessed obvious historical treasures of universal cultural value. Prior to the passage of the Antiquities Act, specific sites like the Serpent Mound could receive protection, but each required a special act of Congress for federal recognition.

The Historic Sites Act of 1935 called for the National Park Service to initiate a National Register of Historic Sites, including the establishment of national historic landmarks. Section Six of the Historic Sites Act calls for protecting "archaeological sites that have produced information of major scientific importance by revealing new cultures or shedding light upon periods of occupation over large areas of the United States." The National Historic Preservation Act of 1966 extends this policy directive to include recognition for Cultural Heritage Sites on private as well as public lands. As of 1985, there are nearly 35,000 Cultural Heritage Sites on the National Register, with as many as 4,000 to 5,000 new sites being recommended for inclusion and addition each year. When a site is listed on the Register, there is no guarantee that it will be preserved, but the site is established as a place worthy of national recognition, which makes it harder to destroy without a fight.

Richard Nixon is a name which has gone down in United States history as being linked with Watergate and the subsequent demise of his presidency, but it should be noted that Nixon struck two important blows for Indian rights. In December 1970, Nixon signed into law the bill which restored to Taos Pueblo ownership the 44,000 acres containing sacred Blue Lake. Then in 1972, Nixon also approved returning Mount Adams to the Yakima tribe.

The Archaeological Resources Protection Act of 1979 took one step beyond previously existing statutes, proclaiming that "existing federal laws do not provide adequate protection to prevent the loss and destruction of archaeological resources and sites resulting from uncontrolled excavations and pillage." It calls for securing protection of archaeological resources for present and future generations, as they are an "irreplaceable part of the Nation's heritage," and seeks to encourage cooperation among all groups interested in archaeological protection.

The bottom line for protection of sacred places according to these statutes is the definition of an "archaeological site." If a place has significant artifacts which are over 100 years old, then it has a good chance of being considered. But what should be done with an area like the Four Corners region, where there is roughly one ancient Anasazi Indian habitation site for every ten square acres of land? Or Marin County, California, where there are old middens of clam and oyster shells every mile or two along the shoreline of San Francisco Bay and the Pacific Ocean? Do these middens represent archaeological resources even though they are ancient garbage dumps? One frustrated Marin developer, who had unearthed a midden right where he wanted to build a waterfront office complex, testified at a public hearing that he was considering hiring a "consulting shaman" to join his crew to determine sacred sites in advance of any development activity. (In Hawaii, incidentally, some developers do hire kahunas for such purposes.)

This brief review of legislative actions and judicial procedures yields important insights into our cultural paradigm and its biases. People may talk about sacred places with knowledge and reverence, but the actual preservation of these places ultimately rests with laws, public policies, and their implementation. According to the legal definition, sacred places exist only if they are used in the ongoing practice of a traditional religion, or if they possess artifacts 100 years old or older. (Incidentally, the status of more than one place has been helped along by people who have quietly buried old pottery shards in the dark of night.) But even if a place is used for ceremonies and does have artifacts, it still must be shown that preservation of the place for its sacred values is the "highest use" for it. One witness, who appeared before the hearings concerning the use of Point Conception for a liquid natural gas plant, said, "Most importantly, it must be kept in mind that the choice is between possible damage to some artifacts and the rejection of a much needed gas project to serve the needs of 22 million people in California."[6]

People find peace of mind and meaning through understanding their heritage in human history and in the land. Carl Jung wisely said that we cannot move into the future with certainty of cultural sanity and ecological stability unless we are grounded in the past and in the Earth where we live. Sacred sites can and do represent a fundamental element in the preservation of human heritage. But their value is much greater than that of a geographic museum. Whether they have artifacts or not, sacred places are religious sites with the potential to move the human mind into those spaces which are wellsprings of creativity, health, and vision. Until we have a living spirituality which is rooted in the Earth and in all the tribes of nature, we will never really achieve ecological harmony.

Across the United States and around the world, sacred places are on trial. Assume for a minute that a hearing has been called before a land commission which wants to know why such a place is so valuable. Why is a sacred place in nature the highest possible use for a particular location? The defense begins by calling attention to the existing statutes on Indian land law, and by citing reports about people having had unusual experiences there. Both of these statements of fact help, but in themselves don't constitute any kind of guarantee of preservation. It is possible, however, to pull in more evidence to support the place's uniqueness and value.

One strategy for supporting this position is to assemble a group of well-respected people who will step forward and give testimony on the merits of the issue. One could even look through history for some "character witnesses" to speak out on sacred places. The following statements indicate the enduring value of the power of special places for the human species.

TESTIMONIALS TO THE POWER OF SACRED PLACES

Seneca, a Roman stoic philosopher who lived from 3 BC to AD 65:

"When you find yourself within a grove of exceptionally tall, old trees, whose interlocking boughs mysteriously shut off the view of the sky, the great height of the forest and the secrecy of the place together with a sense of awe before the dense, impenetrable shades will awaken in you the belief in a god. And when a grotto has been hewn into the hallowed rock of a mountain, not by human hands but by the powers of nature, and not too great depth, it pervades your soul with an awesome sense of the religious. We honor the source of great rivers. Altars are raised where the sudden freshet of a stream breaks from below ground. Hot springs of steaming water inspire veneration. And many a pond is sanctified because of its hidden situation or immeasurable depth."

Zangshu, the Burial Book of Quo-pu (AD 276-324) a classic work of Chinese geomancy, in Parabola *3, issue 1 (1978):*

"At a true Cave there is a touch of magic light. How so, magic? It can be understood intuitively, but not conveyed in words. The hills are fair, the waters fine, the sun handsome, the breeze mild; and the sky has another light; another world. Amid confusion, peace; amid peace, a festive air. Upon coming into its presence, one's eyes are opened; if one sites or lies, one's heart is joyful. Here the chi gathers, and the essence collects. Light shines in the middle and magic goes out on all sides. Above or below, to right or left, it is not thus. No greater than a finger, no more than a spoonful; like a dewdrop, like a pearl, like the moon through a crack, like the reflection in a mirror. Play with it, and it is as if you can catch it; put it off, and it cannot be rid of. Try to understand! It is hard to describe.''

George Winthrop Young, remarking of his visit to Delphi in The Influence of Mountains Upon the Development of the Human Intelligence, *(Glasgow, Scotland: Jackson and Co., 1957), p. 26:*

''To most of us it comes as a surprise to discover that the impression of sanctity or divinity, which we expected to receive from the cascade of splendid statuary, the ruined temples and shrines descending upon the shattered terraces and ledges of masonry, does not emanate from them, but belongs to the penetrating emotion of the great mountain scene itself.''

J. Newcomb and G. Reichard, in Sandpaintings of the Navaho Shooting Chant. *(New York: Dover Publishing Co., Inc., 1975):*

''Locality is of the greatest importance to the Navaho. Names of people, of animals, of dangers, names of arrows, of lightnings and plants, have power when known and used properly. Even so names of places are charms. As the modern writer or dramatist gives his work setting, so also does the Navaho myth. Whenever a protagonist meets someone who is more powerful, the first question he must answer is 'where are you from?' ''

Chief John Snow, in These Mountains Are Our Sacred Places *(Toronto: Samuel Stevens, 1977), p. 3:*

''We talked to the rocks, the streams, the trees, the plants, the herbs and all nature's creations. We called the animals our brothers. They understood our language; we understood theirs. Sometimes they talked to us in dreams and visions. At times they revealed important events or visited us on our vision quests to the mountain tops.''

Vine Deloria, Jr., in God Is Red *(New York: Grosset and Dunlap, 1973), p. 294:*

''The major step to be taken to understand religion today is to understand the nature of religion as it occurs in specific places. There is a reason why shrines exist over and above the piety of the uneducated religious person who has visions while tending sheep. . . . If this concept is true then economics cannot and should not be the sole determinant of land use. Unless the sacred places are discovered and protected and used as religious places, there is no possibility of a nation ever coming to grips with the land itself . . . [and] national psychic stability is impossible.''

Photo 20. *Grandmother & Her Basket, Pyramid Lake, Nevada. Photo ©*
1990 by Cindy A. Pavlinac.

Carlos Castaneda, in The Journey to Ixtlan *(New York: Simon and Schuster, 1972):*
"Fix all this in your memory. This spot is yours. This morning you *saw*,
and that was the omen. You found this spot by *seeing*. The omen was unexpected,
but it happened. You are going to hunt power whether you like it or not. It
is not a human decision, not yours or mine. Now, properly speaking, this hilltop
is your place, your beloved place; all that is around you is under your care. You
must look after everything here and everything will in turn look after you."

Stanislav Grof, M.D., in personal correspondence (1982):
"I have myself no doubt about the reality of 'power spots.' One of them
is certainly the place where Hot Springs Creek at Esalen forms a waterfall and
joins the Pacific. Several Mexican and North American shamans whom we have
invited to our workshops identified it as such, quite independently. My wife,
Christina, and I have been conducting workshops here for some time using that
area, and we have seen such intense transformative reactions in people while in
contact with this area that they can hardly be explained as results of our inputs."

Lama Anagarika Govinda, in "Sacred Mountains," the foreword to W.Y. Evans-Wentz,
Chuchuma and Sacred Mountains, *edited by Frank Waters (Chicago: Swallow Press,*
1981), p. xxix:
"There are mountains which are just mountains and there are mountains

with personality. The personality of a mountain is dependent upon more than merely a strange shape which makes it different from other mountains . . . Personality consists of the power to influence others, and this power is due to consistency, harmony and one-pointedness of character. If these qualities are present in an individual in their highest perfection, he is a fit leader of humanity, be he a ruler, a thinker or a saint; we recognize him as a vessel of supramundane power. If these qualities are present in a mountain, we recognize it as a vessel of cosmic power and we call it a sacred mountain.''

D.M. Dooling, in "Focus," Parabola 3, issue 1 (1978), p. 3:
''The scalp prickles when we pass a certain ancient doorway; we shiver, spinechilled, in such a spot as the ceremonial cavern at Bandelier; the voice drops to a whisper at Chartres. . . .

''When we examine our own experience as well as the records left to us in earth and stone, we see that sacred space is not just any space; it must be defined by something and contained by this definition. It is enclosed by boundaries which are not necessarily walls and a roof; its boundaries are the boundaries of power.''

Swami Nirvedananda, in Hinduism at a Glance *(Calcutta, India: Friends Publishing Co., 1968), pp. 204-205:*
''God manifests Himself as nature . . . the rivers and mountains are the bodies of their presiding deities who are worshipped by the Hindus. . . . The atmosphere of these places is congenial to realization. All-pervading God appears to be thinly-veiled, as it were, in these areas, so that a little search may lead one up to Him.''

Resolution 12, First World Congress on Cultural Parks, Mesa Verde, Colorado, October 1, 1984 (published by US/ICOMOS, Washington, D.C.):
''Preservation and conservation of cultural property should be one of the major concerns of parks, cultural and natural reserves and museums in all nations. Archaeological sites, including rock art sites, should be recognized as truly international cultural resources, protected and interpreted and made available to the public in consultation with native peoples who may be the guardians of such sites.''

Walter Jeske, in Toward an Action Plan: A Report to the Intergovernmental Conference on Environmental Education *(Washington, DC: U.S. Department of Health, Education, and Welfare, 1978):*
''In 1977 the United Nations Environment Programme Tbilsi Conference called for 'improvement of the quality of life everywhere, including safeguarding the holy places.' ''

Photo 21. *Mount Baker, the sacred mountain of the Lummi Indians of northwestern Washington. Author photo.*

IN SEARCH OF THE SIGNIFICANT DIFFERENCE

These voices, and many, many more of like mind, historically and today, share the belief that at certain places on the face of the Earth there is a spiritual ambiance or power which can and does move human minds into transcendental states. Society has mountains of data about stimulus and response, child development, sexuality, and psychopathology. There are public opinions on just about everything under the sun, but next to nothing is written in psychology books about the urge to make pilgrimages to sacred places, even though most people do it. The case histories provided earlier speak only too clearly on the power of place to move people's minds. The pages of children's fairy tales abound with magical places, like Winnie-the-Poo's "thinking spot," and Brer Rabbit's "laughin' place." Sacred places seem for Americans to live only in other cultures or in children's literature. It's a strange culture that knows more about the "G spot" than the power of Lourdes to heal.

In other times and cultures, life and reality were rooted in feeling and sensing. From early childhood, people learned to recognize the periods of the moon, the approach of a thunderstorm, and the power of place in their bodies. Maybe it was modern, from the-neck-up religion that caused people to lose their senses. Maybe it was mechanistic science, which required external, objective proof for the existence of everything, that convinced modern people to dismiss emotions and intuitions in favor of logical rationality. Maybe both religion and science are the culprits, for the chief problem of modern society is its loss of the ability to feel. This psychological bias has had a tremendous influence on our science and its offspring technology.

"A psychological interpretation of science begins with the acute realization that science is a human creation," observed Abraham Maslow. "Its laws, organization, and articulations rest not only on the nature of reality that it discovers, but also on the nature of human nature that does the discovering."[7]

Whether scientist or reindeer herder, we must all choose from an enormous array of environmental conditions that which we will be conscious of at any one time. If a person's day is spent watching animals grazing on the Arctic tundra, he or she will become acutely aware of their moods and behavior as well as the passing weather conditions. A slight indentation in the ground or a few bent blades of grass, which the untrained eye might not even notice, can tell stories of great importance to the Bushmen, the Sami, the pygmies of the Congo, or the Australian Aborigines. On the other hand, few hunting and gathering peoples would do well devising a plan to build the Golden Gate Bridge.

People choose to pay attention to certain things out of personal and cultural need, but they also direct their awareness because of cultural prohibitions, and censor their spoken words even more. Until the Civil Rights Movement, people seldom talked about racial prejudice, even though it was rampant and blatant in many areas of the country. When the Sexual Revolution mushroomed in the late 1960s, newspaper columnists began to talk about feelings and subjects that just a few years earlier would have resulted in expulsion of students from college campuses. An awareness of Westerners' difficulty in owning and expressing feelings has resulted in a fantastic explosion of a the human potential movement, treating a problem which was not even acknowledged as existing as recently as a decade or two ago. The next veil to life which may be lifted is humanity's avoidance of its feelings about nature.

The technological growth of the twentieth century is partially attributable to Westerners' almost obsessive application of mechanistic science. The increasing complexity of the language and thought of science has in turn created a new priest caste: the white-coated scientist, who fills a social void once held by spiritual seers, shamans, and sages. One could liken this societal process to people locking themselves in one room of an apartment building called the mind, and filling the room with computers. But now the foundation of the building is crumbling. When someone stumbles into the elevator and travels to another floor, society worries about his or her sanity. Western culture seeks to keep the room temperature constant, while outside, the greenhouse effect is warming things up. Worst of all, as people begin to see that new technologies are developed to do just about anything, they discover that the electric power supply to the beloved computer may be shut down by energy shortages. Isn't it about time modern people got down to Earth again? Technological development unconnected to nature and unaware of its consequences for people and nature is almost certain suicide.

In perception psychology, research people are frequently asked to discriminate between two objects or conditions. To judge the acuity of a person's perceptions, researchers look for the smallest difference between things that a person can perceive. This is commonly called the Just Noticeable Difference or JND. The identity of a sacred place is based on its ability to be recognized as significantly different from another place, although, as Black Elk wisely said, any place can be sacred. The previous chapter contains a lot of material which attests to the specialness of certain places. However, not everyone feels this unusualness about a place. Is it possible that science could help shed light on sacred places by providing objective measures to help confirm that these places are different in reality and not just in the imagination?

The Significant Difference

If one walks into a coliseum hours before a rock concert is scheduled to begin, the space doesn't affect that person the same way it does a few hours later when the place is jammed with bodies dancing in time to a sensuous guitar solo which screams above a driving keyboard melody and a thundering set of drums. If the personal charisma of a Bob Dylan or a Grateful Dead band is thrown in, the result becomes a more spirited gathering than most religious services. The "vibes" in the place take over, and either one leaves, or stays and is swept up in the ambiance, becoming played like a human instrument.

One of the greatest revolutions in modern psychology was B.F. Skinner's stimulus-response theory of behavior. He showed that putting rats or pigeons in boxes and controlling their environments enabled their behavior to be simplified. He concluded that all behavior can be explained in terms of stimulus-response terms and concepts. His discoveries were especially well-received in academic circles, for he made psychology very quantifiable, so that it appeared scientific in a mechanistic sense. This proved to be a great blessing for getting grants, because psychologists could finally talk to other scientists using the language of numbers, and they could be understood. Realizing how Skinner's model could get them rewards more easily and consistently, the behavioral scientists, like mice in Skinner boxes, adopted his paradigm with gusto, perpetuating its myopia of the complexity of human motivation.

In contrast to Skinner's simplification model of behavior, Kurt Lewin proposed a "field theory" for behavior.[8] Lewin said that a person's behavior is a function of the interaction between the person and the surrounding environmental field, as well as any single part of this field. Echoing Jean Piaget's concept of behavior arising from a "continuity of exchanges" between people and their environments, Lewin talked about real life and not the Skinnerian dream of a nice, simple, controllable reality.[9] At no time in human history prior to Skinner is there any notion of human behavior being so simplistic. This says that either Skinner was the next Christ, or that his model worked so well because it played into the neurosis of our times: mechanism.

In contrast to mechanistic scientists who study things under controlled conditions only, naturalist scientists learn to watch the entire world with carefully trained eyes and instruments and to gather data. They believe that if they can perceive well enough, patterns and laws of nature will emerge from their data which will explain what is going on. As physics has moved from mechanism to more of an organic wholism in the last few decades, the idea of a pattern language of all living things has evolved, thanks to people like David Bohm, Gregory Bateson, and Fritjof Capra.

We exist in a field of environmental forces, visible and invisible, subtle and gross. Hans Jenny created a way for us to begin to understand why some environments move us so. Jenny placed fine particles such as iron filings and light powders on very smooth surfaces and played his violin nearby. It is known that sound creates a disturbance in air molecules as it travels through space. What Jenny found was that each note he played activated the tiny particles nearby, leaving a special "signature" pattern in the particles as an expression of the wave patterns created by the sound. Not only were the patterns unique, but they often took on haunting organic shapes, sometimes resembling shells, honeycombs, colonial organisms, and jellyfish. To his delight, Jenny found that many of the patterns took on the lattice structure of spiritual mandalas drawn by religious adepts who spend many, many hours chanting certain sounds.[10] His work demonstrates how perceptual faculties can be developed to yield results which we have been led to believe can only come through mathematical calculations. Michael Murphy, founder of the Esalen Institute, has been studying mystical perceptions for years and now feels that many scientific concepts like atoms and molecules were first recognized by spiritual teachers decades and perhaps centuries before modern science "discovered" them.

Of the common quality of these forms, Lawrence Blair suggests that "the same geometrical and vortical forms occur because these symbols represent an underlying order of the physical universe and the human consciousness. Symbols are seen at a deeper level of vision, not merely as abstract ideas, but as actual ciphers of the vibrational music which knits us all together."[11]

When Steven Halpern undertook his studies of the healing work of the world, he found that various rhythms, notes, and melodies work not just because of the charisma of the musician, but because of their field patterns and their interaction with the field patterns of the listeners. You can test this for yourself by first playing music which you like, and then music which you detest, and testing your muscle strength with each type.

Music works on and in people because we aren't solid mass. Our bodies are instead great conventions of whirling atoms which somehow find kinship to form molecules, and which then clump together into tissues, bones, and blood. Throughout our bodies there is a great amount of empty space, which allows other environmental forces to move through us, as well as giving our ever-moving molecules the ability to form new harmonic alignments. As pointed out earlier, rock music is usually played in the keys of C, D, or E because it works on our primal lower selves, and the subconscious themes of sex, power, and pleasure which are evoked stimulate us to action, in contrast to the cerebrality of much of modern life.

At a rock concert, the massive amplifiers raise the amplitude of the sound so that our bodies become played themselves. People poetically refer to the "music" of the Earth. Some people suggest that the melodies which seem to arise from special places are simply due to inspiration linked to evocative physical forms in nature. However, research suggests that the fields of some places are strong enough to actually "play" us.

The needle of a compass on a flat, horizontal, non-metallic surface will align itself with a north-south polarity in response to the Earth's electromagnetic field. People cannot hear, taste, touch, smell, or see this field, but the compass proves the field's existence by providing an external, reliable, objective measurement. If a metal object like a pocket knife or a hammer is placed near the compass, the needle moves, indicating the interaction of two fields which people do not perceive. Life itself is made up of spiderwebs of interacting fields like these.

Navigational charts for boats or airplanes note "magnetic deviation zones" for certain areas. These warnings tell navigators that local geological formations have magnetic qualities strong enough to cause a compass to deviate from reading true north. One of the greatest deviation zones in North America is at Guelmes Island in Puget Sound, where deviations as much as fifteen degrees can be expected.

The compass helps point out a difference in the environmental fields of places like Guelmes Island, San Luis Obispo, and Gold Beach, Oregon, which all have strong deviation zones. Indians of the Northwest speak with respect of the spirit of Guelmes Island and some of the other spectacular islands in Puget Sound. Could it be that the locally strong magnetic fields have something to do with these perceptions? We as humans say that we cannot sense such subtle field conditions, but is this true for our species, or because we have been conditioned not to pay attention to such subtle environmental stimuli?

Special Fields at Sacred Places

The Earth has a bipolar electromagnetic field which normally has a positive charge of 120 to 150 volts per meter intensity. In response to the ever-changing universe, the field also varies on day-to-day, monthly, annual, and eleven-year cycles. The eleven-year cycle is linked to linked to solar activity. This field intensity also varies according to time, location, altitude, weather conditions, and atmospheric phenomena like the northern lights. The strength of the field ranges from .2 to .7 gauss, with an overall average of .5 gauss. Waves pulse through the field with a period ranging from 0.1 cycles per second, or "hertz," to 100 cycles per second, such as immediately preceeding a thunderstorm or during earthquake activity.

These electromagnetic aspects of the Earth's field are not static. They fluctuate according to local geology conditions, meteorology, and disruptions of the field such as underground nuclear testing. Often, localized fields can perform amazing feats, according to science writer William Corliss of Glen Arm, Maryland. Through many years of work with the United States government as a science writer, Corliss has amassed a wealth of data from reputable journals about anomalies—unusual natural phenomena—on which he now reports through his publications of the Sourcebook Project.[12] The following is a brief, illustrative listing of some of the more spectacular electromagnetic field peculiarites which Corliss has found:

1. Electrical sparks arching upwards for several meters from gypsum dunes in White Sands National Monument in southeastern New Mexico. This sighting occurred as a thunderstorm passed over the site (*Nature* 240:143, 1972).

2. A moving, ground-level, patch of blue-white light accompanied by a sudden calmness in the air, a marked change in temperature, and the odor of ozone, all noted during a period of intense electrical storms in Yellowstone National Park (*Natural History* 59:258-259, 1950).

3. A glowing, blue-white light "dancing" on the top of the Great Pyramid in Egypt (*Meteorological Magazine* 73:96, 1938).

4. Visible luminous light rays and glows seen on top of the Andes Mountains during dry spells. These Andes Lights occur with local phenomena such as audible sizzling, popping, and, crackling (*Scientific American* 106:464, 1912).

5. "Brush-like" discharges of electrical energy coming from the tops of mountains on the island of Madeira off the coast of Portugal, seen by passing ships (*Marine Observer* 25:95-96, 1955).

6. Mountaintop glows and lights similar to the Andes Lights reported in mountainous regions of the Swiss Alps, Mexico, and Lappland (*Weather* 25:350, 1971).

Conditions like these were well known to crewmen of sailing ships. Frequently, just before an electrical storm at sea, a bluish-white glow would appear along the yardarms of the ship, dancing along the wooden spars and rigging as if a spirit were at work. As it was a forerunner of approaching storms, this glow was named Saint Elmo's Fire, in honor of the martyred Italian patron saint who is the guardian of fishermen.

The presence of Saint Elmo's Fire on a ship is a warning of the environmental build-up of electrical energy. To the naked eye, lightning seems to come down from the heavens. Actually the visible flash occurs when a force in the heavens connects with an opposite charge in the earth. If a person is aware of the tension in the air just prior to a thunderstorm, this is an indication of his or her awareness of electromagnetic energies.

Many of the world's sacred mountains are known for displays of unusual lights, glows, and halos. Sorté Mountain in Venezuela is frequently said to have spectacular natural light shows over it, with flares and veils not unlike the northern lights. Mount Banahaw in the Philippines has similar light displays, and

Figure 8. *Environmental Field Anomalies. Reprinted with permission from* Handbook of Unusual Natural Phenomena, *by William Corliss (Glen Arm, Maryland: The Sourcebook Project, 1977).*

Sparks Radiating from Gypsum Dunes. A static electricity phenomenon of desert areas.

Earthquake Lights. Beams of "light" are sometimes reported radiating upward from the Earth along earthquake fault lines immediately prior to a quake.

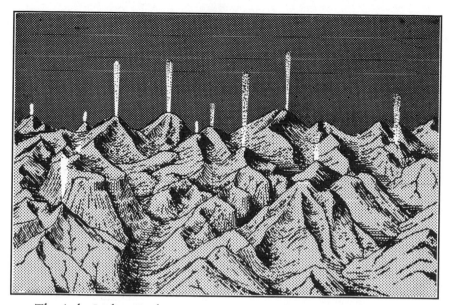

The Andes Lights. "Lights" are sometimes reported shooting upward from the peaks of the Andes Mountains of South America during dry spells right before rain.

Mount Omei in China is famed for the Wenshu Lights which periodically are seen on and around its slopes. In the United States, the entire Colorado Plateau region receives more lightning strikes than any other area in the United States. Reports of sparks jumping into the air in New Mexico, halos around high peaks in Colorado, and extraordinary static electrical fields in Utah are common, and illustrative of the energetic powers of the region.

Other unusual nature phenomena include "foxfire," "ball lightning," and "will-o'-the-wisps," which are moving luminescent lights that seem to have a will and intelligence of their own. In some parts of the United States, such sightings appear over swamps in early spring. These may be attributed to marsh gases generated during winter months that are released as lakes turn over and winter ice thaws. However, I've talked with several people, including my father, who have seen will-o'-the-wisps, and they speak of golden, glowing objects about the size of basketballs which move through marsh areas and fields as though they were animals stalking their prey. If investigators gave these reports more credibility and devoted some serious research to unraveling these occurrences, they might find whole new classes of natural phenomena which could shed light on new dimensions of nature's magical workings.

As underground geological strata move and shift, strong energetic discharges occur along earthquake fault lines, which frequently lie near sacred places. For centuries, the Chinese have used observations of animal behavior as a way to anticipate earthquakes, a thesis in which modern science is giving increasing credibility. Research to date shows that, prior to large earthquakes, zoo animals refuse to go into their underground burrows; insects become hyperactive and swarm; cattle seek out high places; birds leave normal habitats and mill about restlessly; and livestock become agitated.[13] Modern science tends to look for obvious abnormal behavior close to known fault lines, but actual animal awareness of impending quakes may be sensed much farther away. Immediately prior to the horrible quake in Armenia in December 1988, there were reports from people in several parts of the United States who noted unusual animal behavior.

Psychologist Michael Persinger of Laurentian University in Ontario has been examining the effects on humans of exposure to strong electromagnetic discharges such as occur along "hot" fault lines. According to Persinger, the power of intense fields generated in geologically active areas is strong enough to activate in people "dream-like imagery, terror, perceptual changes, depersonalization, vestibular alterations, auditory sensations, and profound meaninglessness."[14] Persinger further says that many UFO sightings are reported along fault lines. He links these reports to local strong fields, proposing that earthquake discharges entrain human minds to create perceptual conditions which favor UFO observations. Here again, the issue of what people are actually seeing remains a matter for much more serious study, for there are a number of sane people who most certainly have seen unidentified flying objects. What is most important is that scientific data does support the conclusion that perceptual anomalies frequently occur along fault lines, showing one way in which natural phenomena can shift gears in our minds.[15]

Fault lines represent one Earth force which affects the mental functioning of living beings, but they are not the only one. There is a growing amount of data which shows that many different kinds of electrical, magnetic, and electromagnetic fields entrain animal minds. This in turn, influences the animals' health and behavior.

It is now fairly clear that birds, insects, fish, and plankton orient themselves to the Earth's magnetic field using built-in compasses to aid navigation, especially during long migrational travel.[16] Plants, too, can grow in relation to magnetic fields. This is called magnetotropism. One of the best examples of plant magnetic orientation is the rosinweed, or "compass plant," *Silphium lacinatum*, of the Great Plains. The leaves of this member of the sunflower family grow off the stem at right angles to each other, each vertical line pointing toward one of the four directions.

There is ample data to show that standing next to an active fault line or exposing oneself to strong fields in work settings can definitely influence health and behavior. But what about subtle fields? Can people be like the animals and the compass plant? The normal field strength for the Earth is .5 gauss. The average overall United States field strength is .6 gauss, while Holland's field strength average is .2 gauss. These fields seem so weak that it is hard to believe they could have any human consequences. However, Dutch meteorologist Solco Wolle Tromp, in the spirit of a true scientist, blindfolded people and placed them in front of a laboratory device which generated weak electromagnetic fields. Tromp found that people are quite capable of discriminating field intensity changes as low as .001 gauss.[17]

In another experiment, Yves Rocard, a physics professor at the Sorbonne, found that people could detect changes as small as .3 milligauss. Recall that the Earth's field is an average of .5 gauss, which is 500 milligauss.[18] These results are supported by William Tiller at Stanford University. He reports on one subject who was able to find an electric wire with only a one microamp current running through it buried several feet underground.[19]

Professor Robin Baker of Manchester University in England goes one step farther. He believes people can detect the directions of the compass, just like bees, birds, and the compass plant. To test his thesis, Baker took some of his zoology students, blindfolded them, and drove them into the countryside. He then had them get out of the car and he asked them to point toward the direction of the university. He reports, "While still blindfolded, their estimates of home direction, particularly the descriptive estimates of north, northeast, etc. were unusually accurate, but when the blindfolds were removed the subjects became disoriented."[20]

Baker's findings are supported by the work of Frances Nixon of British Columbia, who proposed the thesis that all healthy people have a built-in navigational system which orients them to the Earth's magnetic fields. She reports that, with a little practice, most people can sense the direction of their place of birth, as well as the directions of the compass, unless they have suffered head injuries, electrical shocks, or brain damage due to certain chemicals. Using a variety of physical exercises which "cleanse" a person's field, Mrs. Nixon and a number of doctors who have learned her Vivaxis system report that when people recover their ability to sense their direction of birth, they almost always become healthier.[21]

I personally visited Frances Nixon several years before her death, and found her to be one of the most sensitive and wise adepts of Earth energies I have ever met. On one occasion, to prove her awareness of fields, she allowed herself to be blindfolded and then she proceeded to walk around the room, telling me where all the electrical outlets were and whether they had appliances plugged into them—with 100 percent accuracy.

Frances Nixon developed her awareness of natural fields through having the keen eyes of an artist, (which was her original profession) and through living close to nature on tiny Thetis Island off the coast of Vancouver, British Columbia. Whereas most people are conditioned to block off such impressions, she developed them into a healing gift, showing the rest of humanity what we are capable of sensing. For most of us, such field awareness is unconscious. We simply allow our intuition to guide us to places which feel good to us, like dogs finding the most comfortable place in a room or cattle settling down in certain areas of the pasture.

In addition to its strength, a field can also be described in terms of its periodicity. The total range of the Earth's field is .1 cycle per second (hertz) to 100 cycles per second. The overall norm is 3 to 14 cycles per second, which is called the Schumann Resonance. Waves in this frequency include the brain-wave frequencies which are known to be associated with health, relaxation, and the formation of creative imagery.[22] Studies have shown that 10-hertz electrical fields control human circadian rhythms and influence reaction times, as well as entraining people into creative relaxation.[23] Many people report feeling refreshed and relaxed after visiting certain sacred places, including places which are not close to known fault lines and which have fields that lie within the Schumann Resonance range. Natural field strength most certainly may aid perceptual shifting, but clearly gross field anomalies are not necessary for the mind to transcend at a certain place.

My own research with people's sensitivity to clothing demonstrates how fabrics touching the skin can affect consciousness and physical strength. One explanation for this relationshiop is that synthetic substances tend to have a negative electrical field which is in contrast with the normally positive field of the Earth.[24] It has been shown that mental alertness improves under the influence of a positive electrical field. The uneasiness which some people feel when wearing or standing next to some plastics seems to be related to the conflict between the external and internal fields with different polarities. One wonders if living in a world filled with plastics may shift our minds away from states where the spiritual qualities of life are more present.[25] These fields seem very insignificant; however, in the training of yogis and shamans, special dietary and meditational regimens are employed to increase sensitivity and constant awareness of the environments around them. Spiritual adepts also wear special clothing, jewelry, and even hair style designs to keep them more tuned in to sacred dimensions. These techniques may sound ridiculous, but such things shouldn't be dismissed unless one has personally given them a try. People are much more sensitive to the environment than any Western psychology book I've ever seen gives them credit for. The documented fact that healing systems like acupuncture, shiatsu, and chi gung actually work is ample evidence that subtle life energies exist which can and do influence our lives.

One of the most important milestones in developing a modern Western theory for explaining how environmental fields may influence our lives occurred when Yale University professors Harold Burr and F.S.C. Northrup announced their "electrodynamic theory of life" in 1935 in the *Quarterly Review of Biology*.[26] Where there is life, there are electromagnetic fields at work, Burr and Northrup proposed. They suggested the existence of "L-fields," which govern the shape of an organism like the mould for a gelatin dessert.

According to Burr and Northrup, all living things are shaped by these subtle fields. Learning the form and language of these fields could guide us to a much deeper understanding of life itself, as well as how it should be lived. The patterns of L-fields reflect the basic functional structures of organisms, and result in an "energy signature" for each life form, somewhat like the characteristic patterns of powder and iron filings which Hans Jenny created with his violin. These unique fields, L-fields, can be measured in millivolts, have a pure voltage potential, and respond to external and internal fluctuations.

In a later work, A.S. Presman proposed the theory in 1970 that electrical fields operate like L-fields, not only giving structure and form to life but acting as a "communicative function" between organisms and the surrounding environment. Presman proposed three specific communicative functions of fields:

1. In the process of evolution, nature has used electromagnetic fields to obtain information about changes in the environment.

2. Electromagnetic processes are involved in informational connective systems within living organisms.

3. Electromagnetic fields facilitate information exchange among living things.[27]

Research today shows that Burr, Northrup, Presman, and others are correct in the position that all living things have certain electrical components, which are in constant interaction with the surrounding environment in ways that influence health and behavior. In contrast to what might be suspected, it appears that electromagnetic field sensitivity is *greater* for more complex organisms, due to their greater needs for organization.[28]

When bioentrainment takes place, external waves of energy pass through living beings such as people. This creates a dynamic interchange in which, generally speaking, the stronger the external field, the greater the change in the living being's internal fields. So long as there is not a disharmonic antagonism between

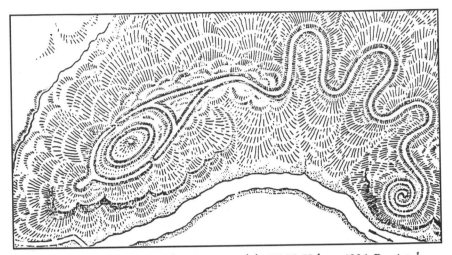

Figure 9. *Reconstruction of Serpent Mound, by W. H. Holmes, 1886. Reprinted courtesy of The Ohio Historical Society.*

the inner fields and the outer fields, the inner fields tend to harmonize with the outer ones. When harmony is reached between two or more vibrating objects, energy is exchanged between or among them. If the human mind-body contains centers of consciousness, that is, chakras or latifae, then, as people travel to various sacred places, the energies of each place merge with their own energies and influence them. According to the unique quality and strength of each external field, special harmonic notes are struck with resonant inner fields. One place activates the head, another the heart, another the genitals, and so on. This is no doubt why there is such a variety of sacred places.

The awe-inspiring Serpent Mound earth effigy in southern Ohio lies on a unique "crypto-volcanic" geological formation. Whether this landform originated from an earthquake or a meteorite striking the Earth, it's clear that it was created by a dramatic upthrusting of subsurface bedrock. No place else in that area can the type of rock which appears at the Serpent Mound be found on the surface.

All around the world, the images of the serpent, the snake, and the dragon symbolize the Earth force, as well as the first chakra at the base of the spine, which is said to contain the "kundalini" or "coiled serpent" energy. Assuming that both the rock strata and the overall ambiance of the Serpent Mound have this very basic Earth essence energetic quality, the fields of the area would harmonize most directly with the first chakra. What better way to express the energy signature of that place than to erect a monstrous serpentine effigy!

Professor Burr first announced his discoveries about the patterns of living fields in 1935, but people have understood the subtle dynamics of bioentrainment

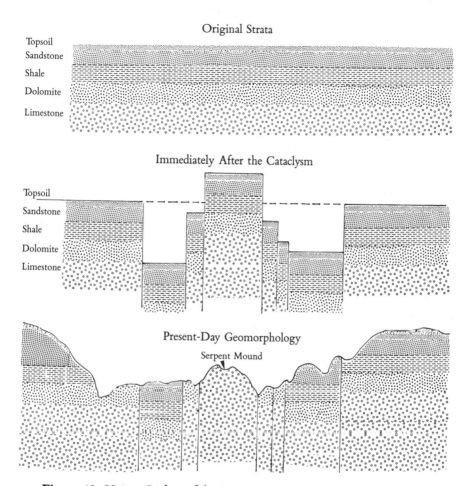

Original Strata

Topsoil
Sandstone
Shale
Dolomite
Limestone

Immediately After the Cataclysm

Topsoil
Sandstone
Shale
Dolomite
Limestone

Present-Day Geomorphology

Serpent Mound

Figure 10. *Unique Geology of the Serpent Mound. The geology of the Serpent Mound is of crypto-volcanic origin. Within a four-square-mile radius of the mound, the layers of bedrock have been broken down into giant chunks, either by an ancient earthquake or meteorite strike. Note how the Serpent Mound itself is perched on top of a layer of deep bedrock that was pushed to the surface. In many cultures around the world, the Earth force and the first chakra have a snake or dragon theme. My sense is that the Serpent Mound design expresses either that a great serpent guards the hilltop, or that at this place the serpent force is very strong and gives birth to many things, symbolized by an egg. It might have been designed as a message to gods in the sky, or simply as an ambitious effigy to honor the Earth force which crystallized ceremonies conducted on this bluff.*

on a visceral level for centuries. The mystical builders of Europe, the Freemasons, constructed the great cathedrals of Europe in accordance with a sacred mystical geometry designed to facilitate the personal experiences of religious worshipers. Each chamber was supposedly designed for the worshipers to understand the quality of the local Earth force, and was created to act as an amplifer for that energy. Each great cathedral, then, is like a giant musical instrument which celebrates the spirit of that place. To test out this theory, musician Sylvia Schecter and a group of friends traveled to a number of the great cathedrals. As they approached each building, they would all become silent. Upon entering the main chamber, they would each quietly go to a separate part of the main sanctuary. Then they would sit and meditate on the space for a time, attuning themselves to the overall ambiance. Then, when ready, they would each raise their hands. On a given signal, all would sing out a note which they felt best expressed the purest harmony with that space. In every case, all members of the group sang the same note, Schecter reports, and for each cathedral, the note was different.[29]

The planning of other chapels, shrines, and temples also employed sacred geometry as well as an awareness of place. Paul Horn's spellbinding recordings of flute music played inside the Taj Mahal and the Great Pyramids expresses the spirit of those places, which is why that music has been so popular. Horn chose to play in those spaces as a result of his spiritual quest and meditation practice, he says, which helped him better appreciate the subtle qualities of the spiritual ambiance of sacred places and opened whole new realms of music potential to him.

Although their original builders are no longer with us, it seems quite clear that the alignments of stones at Stonehenge and at other Neolithic and Bronze Age stone circles of Europe involve astronomical and astrological sightings. The presence of a circle of giant granite monoliths in a grassy meadow is, by itself, evocative for the deepest parts of the human mind. Today, many visitors are reminded of the alchemical mind's genius when they step up to the stones and feel a subtle stimulation. In some cases, people even say a spark of energy leaps from the stones to touch them, as if to initiate them into some ancient order.

In November 1977, a group of about twenty scientists interested in stone circles met at a pub near London to discuss the possibilities of scientifically monitoring the stones. An archaeologist, John Steele, gave this group the name The Dragon Project, and they began more than a decade of work centered primarily at the Rollright Circle in north Oxfordshire. Using extremely sensitive ultrasound detectors and Geiger counters, and monitoring the stones for 24-hour, monthly, and annual cycles, and they found that, to quote chemist Don Robins, "[the] stone circles do indeed emit anomalously high and anomalously low levels of several forms of radiation."[30] Even more astounding,

Robins says, the radiation pulses in relation to the position of the sun, with the greatest pulsing occurring at the equinoxes. When these data were published, other scientists in Europe wrote to The Dragon Project to share data, for they too were finding unusual things. Two of the most bizarre reports are from groups monitoring the stone circles at Moel ty Uchaf in Wales, and near Uppsala in Sweden. Both groups recorded dramatic fluctuations in Geiger counter readings coinciding with nearby aerial sightings of "fireballs" and UFOs.[31]

Don Robins believes that the locally strong fields which are sometimes record-ed within and around the stone circles are in part due to a unique crystalline lat-tice structure of the stones which traps electrons, increasing the potency of the local field strength. The pulses at the Rollright Circle begin immediately before sunrise, and then continue for two to three hours before dropping back down to lower levels, although still remaining higher than background readings. These locally strong fields reach out as far as 40 to 50 yards from the circle. The timing of the readings with the sunrise seems most likely related to special wave fre-quencies of the morning sun. These frequencies are more centered in the red band of the visible light spectrum, which has the longest waves and is the optimal energy to entrap. Robins, an inorganic chemist, now believes that the standing stones act as a "three dimensional dielectric antenna whose orientation allows maximum energy transduction" at specific times of the day and year. Another member of The Dragon Project, Paul Devereux, has taken infrared photos which show halo-like glows around the stones, similar to the auras we see around holy people.[32] Subsequent checking of the geology in the vicinity of the stone circles shows that nearly all major circles in the United Kingdom are sited within a quarter mile of earthquake fault lines.[33] This suggests that the stones draw energies from both the sun and the Earth to create religious sites where human minds more easily slip into those precious states of consciousness we call sacred.

Tourists, more than robed Druids, now represent the main body of pilgrims to Stonehenge and its monolith kin. Some believe these stone circles are linked harmonically in a golden chain of light which becomes visible to some minds at special times of the year. It seems ironic that the old religion which built these stones was condemned, and yet people still flock to the circles in such great numbers that they have to be fenced off to prevent them from being loved to death. From the flock of rock and roll groups which Great Britain has spawned, is it any coincidence that the one with the name The Rolling Stones should have become so popular?

Many people today find the Andes working a magnetic spell on them. Perched among the crystal-cold high peaks of South America, once the home of the Inca empire, are flocks of yogis, Tibetan monks, and hermetic Christians who see Chile as the new center of spiritual magnetism; a "New Jordan" according to Padre Ramon Borrega, a Catholic priest who heads the Hermetic Society of the Pacific.

Borrega says that a Tibetan prophecy received in 1947 announced a shifting of the "spiritual light" of the Earth from the Himalayas to the Andes. The light which Borrega speaks of seems metaphorical, but Gemini-flight astronauts and Russian cosmonauts both have reported seeing strange glows and flashing lights while orbiting above the Andes.

Richard Underwood, retired photo-interpretive specialist from NASA in Houston, Texas, confirms that "flashbulb-type lights" were seen by astronauts in the Himalayas and in northern Chile. NASA also has recorded electromagnetic conditions in northern Chile and Argentina, where the main body of new spiritual seekers have gone. NASA reports that the strongest field anomalies in South America tend to occur right where the seekers are settling. Writing on this migration in *OMNI* magazine, Patrick Tiernay says that physicists and astronomers doing research in the Andes frequently feel drawn to meet with the local spiritual seekers, one result of which is a new physics emerging from a blending of meditation, ritual, and research. One of the most noteworthy human examples of this syncretion is Nobel Prize–winner physicist Brian Josephson.[34]

Before the microscope, the germ theory was unproven. With the invention of the microscope with its magnifying power, and the application of scientific methods, germs were discovered, setting the stage for a revolution in medicine. There are now instruments quite capable of detecting subtle fields, but people have been reluctant to apply them to studying subtle issues like the spirit of place. This is partially because Western society still clings to an older paradigm that it doesn't want to release because it is too tidy and manageable. When Westerners are brave enough to look at the fields of life and how they influence people, it will be found that, as physicist Elizabeth Rauscher sums it up, "there are some remarkably similar electromagnetic conditions which seem to occur in both the human mind and the mind of what the Hopi Indians call the 'Mother Earth.'"[35]

Entraining the human mind with strong environmental fields can alter consciousness, but nature has more than one way to help move people into spiritual consciousness. Often, where strong magnetic fields exist, there is also a soft, invigorating ambiance which is the result of an abundance of negative air ions.

Air ions are charged molecules of common gaseous elements in the air which form when uncharged, stable molecules lose or gain an electron due to some disruption. Negative air ions each have an extra electron, giving them a negative electrical charge, while positive air ions each have one less electron than normal and a positive charge. In nature, the causative agents of negative air ions include crashing ocean breakers, waterfalls, pine forests, exposed surfaces of rock rich in uranium, and the summits of mountain peaks, where electrical charges are highest.

An abundance of negative ions in the air interacts with human biochemistry, reducing the level of serotonin in the blood. Serotonin is normally produced in stressful situations as part of the fight-or-flight response of the sympathetic nervous system. In brief doses it activates us, but prolonged high concentrations of serotonin weaken us and make our minds less stable. An abundance of negative air ions reduces fatigue, invigorates us, and improves the protective powers of the mucous membranes of the respiratory system, making us less susceptible to colds and infections.

Positive air ions are created by plastics, poorly ventilated meeting rooms, and synthetic building materials in civilized environments. In nature, many parts of the world know the feel of special warm, dry winds which contain large numbers of positive air ions. These winds are called the *Föhn* in Germany, the *mistral* in France, the "Santa Ana" in southern California, the "Chinook" in Washington state, the *sharav* in Israel, the "sirocco" in Italy, and the *zonda* in Argentina. Typically, when these winds blow, interpersonal tension rises, colds become more common, respiratory infections increase, personal anxiety levels rise, and some people feel depressed and mentally unstable. The relationship between these warm, positive-ion-rich winds and disease is so well-documented that, in Israel, judges will sometimes lessen sentences for crimes committed during a *sharav*.[36]

In studying the local environmental fields of the Colorado Plateau region, where there are so many Indian sacred places, Joan Price and Elizabeth Rauscher have reported an abundance of negative air ions at many of these sacred places, as well as unusually strong positive electrical currents in the ground.[37] They attribute the negative air ion richness they have found at special places to several factors, including evergreen forests, waterfalls, caves, the abundance of electricity in the ground, and deposits of uranium ore. One of their most fascinating finds is that, underlying some of the Four Corners region, there is a labyrinth of caverns which connect with the surface through caves and "blow holes." On a hot summer day, wind whistles out of these surface vents at as much as twenty miles per hour, sometimes creating audible whistling noises. These winds are high in negative air ions because they originate in deep, cool underground chambers with spring waters flowing through them. At night, as surface temperatures drop, air rushes back into the ground, recharging their reservoirs. Being in the vicinity of one of these breathing caves or blow holes is like being near a natural air conditioner.[38] These refreshing desert oases are magical in themselves, but when Elizabeth Rauscher looked more closely at the underground water table in the Four Corners area, she was floored. She discovered that the water in these caves rises and falls with the same rhythmic pulses as those of the Pacific Ocean, hundreds of miles to the west.[39]

Another atmospheric field condition which may be active in the experience of place is the presence of certain gases which are released by geological and geochemical processes. After a thunderstorm passes, for example, there is the sweet smell associated with ozone and negative-ion-rich air. As Chinese barefoot seismologists trek through the countryside looking for any signs of impending earthquakes or volcanic eruptions, they also test the scent of places. According to University of Washington biophysicist and veteran volcano watcher Steve Malone, distinctive gaseous ions are commonly released along earthquake fault lines.[40] One such gas which is often associated with artesian water is hydrogen sulfide, which smells like rotten eggs. Atmospheric gases interact directly with human biochemistry through the mucous membranes of the nose and respiratory system, giving the gases quick and direct access to the brain, as anyone knows who smells perfume. Such odors can be triggers to consciousness changes, providing other environmental factors are supportive.

In the Chinese geomancy system, an abundance of the life-force energy, chi, is said to be directly associated with special places. Is chi a combination of negative air ions and electromagnetic fields, or is it something else? Frankly, we don't know, which is embarrassing considering the success of acupuncture and the growing acceptance of the use of geomancies like feng shui to make human life better. Psychiatrist Wilhelm Reich proposed that there was a life-force energy called "orgone," which was like chi. He was placed in prison by the FDA in the 1950s and died there, accused of being a fraud because he claimed that manipulating orgone could heal people. Reich said he could see and feel orgone. Chinese feng shui practitioners say you can see, feel, and sense chi. Shamans say they, too, can see a life energy. Rolling Thunder tells me that he looks at a person's energy field to help determine his or her health. He says he does this by looking at the person out of the corner of his eyes. The physiology of the human eye is such that we see details and colors best by looking directly at things, because the cone cells in the center of the retina are specially suited for this kind of work. However, rod cells are located more along the periphery of the retina, and they are better at seeing patterns. It is through developing this ability to see patterns that Indians make good trackers and possibly also see life energies. Only with the invention of the printed word and other modern media have people come to use their intense visual focus faculties so much, as opposed to scanning the overall environment to look for changes and then to check out what they are.

At any given time, there are so many different forces at work in the atmosphere of a place that to single out any one of them and say it is the reason for the specialness of a place is probably impossible. It seems very clear, however, that places have ambiances which can alter our moods and change our plane of awareness. Perhaps one of the reasons why modern Westerners have been so slow to seriously study the subtle atmospheres of places is that they have lost touch with their value, being blinded by modern materialism amd mechanical models of reality. People laughed at Edgar Cayce when he said that natural uranium ore had healing values. At the time, uranium was seen only as a source of radioactivity and a resource to use to make a bomb. Now it is known that uranium ore stimulates the production of negative air ions, and some feel it may be a useful element in certain cancer therapies. Like wearing sunglasses, the world looks different according to which paradigm you choose.

Healing Waters

In 1858, a fourteen-year-old girl named Bernadette reported the first of seventeen visions of the Virgin Mary at the location of the modern grotto of Our Lady of Lourdes in France. Today, more than four million people visit Lourdes each year to see this shrine, which has become so well known for its healing powers. Spiritual healer Olga Worrall told me that her husband Ambrose, who was an engineer, took samples of the water from the spring at Lourdes and could find nothing unusual in it. This was in the late 1970s. Perhaps new chemistry would find something he did not, because the healings go on at Lourdes regardless of whether or not they defy rationality. However, there is no question that water can be a powerful healing element, especially water which comes from springs which have a high content of beneficial chemicals.

In 1884, when Captain Jeff Maltby and a group of Texas Rangers explored the West Texas area looking for cattle ranching sites, they came upon a group of 22 artesian springs near the Rio Grande which were surrounded by a network of well-worn trails. By the accounts of Indians on both sides of the border, Indian Hot Springs was, and still is, a healing place. The strange dreams and visions which people report while visiting this simple spa were noted earlier. It's common knowledge that "desert lights" can also be seen nearby on some nights, and not far away are the famous Marfa Lights which the U.S. Army recognizes but can't explain.

According to Jewell Babb, who learned to use the healing powers of Indian Hot Springs through years of work with the local curanderos, each spring has a special power. Bath Spring and Squaw Spring are good for the liver and general purging. To cleanse yourself, you might drink and bathe in the Sulfur Spring. After a day or two you might feel poorly, she says, but, as with homeopathic medicine, the bad feelings are the poisons being released from your body. She says that if you can make it through this initial purge, you begin to feel better. Squaw Spring nearby is too strong to drink, but bathing in the water is good for women with menstrual problems. Stump Spring, on the other hand, is good for diabetes and asthma.

Around each spring there are colorful muds, mosses, and rocks. Sitting in the black mud of one spring helps to cure some people's insomnia. The mud from Sulfur Spring is supposedly good for skin rashes, and the mosses are used to clear up complexion problems. The whole springs is like a natural medicine chest, if you know how to use it, Mrs. Babb relates.[41]

The number of people who have been helped or cured by visits to Indian Hot Springs is too numerous to dismiss. You could say that the power of the springs is due to suggestion and to being at a retreat space where the pressures of daily life are not so commonplace. A more careful scrutiny of the area, however, shows that Indian Hot Springs is special in several ways. First, it sits on top of the Cabrillo Fault Line, which means that it is subject to electromagnetic field discharges. Also, the springs, the uranium rocks, the nearby Rio Grande, and electricity in the ground help keep the air rich in negative ions. In addition, the waters of each spring are indeed chemically unique. Large amounts of calcium bicarbonate, magnesium bicarbonate, sodium bicarbonate, sodium sulfate, and sodium chloride are present in the springs' waters, making them like epsom salts. The total dissolved solids in these springs are from 20 to 100 times higher than at any of the 40 other natural springs in the area.[42] Especially interesting, though, is the large amount of lithium dissolved in the water system of the springs. Lithium is a commonly prescribed medicine for calming and stabilizing the mind, and some doctors have told me that there is enough lithium at Indian Hot Springs for a drink of it to be like taking a naturopathic remedy.

Reminiscent of what happens at the magical stone circles of England, Mrs. Babb says that if a person sits on some stones beside the pools or in the water, sometimes he or she gets a jolt of energy. She says that some people with piles and constipation have been helped by sitting on certain stones, while women with menstrual problems have been helped by sitting on others. These rocks could be acting like antennas for transmitting underground energies to the surface. Some of the rocks are also high in uranium ore, and Indian Hot Springs in general has natural radiation levels thirteen times higher than the surroundings.[43] Here again is evidence of the Indian belief that uranium is a natural power which is best left in the soil where it can help people and balance life, rather than be turned into bombs.

Before vitamins became so popular and wonder drugs were invented, bathing in hot springs and drinking mineral water were popular as health supports. For a time, these practices slipped away, but as it has been learned that wonder drugs have side effects and that health arises from overall fitness and not from chemical dependency, more and more people have been turning to natural healing methods like visiting hot spring spas. If a person was alone in the West Texas desert and without a doctor, Indian Hot Springs could be a lifesaver if one understood its

Photo 22. *In the foreground, a sign announces uranium mining, while a thunderstorm with more energy than any bomb ever built hovers in the background. Author photo.*

proper use. To show deep reverential respect for such a natural resource would be very understandable, and to call it sacred would not be a difficult next step.

Today there is a tendency to try to commercialize good things and to turn them into profits. The late billionaire Howard Hunt tried to turn Indian Hot Springs into a plush resort, but the development could never get off the ground. Several other people have tried the same thing, but it never seems to become a successful venture. The curanderos simply say that this is either the spirit of the springs or because that the medicine people have put a curse on the springs so that they cannot be overly developed. If modern people could understand the powers of places, they might know the best use of Indian Hot Springs and simply go along with it. Working with the spirit of a place generates the most power and creativity for people who visit it or live there.

Is There a Significant Difference?

If sacred places are to be preserved in the face of conflicting interests, then one argument which can help support their uniqueness is the possible existence of significant differences in air, water, and soil chemistry. Many places do have unique natural features which can be used in defense of their preservation, for if such places were lost, humanity would be stripped of the potential to ever use and enjoy such resources again. In some cases, this approach will help, but it's not foolproof. Suppose a place is studied and nothing is found. One might be looking for the wrong things to prove its uniqueness, and the result would be that this data would be used against efforts to preserve the place.

The value of sacred places is that they are touchstones of consciousness for people. They may serve other purposes, but people act from self interest more often than not. Therefore, along with data on environmental uniqueness must go data on the usefulness of the places for people. One way to develop an understanding of the value of place is to simply study what happens to people when they visit the places. Gathering material on sacred experiences helps, but people can always say that others are lying about having special experiences at various places, and who is to prove them wrong? I would like to see some portable biofeedback-type devices used to study what happens when people visit special places. Tromp's studies have shown changes in personal electricity when people walk across dowsing zones. We may not always consciously sense the power of place, but it is still there working on us at an unconscious level. It also seems likely that researchers could study the behavior of microorganisms, as well as larger animals and plants, in response to place. Magnetotropism is a well-known behavioral response. Westerners could be like the Chinese barefoot seismologists and tell from animals and plants that special places of power exist, for the ancient wisdom of the shamans teaches that the animals know the sacred places best of all. But even if all the data in the world is collected saying that a particular place deserves to be called sacred because of its unique environmental attributes, a zoning board or court could simply say that a higher use for the place would be for another purpose. Sacred places will become safest when people come to recognize the value of the sacred dimensions of life.

INTEGRATING SPIRITUAL LAND VALUES
INTO PRACTICE

At the World Congress on Cultural Parks held at Mesa Verde in 1984, the assembled delegates came up with a series of recommendations which they felt should guide policies and practices of heritage preservation all around the world. One of the most powerful resolutions stated:

> All nations should take immediate action to identify sites, cultures, and their respective ecosystems that are threatened with degradation and loss, and submit relevant nominations for World Heritage Status and World Heritage Endangered List, and also take such actions as may be necessary to protect and preserve such properties and ecosystems, as well as to permit indigenous peoples to maintain their lifeways.[44]

The passage of this statement was met with cheers from those attending, for in many instances sacred places were not faring too well for reasons of exploitation, commercialism, and the erosion of traditional cultural values. For this group to reach agreement on such a resolution was a hopeful sign. Not that long ago, many governments had specific policies calling for the eradication of traditional cultures and their values.

One of the delegates, Glen Morris, an Australian Aborigine, made a passionate statement to the group in response to an Indian complaint about reservations. "You might not like reservations, but they're yours. We don't have any land," Morris said. "It all belongs to the government. My people are just starting to get some of our ancestral lands back, and it's because of the Australian Aboriginal Movement." With these words, Morris opened his jacket, displaying a shirt made of red, black, and yellow cloth. "These are the colors of our flag," he said proudly, and then went on to describe his work as a sacred sites ranger.

Down under, Glen Morris is one of a group of Aborigines hired by the Australian government to act as intermediaries between Aboriginal tribes and the government as new land-use policies are established which honor Aboriginal land claims. Aborigines were stripped of their land rights decades ago, after thousands of years of residency. In recent times, a series of legislative acts have begun to restore land and dignity to the Aborigines, the most important of which is the Sacred Sites Act. According to this act, a Protective Authority is established to evaluate all claims made for sacred places. Seven out of twelve members of the Authority must be Aborigines. Morris and fellow park official Sharon Sullivan said that they have been able to protect some sites with this law, especially "dream treks," which are cross-country trails marked by stones and used by Aborigines in seeking dreams and visions. The stones provide easy markers for the boundaries of the sites. Other places used for initiation ceremonies are marked by elaborate pictographs and petroglyphs, but defining boundaries of the sites surrounding such rock art is not easy, they reported. For ceremonies to occur properly, especially ones like the ritual circumcision initiation, which is the primary puberty rite for Aborigine men, psychological privacy as well as physical space is needed.

In the United States national park system, the director of Indian Affairs works on interpreting Indian heritage through the parks. In addition, Indians are employed at various parks as rangers and cultural interpreters. There is no special job of sacred sites ranger, such as Glenn Morris holds, however. As the present United States law calls for preserving sacred sites, an appropriate next step for implementing American Indian religious freedom would be to create federal jobs equivalent to Morris's position for all federal lands. These sites rangers could serve as links between the Indian community and the federal government. They would develop management policies which would help preserve sacred places as well as interpret them for people from all faiths, the same way that priests in other parts of the world interpret their religious shrines. Calling these people "sites rangers" would help establish the validity of sacred places even more.

On September 29, 1976, California Governor Jerry Brown signed into law AB-4239, which established the California Native American Heritage Commission. This commission is empowered with safeguarding the religious and cultural heritage rights of California Native Americans, including: identifying and cataloging places of cultural significance, developing protective measures for sacred places, and ensuring appropriate rights of access to these sites located on public lands for ceremonial purposes.

The Native American Heritage Commission has nine members, appointed by the Governor, five or more of whom must be elders, traditional people, or spiritual leaders of California Native American tribes or groups. To date, all commission members have been Native Americans. They receive no compensation, but do receive travel expenses, room, and board while on Commission business, and they have a small staff and an executive secretary.

The Commission meets six times per year, on or near Indian reservations. Since California has a rich heritage of more than 50 tribes who once lived in the state, the Commission is very busy. One of their biggest successes to date has been resolving an access problem to Coso Hot Springs, a healing springs site which today is located on the China Lake Naval Weapons Center near Owens Lake, California. Traditionally, Paiute and Shoshone peoples used Coso Hot Springs, but the Navy blocked access to the springs when they acquired the land in the 1940s. Today the Coso Hot Springs has been nominated for the National Register of Historic Sites, and medicine people can gain access to the springs if they make the request through the appropriate channels.

The California Native American Heritage Commission has also prepared a special *Cultural Resources Handbook*, which provides a detailed analysis of existing cultural heritage protection laws. In addition, they work directly with families and tribes to prevent activities which would disrupt burials and other sacred sites, including ceremonial sites, middens, historical habitation sites, grinding rocks (for acorns), holy places, meditation places, ritual gathering places, and works of art.[45]

One of the most unique aspects of the work of the Commission has been a statewide survey to determine sacred places. At first, some tribes balked at complying with this survey, but with the passage of time trust has developed and people have seen positive results from it. This inventory has been especially helpful with protection and access to burial sites, for in California the law says that Indian burials on private property should be made accessible to the relatives of the deceased. The Commission would prefer to simply guarantee access to burials on private lands. However, in their charter is the provision that they may ask the state to buy such lands to enable permanent preservation and access. This is clearly one of the most powerful and enabling statutes for Native American land rights on the books anyplace in the United States.

ENLISTING THE SUPPORT OF THE CHURCHES

The history of the attitude of Christian churches toward American Indians is largely an accounting of a religious war. The depth of compassion for Indians among many of the Pilgrims is expressed in the words of John Robinson, who wrote to William Bradford of Massachusetts in 1623 concerning reports of the killing of several Indians: "Concerning the killing of those poor Indians, of which we heard at first by report, and since by more certain relation. Oh, how happy a thing it had been, if you had converted some before you killed any."[46] Until the passage of the 1924 Indian Citizenship Act, Indians did not have First Amendment protection for freedom of religion and, in most cases, performing ceremonies was forbidden, as the Indians were supposed to have become Christians.

On November 21, 1987, a dramatic act of balance between Indians and the Christian churches took place in Seattle, Washington, at the intersection of First and Spring Streets. On this site, which was once a burial ground and is now paved over, with drums beating and sage and sweetgrass smoke filling the air, representatives of nine Pacific Northwest Christian churches delivered a one-page letter to a delegation of regional Indians led by a Lummi Indian carver, Jewell Praying-Wolf James. The letter was an apology directed to the 26 recognized tribes of Indians, Aleuts, and Eskimos of the Pacific Northwest. It acknowledged the "long-standing participation [of the Christian churches] in the destruction of traditional Native American spiritual practices," and pledged commitment to help right this wrong by active support of the principles and concepts of the American Indian Religious Freedom Act. In contrast to the traditional Christian view of calling the faithful to "multiply and subdue" the Earth, and to destroy the traditional religions, this document asserted that "the spiritual power of the land and the ancient wisdom of your indigenous religions can be, we believe, great gifts to the Christian churches."

As a gesture of good faith, the letter of apology was accompanied by a check for $1,000 made out to the Native American Rights Fund in Boulder, Colorado, an Indian legal advocacy organization.

According to Jon Magnuson, Lutheran campus pastor at the University of Washington and co-chair of the Native American Task Force of the Church Council of Greater Seattle, the idea for the apology was sparked by a letter from Jewell Praying-Wolf James asking the churches to help support Indian human rights and treaty struggles. Wanting to do something more than just send their regards, a select group of concerned clergy went on a retreat to Chaco Canyon and then met on the grounds of Taos Pueblo to sketch out the document. The actual wording came later, after four weeks of meetings by the bishops.

The text of the apology was mailed out to 1800 Christian churches of the region, to be read on Thanksgiving Day. A simultaneous reading took place on dance floors and at long houses all throughout the Pacific Northwest.

At first the Indians were skeptical, wondering if this was another empty promise. However, cross-cultural communications continued and soon Indians were appearing in Christian churches to preach during services, and white clergy were invited to attend ceremonies which previously no Christian minister had ever attended. In the spring of 1988, the bishops donated another $500 to buy ten elk skins to use for new drumheads on ceremonial drums used to conduct sweatlodge ceremonies in Washington state prisons. As this book is being written, I'm told of joint actions between Indians and Christians of the Pacific Northwest to stop a developer from building a resort on a site where there are Indian burials, and a major conference on Indian treaties and the Christian churches is planned for 1990 in Seattle.

The full text of the letter of apology is reproduced at the end of this chapter to demonstrate what can be done when religions honor their common heritage to the land and when Christian churches show respect for indigenous Earth wisdom of the Indian people. Land use is ultimately a matter of human attitudes and values, for laws, like prophecies, are always subject to reinterpretation. If more institutions and organizations would follow the leadership of these brave Christian clergy, the American Indian Religious Freedom Act would take on a new potency and the sacred places of North America would have more support and respect to help keep them safe.

One example where one can begin to see an acknowledgment of sacred places as having universal spiritual value comes from United States Forest Service environmental impact statement prepared for a proposed ski development on Mount Shasta. After reviewing traditional tribal uses of the mountain, the report says, "Several locations near Panther Creek have been used for 'medicine sweats' or purification rituals. Some of these have been performed by Native Americans without any special tribal affiliation or endorsement. Some spiritual/religious groups which place great significance on Mount Shasta also participate in similar activities."[47]

Figure 11. *Letter of Apology from Christian Churches of Seattle, Washington, to Aleuts, Inuit & other Native Americans of the Pacific Northwest. Reprinted courtesy of the Native American Task Force of The Church Council of Greater Seattle.*

A PUBLIC DECLARATION

TO THE TRIBAL COUNCILS AND TRADITIONAL SPIRITUAL LEADERS OF THE INDIAN AND ESKIMO PEOPLES OF THE PACIFIC NORTHWEST
In care of Jewell Praying Wolf James, Lummi

Seattle, Washington
November 21, 1987

Dear Brothers and Sisters,

This is a formal apology on behalf of our churches for their long-standing participation in the destruction of traditional Native American spiritual practices. We call upon our people for recognition of and respect for your traditional ways of life and for protection of your sacred places and ceremonial objects. We have frequently been unconscious and insensitive and have not come to your aid when you have been victimized by unjust Federal policies and practices. In many other circumstances we reflected the rampant racism and prejudice of the dominant culture with which we too willingly identified. During the 200th Anniversary year of the United States Constitution we, as leaders of our churches in the Pacific Northwest, extend our apology. We ask for your forgiveness and blessing.

As the Creator continues to renew the earth, the plants, the animals and all living things, we call upon the people of our denominations and fellowships to a commitment of mutual support in your efforts to reclaim and protect the legacy of your own traditional spiritual teachings. To that end we pledge our support and assistance in upholding the American Religious Freedom Act (P.L. 95-134, 1978) and within that legal precedent affirm the following:

1) The rights of the Native Peoples to practice and participate in traditional ceremonies and rituals with the same protection offered all religions under the Constitution.

2) Access to and protection of sacred sites and public lands for ceremonial purposes.

3) The use of religious symbols (feathers, tobacco, sweet grass, bones, etc.) for use in traditional ceremonies and rituals.

The spiritual power of the land and the ancient wisdom of your indigenous religions can be, we believe, great gifts to the Christian churches. We offer our commitment to support you in the righting of previous wrongs: To protect your peoples' efforts to enhance Native spiritual teachings; to encourage the members of our churches to stand in solidarity with you on these important religious issues; to provide advocacy and mediation, when appropriate, for ongoing negotiations with State agencies and Federal officials regarding these matters.

May the promises of this day go on public record with all the congregations of our communions and be communicated to the Native American Peoples of the Pacific Northwest. May the God of Abraham and Sarah, and the Spirit who lives in both the cedar and Salmon People be honored and celebrated.

Sincerely,

The Rev. Thomas L. Blevins, Bishop
Pacific Northwest Synod —
  Lutheran Church in America

The Rev. Dr. Robert Bradford,
  Executive Minister
American Baptist Churches of the Northwest

The Rev. Robert Brock
N.W. Regional Christian Church

The Right Rev. Robert H. Cochrane,
Bishop, Episcopal Diocese of Olympia

The Rev. W. James Halfaker
  Conference Minister
Washington North Idaho Conference
  United Church of Christ

The Most Rev. Raymond G. Hunthausen
  Archbishop of Seattle
Roman Catholic Archdiocese of Seattle

The Rev. Elizabeth Knott, Synod Executive
Presbyterian Church
  Synod Alaska-Northwest

The Rev. Lowell Knutson, Bishop
North Pacific District
  American Lutheran Church

The Most Rev. Thomas Murphy
  Coadjutor Archbishop
Roman Catholic Archdiocese of Seattle

The Rev. Melvin G. Talbert, Bishop
United Methodist Church —
  Pacific Northwest Conference

Sacred places exist in nature with or without modern people's recognition of their existence. Modern society can honor and respect them, ignore them, or say that they simply exist for other people. If we choose to honor and respect them, and fall into harmony with their power and spirit, the spiritual dimensions of our lives will be enriched. It appears clear that sacred places are touchstones of health, well-being, and creativity, and when we fail to honor their power, our lives become empty and the ecology is less respected. But once the power of the land has become a part of our consciousness, our lives change. Suppose our entire modern society accepts the value and importance of sacred places to all of us. How would life be different?

ENDNOTES

1. Federal Agencies Task Force, *American Indian Religious Freedom Act Report* (Washington, DC: United States Department of Interior, August 1979).

2. Ellen Sewell, "The American Indian Religious Freedom Act," *Arizona Law Review* vol. 25, no. 1 (1983) pp. 429-453.

3. Federal Agencies Task Force, *American Indian Religious Freedom Act*, p. 52.

4. Sewell, "The American Indian Religious Freedom Act," *Arizona Law Review.*

5. Sewell, "The American Indian Religious Freedom Act," *Arizona Law Review.*

6. Federal Energy Regulatory Commission, "Initial Decision Approving South Alaska Liquified Natural Gas Project, Including Siting of Facilities Near Point Conception, California, to Regasify Indonesian and South Alaskan LNG" (August 13, 1979), p. 236.

7. A.H. Maslow, *Motivation and Personality*, 2nd ed. (New York: Harper and Row, Inc., 1970), p. 1.

8. Kurt Lewin, *Field Theory in Social Sciences: Selected Theoretical Papers*, ed. D. Cartwright (New York: Harper and Brothers, 1951).

9. Jean Piaget, *The Child's Conception of the World* (New York: Harcourt, Brace and World, 1929).

10. Steven Halpern, *Tuning the Human Instrument* (Belmont, CA: Spectrum Research Institute, 1978).

11. Lawrence Blair, *Rhythms of Vision* (Boulder, CO: Paladin, 1975).

12. William Corliss, *Handbook of Unusual Natural Phenomena* (Glen Arm, MD: The Sourcebook Project, 1977). (This is one volume of several, plus a wonderful newsletter that Bill Corliss produces as part of the sourcebook.)

13. C.G. Anderson, "Animals, Earthquakes, and Eruptions," *Field Museum of Natural History Bulletin* 44:5 (Chicago): pp. 9-11.

14. Michael Persinger, "Geophysical Variables and Behavior: IX. Expected Clinical Consequences of Close Proximity to UFO-Related Luminosities," *Perceptual and Motor Skills* 56 (1983): pp. 259-265.

15. G.L. Playfair and S. Hill, *The Cycles of Heaven* (New York: Avon, 1979). See chap. 8.

16. J. Gould, "The Case for Magnetic Sensitivity in Birds and Bees (Such As It Is)" *American Scientist* (May/June 1980): pp. 256-257.

17. S.W. Tromp, *Psychical Physics* (New York: Elsevier, 1949).

18. Yves Rocard, *Le Signal du Sourcier* (Paris, France: Dunod, 1964).

19. William Tiller, "Some Energy Field Observations of Man and Nature," in *The Kirlian Aura*, ed. S. Krippner and D. Rubin (New York: Doubleday, 1974), pp. 92-136.

20. Robin Baker, *New Scientist* 87 (1980): pp. 844-846.

21. Frances Nixon, *Mysteries of Memory Unfold* (Chemanius, B.C., Canada: Magnetic Publishers, Inc., 1977).

22. William Tiller, "Some Energy Field Observations of Man and Nature" in *The Kirlian Aura*.

23. William Tiller, "Some Energy Field Observations of Man and Nature" in *The Kirlian Aura*.

24. James A. Swan, "Environmental Energies: Effects on Health and Well-Being" (Paper presented at First Regional Congress, American Association for Social Psychiatry, Santa Barbara, CA, 1977).

25. R.W. Carson, "Anti-fatigue Device Works by Creating Electrical Field" *Product Engineering* (Feb. 13, 1967).

26. H.S. Burr and F.S.C. Northrup, "The Electrodynamic Theory of Life," *Quarterly Review of Biology* 10 (1935), pp. 323-333.

27. S. Krippner and S.A. Drucker, "Field Theory and Kirlian Photography: An Old Map for New Territory," in *The Kirlian Aura*, pp. 85-91.

28. A.S. Presman, "The Role of Electromagnetic Fields in Vital Processes," *Biofizika* 9 (1964): p. 13.

29. Related to the author by Sylvia Schecter, October 1980.

30. Don Robins, "The Dragon Project and the Talking Stones" *New Scientist*, Oct. 21, 1982, p. 166.

31. Don Robins, "The Dragon Awakens," *The Ley Hunter*, no. 87 (1979-80): pp. 3-7.

32. P. Devereux, "Is This the Image of the Earth Force?" *The Ley Hunter*, no. 87, (1979-80): pp. 8-9.

33. P. Devereux, *Earth Lights* (London: Turnstone Press, 1982).

34. Patrick Tiernay, "Chilean High," *OMNI*, October 1983.

35. E. Rauscher, "Working With the Earth's Electromagnetic Fields," *Proceedings of Keynote Speeches at the Spirit of Place Symposium, Sept. 8-11, 1988* (Mill Valley, CA: The Institute for the Study of Natural Systems, 1989).

36. F. Soyka and A. Edmonds, *The Ion Effect* (New York: E.P. Dutton and Co., 1977).

37. J. Price, The Colorado Plateau Project, Santa Fe, New Mexico.

38. D. Sartor, "Meteorological Investigation of the Wupatki Blowhole System," *Plateau: Quarterly Journal of the Museum of Northern Arizona* 37, no. 1 (Summer 1964).

39. E. Rauscher, personal correspondence, 1985.

40. S. Malone, personal conversation, 1979.

41. P.E. Taylor, *Border Healing Woman: The Story of Jewell Babb* (Austin, TX: University of Texas Press, 1981).

42. J. Hoffer, "Thermal Water Occurrences in Trans-Pecos, Texas," *Texas Journal of Science* 30 (Dec. 1978).

43. This research was done by Phillip Sampler and is reported in *Border Healing Woman* by Pat Ellis Taylor.

44. Reported in "World Heritage," the Newsletter of the United States branch of the International Council on Monuments and Sites, Washington, D.C. October 1, 1984.

45. N. Evans, "The Native American Heritage Commission and Energy-Related Issues," April 23, 1981. Available from the Native American Heritage Commission, 1400 Tenth Street St., Sacramento, CA 95814.

46. W. Washburn, *The Indian and the White Man* (New York: Anchor-Doubleday, 1964), pp. 176-177.

47. United States Department of Agriculture, Forest Service, Pacific Southwest Region, *Final Environmental Impact Statement: Shasta-Trinity National Forests* (San Francisco, CA: United States Govt. Printing Office, 1988), p. S-17.

FIVE

Minding the
Spirit of Place

"Profane man is the descendent of 'homo religiosus' and he cannot wipe out his own history . . . because a great part of his existence is fed by impulses that come to him from the depths of his being."

MIRCEA ELIADE[1]

A totally rational society, composed entirely of characters like Spock on the "Star Trek" television series, cannot exist in real life. When people deny their real selves for any significant period of time, the result is tension, anxiety, then hatred, and, as Mircea Eliade points out, at our roots we are still a very primal species. Nowhere today is this more apparent than in American Samoa.

Strolling along a beach in Pago Pago, if one should happen to overhear a conversation between two Samoan lovers, one might hear the word *Anu'u* spoken, usually in a suggestive, flirting tone. Anu'u is a tiny island, less than a square mile in total area, which lies just off the eastern shore of the main island of Tutuila. Samoan myths tell of a day long ago in mythic time when three mountains on Tutuila got into an argument. The two larger mountains, Olotele and Olovalu, began to dominate the third, Olosega. In dire straits, Olosega called out for help to his friend the octopus. The devilfish came and wrapped his tentacles around Olosega, pulling and pulling until Olosega broke free from Tutuila and fell into the sea. The octopus then began towing Olosega to a new home—as an island in his own right in the Manua group some 63 miles away. Just as Olosega pulled free from Tutuila, a rock broke off the fleeing mountain's side. At first the rock floated in the ocean like a coconut, but then it took root and grew into the tiny island which today is known as Anu'u.

This is the story that the history books tell, but they were written by the Christian missionaries. Nothing in this myth is at all suggestive of the sexual innuendos I detected in reference to Anu'u, and so I asked members of the *aiga* (Samoan extended family) where I was staying if they could tell me more. At first I received silence, followed by some muffled chuckles, and no more. Then one day I was walking along the beach when the daughter of one of the chiefs who had heard my question looked at me and said with a foxy smile, "You wanna know about Anu'u?'' She was barely fifteen, had long black flowing hair, and was the archetype of the Samoan girls Margaret Mead wrote about in *Coming of Age in Samoa*. ''This is a special story only Samoans talk about,'' she said, and then began by drawing pictures in the sand with her bare foot.

On Anu'u there is a special sacred palm tree which all Samoan girls and boys learn about when they are growing up. They say that a long time ago a young girl was swimming out in the surf when she found an eel, which became her pet. This girl played with the eel all day long in the warm ocean water, and they became very good friends. Then, when she got older and began to become a woman, the *matai* (Samoan chiefs) came up to her and told her that she must give up this eel. She cried, but in Samoa the word of the matai is law, and so she agreed. The matai told her to kill the eel and bury it in the sand, which she did with great sorrow. Then, to her amazement, from the grave of the eel sprang a palm tree. The tree grew like Jack's beanstalk, straight and tall, with a thick crown of leaves at the top and some big, black coconuts hanging beneath it. The matai then told her she must learn to climb this tree with her eyes closed, and that when she touched the coconuts she would find great pleasure.

On the same island of Anu'u there is also a special pit filled with warm, bubbling, brown mud, my storyteller related with a giggle. Boys must learn to pick up a large tree trunk, carry it to the pit, and then throw the tree trunk just as far as they can into the pit. Then, to show their manhood, they have to jump onto the tree trunk and hold on, for great bubbles of mud rise to the surface, causing the tree trunk to rise and fall, and giving a ride of great delight.

''A society depends for its existence on the presence in the minds of its members of a certain system of sentiments by which the conduct of the individual is regulated in conformity with the needs of the society,'' ethnologist A.R. Radcliffe-Brown has pointed out.[2] It doesn't take a Freudian analyst to see that the island of Anu'u represents the sexual attitudes of the Samoans, which Margaret Mead shared with the world, helping to trigger the sexual revolution. A mythic theme with these sentiments sets a tone for a culture's sexuality, but it must be translated into the ethics and codes of behavior of the entire cultural system to preserve the original sentiments and make them come to life.

Apparently in old Samoa this was the case. In the days before science and Christianity became the cultural standards, community recreation featured ''night dances'' to honor the spirit of Anu'u. As the sun set in the west, fires were built on the beach and naked old men and women began dancing to the beat of slit log drums. Two lines of people, men in one and women in the other, slowly snaked into a large *fale* (a thatched- roof structure without walls), and there they danced until their bodies glistened with sweat. Then they retreated into the shadows.

Photo 23. *When the people of Samoa dance and sing, their words and gestures weave many elements of nature into the performance, including the harmonies struck with sacred places. Author photo.*

Two new lines then formed by the fire, this time consisting of naked teenagers. They, too, snaked around the fire to the beat of the log drums, moving with the full sensuous physicality of the spirit of Anu'u, the warm trade winds, the gentle ocean waves, and the humid night air. This dance worked up to a frenzy, and then suddenly the ritual leader cried out *aitu!*, which in Samoa means "ghost." As the Samoans believe that ghosts are the cause of bad fortune and illness, no one wanted to get caught by a ghost. So the best place to hide, of course, was in the bushes.[3]

The songs, dances, and stories of old Samoa are filled with sensuality. Samoans believe that the life-force energy or *to'ala* is centered in the pelvis. *To'ala* is also the name for the female sexual organs. If your *to'ala* gets unbalanced and you get sick, you go to a *fo fo*, or traditional healer, who treats you with massage and herbs. In some cases the *fo fo* applies a massage treatment while a chorus of dancers and singers may undulate behind his or her back, serving as a living battery for generating *to'ala* for the *fo fo* to channel into the body of the client, for massage strokes can follow the rhythm of the dancers.

Even today on American Samoa one is reminded of these sensual values while driving around the island, for on each auto license plate there is the slogan *motu o' fiafiga*, which means "the islands of pleasure." The friendly trade winds, the inviting warm ocean, the swaying palm trees, the abundant rainfall, and the lush tropical foliage speckled with brilliantly colored flowers all carry this theme, making the pace of life sea-turtle slow. However, if one drives up to the modern L.B.J. Tropical Medical Center on Tutuila, one comes upon a startling sign: Hypertension Clinic. Physicians today say that as many as 65 percent of all Samoans suffer from stress.

Stress and hypertension are normally associated with a hard-driving lifestyle, living in urban areas, and driving on crowded freeways. None of these exist in Samoa. The population has grown considerably, from 6000 in 1900 to 32,000 today, but there is still is plenty of room. In the warm climate, shelter is not a problem, and every Samoan is part of a large extended family, the *aiga*, which means that homelessness does not exist. Neither does starvation. The warm tropical waters abound with fish and shellfish, and on land, bananas, papayas, breadfruit, and other fruit grow everywhere. There are also fields of taro and sweet yams, as well as pigs and chickens scurrying about. With an average annual rainfall of 144 inches, the joke is don't stand in any place too long or the plants will start to grow on you.

It would seem that Samoa is still "the islands of pleasure," but the bloated bellies and bloodshot eyes of the people sitting in the waiting room of that clinic tell a different story. Physicians say that Samoans also have considerable problems with kidney stones. The kidney is the organ of fear. Beer sellers are happy; they report that Samoa has the second highest per capita consumption of beer in the world, only surpassed by Germany. Nurses and social workers talk about domestic violence and battered children.

The problems in Samoa are in many respects similar to those on Indian reservations, or in other places around the world where traditional cultures and modern society struggle for control of people's minds. In a traditional society, everyone has a job; there is no unemployment. Switch to a cash economy, and unemployment soars. Except for sports and dancing, the traditional Samoan culture has few direct translations into successful occupations in modern society. Old role models die. No longer is the mark of a man how good he can paddle his canoe and catch fish. Today the tuna are caught in big purse seines, canned, and shipped to the mainland. Working at the canneries has become a substitute for catching one's own food. Instead of fishing or hunting for food, one gets a job and uses money to buy New Zealand sausages and turkey tails, Australian canned corn beef, or the usual array of packaged foods which supermarkets on the mainland have.

These standards have come in with modern mainland values being promoted through the government (American Samoa is a United States Trust Territory which until very recently has been run by the Department of Interior, and still is under Interior jurisdiction), the military, and the churches. Thanks to an attempt to "bring Samoa into the twentieth century overnight," in the front of each classroom is the ultimate teacher: the television set. Samoans are great at mimicry, and so they have learned over the years that people who know how to best imitate the white people tend to get jobs. To get ahead, the *aigas* pool their money and buy television sets. Driving through the jungles at night, one sees the blue glows of Samoan "fireflies," not fires. Instead of the people dancing and singing, they sit quietly, watching, trying to understand modern society by seeing two-week-old, tape-delayed programs from network television on Hawaii. They watch and try to learn, and the old glow inside them which was fueled by sacred places and their myths dwindles. Instead, they seek the glow without, in the television set, looking through eyes clouded with fear, confusion, and anger. Hypertension arises from the denial of self, regardless of the pace of life.

The island of Anu'u is not just a spit of coral with a few palm trees and a mud pit and some sexual stories. It represents one of the most important of all human mechanisms to tie culture to nature—mythic place naming, or *landa nama* as Ananda Coomaraswamy called it.[4] In the land of the Navajo, all sacred places and many other landforms are associated with mythic stories, heroes, and heroines, so that wherever the Navajo go they are reminded of the sentiments which shape their culture. The Norse also mythologized the landscape, as do the Hindus of India, who associate their sacred places, *pithas*, with parts of the body of the Mother Goddess, Sati. The practice of *landa nama* not only helps people remember their myths, but it guides them to live in a world where both the mythic dimension and the profane dimension exist together, making *skalalitude* and its cultural equivalents elsewhere normal consciousness. In Samoa, nature is a strong force, and the mythic meanings are still living in the unconscious, but to recognize and live the myths is now taboo. The fires that burn brightest now are the inner flames of suppressed rage.

Myths make great children's entertainment, but they are much, much more. They are the guiding, organizing, and energizing symbols of life, touching us as people at our very core, keeping us in contact with the roots of being human and alive. Psychologist Rollo May writes, "The process of myth forming is essential to mental health, since myth is man's way of constructing interpretations of reality which carry the values he sees in a way of life; and since it is through myth that he gets his sense of self identity, a society which disparages myth is bound to be one in which mental disorientation is widespread."[5]

In Samoa today, even though the senses are constantly teased by the powerful sensual qualities of tropical island ecosystems, being successful as a human being means to deny nature within and nature without. The Samoans' anxiety comes from not knowing which world to focus on. People in the continental United States do the same thing, but they have become more calloused, having mastered certain skills which can be turned into more money than any Samoan could ever earn. Americans work so they can recreate, which really means recover. Among many cultures, recreation as Americans know it is unknown, for life itself is more of an organic whole and is without any need for special regenerative time except for ceremonies and rituals, which are much more wholistic than what Americans call "recreation." People suffer more in Samoa because the blindness of modern society is more apparent to their bodies and minds, which still know how nature should feel. Also, Samoans don't have enough money to escape.

One of the chief culprits for the "gift" of modern socialization is the contemporary school system. George Leonard writes:

> We have been taught in school that increasing human control of the non-human world has brought us leisure and art and culture and freedom from want. We have not been taught that control over nature has also meant an equivalent control over human beings. We have not been taught that whatever we have gained in dominance has been paid for with the stultification of consciousness, the atrophy of the senses, the withering away of being. We have not been taught because the whole business of being taught itself is part of the price we have paid and are still paying.[6]

When people spend years in school learning facts and skills, the product more often than not is a deeper nagging emptiness which they seek then to avoid through work, television, drugs, and superficial travel. Instead of discovering who we are and what our dreams mean, and playing with our creative potential to build a sound foundation of self, we learn through fear that if we get good grades we will make more money, and that is the ultimate source of success and happiness. If we feel tired, lonely, or bored, the answer to the problem is to buy something. As the promotional literature arriving with my monthly charge-card bill says, "A fresh selection of products to brighten your midwinter mood."

Modern technological sophistication still supports the consumerism habit, but like people addicted to alcohol or cocaine, Americans are needing to consume more and more energy and resources just to keep their cravings satisfied.

The people of Samoa are like canaries in the coal mine, showing people the future if they persist in following the present path of modern society toward self-destruction caused by avoidance of self and kinship with nature.

This is not a new condition in the United States. When Carl Jung first visited America in the 1920s, he remarked, "In America there is a discrepancy between conscious and unconscious that is not found in Europe, a tension between an extremely high level of culture and unconscious primitivity." Jung attributed this conflict not just to modern technology, but to the failure of Americans to recognize the need for achieving a mental harmony with the places where they live. In therapy with troubled Americans, Jung found that, when his clients began to have dreams containing Indians, serious healing was taking place. Jung said the meaning of this was that Indians are in harmony with the place where they live, and that in all of us there are deep roots which seek to achieve geographic harmony to stabilize the psyche, like the roots of a tree. For this reason, Jung made the recommendation that American society should seek to take on "the soul of the Indian" to find true peace.[7]

Jung's "Indianization" thesis receives strong support from the wisdom of the Hopi Indians, who are known for their expertise in prophecy. In 1964, Hopi elder Thomas Banyacya attended a special elders' meeting held at one of the high mesas of Arizona. At that meeting, one of the elders spoke of a special sacred rock where a most important ancient prophecy was etched in stone as a petroglyph. Banyacya and the elder went off in search of this rock and eventually found it. With the utmost care they scraped away the lichen and mosses, revealing an ancient rock art carving which describes the history of North America and gives all members of modern society a chance to understand the choices they face for survival.

According to Banyacya, who has often served as the spokesperson for Hopi messages and wisdom, the symbols tell the following story:

Once red and white people lived together as brothers and sisters. Then they were separated and the red people came to North America, where they settled. A time came when red and white people came together again, which is shown by the vertical line with the cross at the bottom. If the white people came bearing the symbol of the cross, which means Christianity, then the two could not live together, which has been the case. During this time of separation, two major world wars would occur. Finally, the continent would be faced with a choice. People would have to learn to live in harmony with the land, in peace like the Hopi, or there would come a terrible war, indicated by the wavy line going upward.

This time of choice would be apparent, the prophecy says, when certain signs came. One is that people would live in the sky. Skylab, the elders believe, fulfills

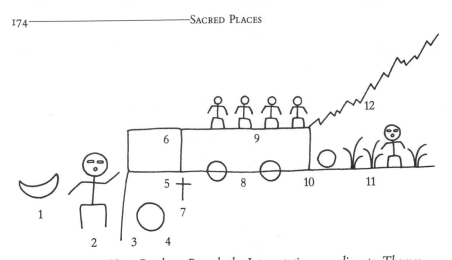

Figure 12. *Hopi Prophecy Petroglyph. Interpretation according to Thomas Banyacya: Time passes from left to right, beginning with the emergence of this world (1), aided by the Creator (2). Once, all the people lived together, hence a circle (3). Then white and red people split apart (4). The Hopi kept a tradition of close contact with the Creator and spirituality—the lower line (5); the white people went off to develop the power of invention—the upper line (6). The two would come together again, but if the white people came under the sign of the cross, it would not be possible to live as brothers and sisters (7). Two world wars would come to pass— the two circles (8). After this would come a time of the appearance of the "purifiers," powerful people who would change things and shake people up—shown by the four people on the upper line (9). Then we as all people would face a time of decision (10): to return to the land and the spirit of the place where we live, where the Great Spirit will walk among us and we will live again as brothers and sisters—the lower line (11); or to destroy ourselves—the upward-waving line (12). Rendering of petroglyph based on presentation by Thomas Banyacya.*

this prophecy. Another sign is that a spiritual man from the East would come to Hopiland and "dance in the sacred circle with the blue star kachina." This prophecy was fulfilled when the various gurus from India began coming to North America. In keeping with Jung's prophecy, another sign of the times prophesied by the Hopi was that white people wearing long hair and beads would come as brothers. When the hippies turned on, tuned in, and dropped out, they released their culturally conditioned ego consciousness and began to harmonize with the land, resembling Indians.

The hippie movement has blossomed and passed, and was followed by the human potential movement, which explored all the ways that people might be, as well as who we are. In the 1980s we saw more and more people looking for a new religion and spiritual psychology rooted in nature, which could give stability and a foundation on which to build a cultural system.

Each of us is descended from people who worshipped nature, and the symbols, forms, and energies of our ancestors reside somewhere in our personal unconscious as well as our collective unconscious, waiting for us to tap them and awaken human resources to renew our primal roots of well-being. To recapture them, it may be useful for modern Westerners to participate in shamanic rites from other cultures, but ultimately we must build a new type of religion and culture which "minds the earth," as Joe Meeker puts it, respecting life as it is and not seeking to dominate, control, and ignore living things.[8]

The challenge of our times is to "reinvent the human at the species level," says Thomas Berry, and in developing a new social architecture we will have to begin by facing the arrogance and egocentrism of modern science and technology with appropriate humility. Lewis Thomas reminds us of this when he says, "The only piece of scientific truth about which I feel totally confident is that we are profoundly ignorant about nature."[9]

This doesn't imply that technology per se should be dismissed as being evil, for it isn't. Technology is an extension of the human mind. When humans hold a false illusion about life, it may work for a time, but eventually the truth comes leaking out. Fueled by the myth that people can do and be anything they want to be, we often act out infantile fantasies without appropriate reality testing.[10] Once, when science and spirit were still married, the training of the forerunners of modern science had to go through intensive personal exploration and growth as well as to learn skills and methods of manufacturing and manipulating things and people. This gave them a firm foundation to create from a sense of inner self-awareness and peace. One of the biggest mistakes of our present technological world is to think that we have done away with magic, sorcery, witchcraft, and parapsychological matters by focusing on objectivity. Magic is a matter of ritual acts of communication. The advertising industry practices not-so-white magic quite a bit. Sorcery involves influencing things at a distance, which is the work of all planners. Witchcraft is a matter of controlling the ambiance of minds and places, which is the realm of the cosmetic industry and interior designers. While scientific psychology may try to deny the validity of psychic matters, intuition is the root of success for all good athletes, businesspeople, musicians, and parents. For nearly twenty years I have worked with shamans, sorcerers, witches, and psychics. Some of the blackest psychic forces I have encountered have been scientists, doctors, and salesmen, because they are consciously unaware of how they are practicing magic; they do not have an understanding of what they are doing.

Right now modern society is in a time of balancing. Since the late 1800s, there have been massive advances in science and technology, largely without ample consideration of their environmental consequences. The next wave of technology must concentrate more on asking ourselves whether we should do something and what the consequences are of our actions, rather than simply on what we are capable of doing. The past twenty years have taught many people that self-awareness is the key to personal growth. Now we have to expand this concept so that we do to our environment what we do to ourselves to grow. Monitoring should become at least as important as manufacturing if modern people are to create a society which acts as an aware person does.

The technologies which modern society desperately needs are those which operate in harmony with nature, as well as human nature. To create them, modern people will need to rework the way they think, solve problems, educate, and relate to each other. As John Naisbitt suggests in *Megatrends*, ''Whenever new technology is introduced into society, there must be a counter-balancing human response.''[11]

Many people become skeptical when it is proposed that a new social system be quickly invented, but the rate of change in the past century shows that people are capable of very rapid alternation in just a few short years. In the late 1800s, 90 percent of the population was employed directly or indirectly in agriculture. Today, less than 3 percent of people are professional farmers. As recently as the late 1950s, 65 percent of the workforce was working in manufacturing. Today, as cybernetics, robots, and automation take over manufacturing jobs once performed by human hands, some 65 percent of the population is employed in the computer field and the generation, communication, storage, and processing of information.

Naisbitt suggests that the ''high-tech'' side of the ledger needs to be balanced by an equally sophisticated ''hi-touch'' human-potential realizing process. Initially this may mean yoga and aikido as physical activity, meditation for relaxation, and biofeedback and mental imagery for healing. But this is just the beginning of something much more profound.

When Earth Day first came into being, people clamored for suggestions about what actions they could take to help the environment. In response, they were given lists of dos and don'ts, ranging from not driving so much, to not using colored facial tissues, to putting bricks in the toilet tank. In short order, many people complied, and change began. But despite nearly two decades of increased environmental awareness, modern society is still polluting the oceans, destroying the tropical rainforests, poisoning the soil, and generating mountains of garbage. The real environmental consciousness is yet to come into being, and part of the reason is the matrix of the socio-cultural system of modern culture.

Psychologist Herbert Kelman suggests that attitudes change and develop through three different paths:

1. COMPLIANCE. A person or group accepts influence from another person or group because they hope to achieve favorable reactions from the other, such as getting approval or rewards, or avoiding punishment.

2. IDENTIFICATION. An individual or group adopts a behavior of another to join the norms of that group or other person. This establishes some kind of mutually supportive relationship. Change in this case comes not from coercion or promised reward, but because the person wants affiliation.

3. INTERNALIZATION. This is a behavioral and attitude change which arises from within a person or group, as the result of careful consideration of things and of judging "What's good for me?"[12]

Compliance is what happens when laws are created or rules are laid down by a person in authority. Its success depends on the "carrot" of rewards, or the "stick" of fear of punishment. If a society requires heavy amounts of compliance, its people will have less control over their lives, and beneath their compliance may lie hatred. Identification involves membership and is part of group formation, as well as human development. Like compliance, however, it is heavily dependent on external conditions rather than internal needs and desires. If society as a whole works this way, it makes people very malleable and insecure, for it supports fads and charismatic people of all persuasions who easily move others to follow their whims.

When people's actions spring from a clear motive of doing what is good for them—"follow your bliss" as Joseph Campbell advised—they are acting from a sense of internalization. Maslow's research on self-actualizing people shows that humans are not greedy, impulsive creatures deep down, but compassionate beings who love nature as well as human nature. These messages have been buried inside of us for a long time, and they are overdue to come out as the wellsprings of a new society. For internalization to occur, however, we must be able to access and appreciate the roots of the experience of being human and to keep these roots alive and renewed.

The research presented in this book supports the ancient thesis that sacred places in nature exist and have the capacity to enable our minds to transcend time and space, plugging us into ourselves and the universe in a way which gives meaning, purpose and health to life. The real meaning of the word "recreation" is a regenerative experience which occurs as people interact with sacred places. Modern people can begin the process of honoring the sacred places by understanding them and making pilgrimages to them, but that is only a start. To keep the sentiments of these places alive and pulsing through people's lives, modern society has to develop a social structure which bows to the power of nature and works with what is, rather than ignoring or trying to dominate it.

It would be a mistake to think that we as individuals are doing all we need to do about honoring the power of spiritual sites by just shelling out a few dollars a year to pay a group to act for us to protect sacred places, as we do now with environmental organizations. An ecological conscience can only emerge from an internalized acceptance of the value of sacred places in nature and an adjustment of our personal and collective behavior to honor, protect, and use them.

The attitude of modern society toward issues like the environment has been all too often one of compartmentalized humanitarianism. Suffering from well-informed futility due to information overload from the media, we take out our checkbooks and give money to such and such a group to act as our conscience, but then, having sent off our money, we go to work in a totally air-conditioned building, surround ourselves with plastic, and fill several garbage cans a week with junk that we are too busy to recycle. It's great that there are so many good nature shows on television now, but I really worry that in a few years people will come to think that nature is something you only to be seen through a television and not something to experience in person. Will our grandchildren know wilderness only as a rerun?

A society exists as the result of multiple sentiments and agreements which are translated into thoughts, actions and structures. The roots of these patterns of interaction and thought are myths, legends, and values. Like within the personality of an individual, the extent to which there is unity in thought and action within a society is a reflection of how well the individual elements are interlinked and mutually reinforcing.

Assume for a minute that all people agree on a primary goal for the world of tomorrow of living in harmony with nature and honoring sacred places which serve as touchstones for our sentiments of kinship with the natural world. Actually having this happen would require a whole set of cultural elements working in concert to preserve and express natural harmony. Right now, modern society has considerable disharmony with nature. So, what follows is a brief look at some of the basic functional elements of modern culture and an examination of them in terms of the harmonizing roles they can play.

THE HARMONIZERS

1. Diviners. The need to see into the future and determine the truth in situations is essential for planning and carrying out our lives. Each day the weathermen forecast the future, as do the stock analysts, political analysts, market researchers, public health research teams, and game biologists. Divining is an essential social skill, and it has a long and rich tradition. In Christopher Bird's classic study of soothsaying, *The Divining Hand*, he lists forecasting methods used by peoples down through history, including aeromancy (interpreting atmospheric pressure, as in a barometer); austromancy (studying the winds); belomancy (shooting arrows into the air or at a target); ceromancy (dropping hot wax into water); cleromancy (throwing dice); crystallomancy (reading crystals); halomancy (using salt); hepatoscopy (analyzing the entrails of dissected animals); lithomancy (reading stones); moleosophy (examining moles on the body); oenomancy (watching the appearance of wine poured in libation); ophiomancy (the behavior of snakes); spedomancy (studying ashes); uremancy (interpreting urine); xylomancy (predicting with dry sticks); and zoomancy (observing animal behavior).[13] To this list, each of us could add other forecasting strategies, including observing the width of a woolly bear caterpillar's middle stripe as an indicator of the severity of the coming winter; contemplating tea leaves; evaluating the lines on

A—TWIG. B—TRENCH.

Figure 13. *Early Uses of Dowsing & Divining. This portrayal of prospecting for metals is reprinted from* De Re Metallicus *by George Agricola, 1556, courtesy of the University of Washington library.*

a person's hands; reading the I Ching, tarot cards, and astrological charts; and using complex computer simulation models.

Today, as a result of modern society's love affair with mechanistic science, Western culture favors mathematical models for future forecasting or personality diagnosis, although astrology remains the most popular divining method in the world, and everyone has an intuitive function, whether they are aware of using it or not. Modern people have replaced finding the truth through inner recognition with seeking truth through external objective measurements, thus giving up a precious ground of human self-confidence and awareness. The Sufi saint Ibn el-Arabi of Spain proposed that there are three kinds of knowledge. The first kind, intellectual knowledge, the forte of academicians, results from collecting facts. It can be organized into systems, but it may have nothing to do with reality or wisdom. The second is the knowledge of states, which includes recognizing emotional states and mystical experiences. This domain has value, he counseled, but it is the beginning, not the end, of real knowledge. The third kind of knowledge is the "knowledge of reality," with which a person can perceive what is right, true, and beyond the boundaries of thought and the senses. "The people who attain the truth," Ibn el-Arabi advised, "are those who know how to connect themselves with the reality which lies beyond . . . both intellectualism and romanticism."[14]

In a world more in tune with the wisdom of sacred places, developing one's intuitive faculties is of the utmost importance. In traditional societies, people know of impending storms, hurricanes, earthquakes, and natural diasters because of their dreams, visions, and intuitions. We each have the capacity to be more intuitive and part of coming into greater harmony is to prize and develop this intuition, for it arises from an awareness of the totality, which ultimately is nature. It is quite clear that some people do have profound experiences at sacred places which reveal truth—past, present, and future. A culture more in touch with the power of the sacred place would pay more respect to this potential and to the people who best understand it—the shamans. Both the vision-quest tradition as practiced by many Indian tribes and the understanding of dreams should be required subjects in school, just like math, computer proficiency, and writing. Modern society might also employ shamans as consultants to planning and scientific research, asking for their input in the creative process of guiding humanity toward the future, as well as in unraveling the problems of the times. For example, modern medicine is presently spending millions seeking a cure for AIDS. In contrast to laboratory methods, several shamans have suggested to me that their approach would be to be flown to the physical site of the origin of the disease, so that they might conduct dream ceremonies and speak with the spirits and the animals to determine what they might have to say. The cost of such a project would be miniscule compared to what other research costs, and it seems likely that the results could be very rewarding.

2. Symbolizers. The language of the unconscious mind is symbolic. Down through the ages, whoever or whatever controls the symbols of a culture is frequently the force which structures its norms and paradigms. The master symbolizers of modern times are the media and the advertising industry. They seek to motivate people to buy what they are selling by convincing us we are not happy, sexy, adult, or complete without what they have to offer. They thrive on our insecurity, helping it to exist by constantly reminding us of what we do not have. Instead, if we could all be more whole, self-satisfied, and filled with the symbols of nature for our identities, advertising as it exists today would have to change.

When I worked with the government of American Samoa to develop their environmental health education plan, we decided to bring back the old wise animals as educators. So, today, like in the days of old, the shark and the turtle are again valued as wise beings, not only because of the old myths but because, like Smokey the Bear and Woodsy Owl, they are now characters who communicate ecological and public health information. Using such symbols to convey sentiments has a double value, for they both educate and remind people of the attributes of animals as wise beings, which helps to preserve some of the old sentiments of traditional Samoan culture. When I was hired, I had to agree that our plan would be *fa'a Samoa*, which means the "Samoan way." More tribes should consider such a guiding standard for contracting outsiders, requiring assistance to support cultural heritage and not change it. Another outcome of the Samoans taking more control over their own education and culture-building process is that all Samoan schools now teach units on parapsychological perception. The units include the latest research on telepathy, clairvoyance, and precognition. Students test themselves for various abilities, and considerable sharing of the elders' abilities and folk tales is done. The denial of such faculties is a prime cause of modern people's loss of harmony with nature and our denial of the power of place to charge our minds and bodies with inspiration and meaning.

As a way of building community spirit, each community today ought to have some special place it honors, using symbolic natural characters in story, song, and dance to build positive sentiments about the spirit of that place. This is already done with athletic team mascots, but the idea needs to be connected to geographical places in order to build the positive associations needed to link us to places of power for identity and spirit. Each community might consider contests to develop a symbol which is an expression of the spirit of that place. From such a symbolic root, myths and stories could be generated which reflect community values. This set of sentiments could in turn be translated into an annual festival to celebrate the spirit of that place. If a community's identity is symbolized by a mountain, or a species of tree or flower, the preservation of that part of nature will be a lot easier.

3. Entertainers. Originally, poets, actors, bards, and clowns were the people who inspired communities, brought them together, preserved the history, made the myths come to life in ritual, and praised or criticized the social norms. All public entertainment is a form of ceremonial art, but the extent to which the power of ritual is actually used in a positive fashion by entertainers is miniscule compared to what it could be. The potential power to use the arts on behalf of the environment goes beyond fundraisers; it offers a direct link to the human soul. In the words of Joseph Campbell, whose book, *The Hero with a Thousand Faces,*[15] was a primary guiding force for George Lucas's *Star Wars* trilogy:

> The harmony and well-being of the community, its coordination with the harmony and ultimate nature of the cosmos of which it is a part, and the integration of the individual, in his thought, feeling, and personal desires, with the sense and essential force of this universal circumstance, can be said . . . to be the fundamental aim and nature of the ceremonial. . . . It is possible that the failure of mythology and ritual to function effectively in our civilization may account for the high incidence among us of the malaise that has led to the characterization of our times as the "Age of Anxiety."[16]

The television set in the average household is on more than seven hours a day. In addition to nature programs and documentaries about new disasters, environmental issues and the love for nature could be themes in soap operas, feature series, comedies, and children's programs. In New York City, a nightclub opened in 1989 called The Wetlands Reserve, which features only entertainment dealing with ecological themes. The more places in which ecologically supportive sentiments and values are expressed, the quicker society as a whole translates them into acts which collectively support these values.

4. Healers. Healing is an art and a science. Magico-religious figures with strong ties to nature for their power—shamans, witches, and wizards—were the first healers. In studying the methods of Navajo shamans, Donald Sander sees four elements central to the successful practice of these traditional healers: (1) a return to the origins and roots of life; (2) confrontation with and manipulation of evil; (3) death and rebirth; and (4) the restoration of the universe.[17] The word "health" in English is derived from the Anglo-Saxon root word "hale," which means "whole." Modern medicine does a great job of attacking infectious forces with chemicals, operating, and setting bones, but it tends to avoid the approach of the traditional medicine person, which is to drive out negative elements that block a person from becoming healthy and whole. In making a person whole, the medicine person calls upon the energies and symbols of nature to enter the client. For a long time, modern medicine has laughed at such ideas, but the development of the "core shamanism" methods of Michael Harner, including journeying for power animals and finding plant allies, has shown widespread beneficial value for helping to heal mental and physical dis-ease. This shows us how nature is and always will be the greatest healer.[18] The more modern people can relearn to use natural healing vectors ranging from herbs to hot springs, exercise, ritual, and even pilgrimages to places of power, the better off we all will be. The more a culture as a whole arises from ecologically respectful themes, the easier it will be for each person in that culture to be whole and healthy. It seems no mere coincidence that transcendent experiences at sacred places have a unitive quality. These experiences represent touchstones for the kind of mindset which needs to be translated into all of life.

5. Lawmakers. When the Hawaiian kahuna priests climb to the top of a platform above the black volcanic stone *heiau* (ceremonial stone platform), they chant to seek perfect harmony with reality. Modern people like to think of courts as being places where perfect truth and justice preside, but the actual practice of law is a very subjective system involving personalities and standards beyond what are set out in the law books. One of the key methods for seeking justice in a court of law is the ability to gain recognition or standing. Since people have recognition as members of society, they have legal rights, but so do non-human entities including corporations, municipalities, and trusts. Therefore, why can't natural objects also gain legal rights? wonders attorney Christopher Stone in his fascinating book, *Should Trees Have Standing?* As much as some people might like to think Stone is joking, in recent years both grizzly bears and a species of Hawaiian goose have been given standing by judges in cases where their homelands are threatened with destruction. Some people now argue that the whole Earth should have legal standing, especially if modern science can agree that the Earth is a living being.

In traditional societies, judges normally are spiritual figures, or political figures who rely on spiritual diviners to help them make decisions, for keeping the balance in life is ultimately a spiritual matter. Modern judges, attorneys, and politicians all might benefit from spiritual training linked with the Earth, as well as from making periodic retreats to natural places to contemplate just what balance is. To fully understand an abstract concept like balance you should be able to feel it in your inner self as well as sense and see it in the world around you to translate it into legal actions. William O. Douglas was an example of such an ecological lawmaker, a fact which he readily admitted was linked to his spiritual bonding with nature. He once said, "I hope that before it is too late people will develop a reverence for our rich soils, pure waters, rolling grass country, high mountains, and mysterious estuaries. I hope that they will put their arms around this part of this wonderous planet, love it, care for it, and treat it as they would a precious and delicate child.''[19]

6. Scientists. Chukchi author Yuri Rytkhen was born in Siberia, looking out onto the Bering Strait and the two Diomedes Islands. Considering the evolution of his people, the Chukchi, one of the circumpolar tribes, he writes, ''When we observe, for example, that in the Soviet Arctic shamanism has vanished very quickly, we overlook the fact that it simply has taken on modern dimensions. The shaman was the preserver of tradition and cultural experience. He was meteorologist, physician, philosopher and ideologist—a one-man academy of sciences.''[20]

Once the social role of the scientist was filled by alchemists, shamans, priests, wizards, witches, sages, and Freemasons. Like modern scientists, these practitioners sought truth and order in the world, but used non-linear methods of divining. These seer-scientists fell from their position of trust in society when some of their inaccuracies were exposed by people like Copernicus, Kepler, and Galileo, who used objective methods to expose superstition masquerading as the truth.

As the old soothsayers fell into disrespect, Newtonian physics, Euclidian geometry, and the Cartesian system of coordinates came into being. In an act of philosophic balance, society then leaped ahead to make up for time spent not honoring linearity. But now we cannot afford to embrace the Newtonian-Cartesian model, for as physicist David Bohm has pointed out, this model of reality is ultimately fragmenting: ''The world [according to the Newtonian-Cartesian paradigm] is regarded as constituted of entities which are 'outside of each other', in the sense that they exist independently in different regions of space [and time] and interact through forces that do not bring about any changes in their essential nature.''[21]

Like the theoretical physicists who are now exploring meditation, martial arts, and shamanism in the Andes, Bohm says the ''new sciences'' must return to wholeness by embracing the world as it is, and not how people would like it to be. In his view, Einstein's theory of relativity was the first step toward developing a model of life which is based upon ''unified wholeness,'' a thesis which is in total agreement with the paradigm of ecology that all things exist in systems. Prizing this view, one can see how Spinoza's God, which is a manifestation of harmony in all things, begins to make sense in terms of science as well as metaphysics. The quest for truth becomes the common goal of both spiritual seeker and scientist.

Modern society cannot afford to continue to educate scientists and engineers without making the foundation for their work be a thorough understanding of ecology and self-awareness. The danger of science today is that it operates as if it exists without any overall context or responsibility for its actions. The result is pollution and resource destruction. The new sciences must be holistic, organic efforts to tinker with the forces of nature, rather than systems bending these forces to fit the whims and economic cravings of people. We joke about the "mad scientist," like Dr. Strangelove or Dr. Jekyll and Mr. Hyde, but, in a way, a good deal of what we call science is the result of madness. Why else would people try to build nuclear power plants instead of developing energy technologies based on harmony with natural forces like the sun, wind, tides, and biomass? The invention of nuclear power itself is a manifestation of a certain consciousness rooted in the myth that we can do anything we want without fear of negative consequences. Examples of the myopia of this mindset include Bhopal; Chernobyl; Three Mile Island; the mercury and PCBs in the fish, animals, and people of Michigan; and other toxic nightmares. Another example of such arrogant technology is the gasoline-powered leaf blower. Rakes and brooms, both made of natural materials, can do the same job with less noise, no fumes, no hazard to the user, fewer resources consumed, more efficiency, and more thoroughness. But, seduced by power and speed, people keep buying and using these miniature tornadoes. Tiburon, California, has recently banned the use of leaf blowers, a move which hopefully other cities around the world will follow.

So many important scientific discoveries have come from dreams, visions, and mystical insights that it seems fruitful to consider increasing the chances of such experiences by putting scientists out on vision quests or dream treks to help their thinking remain creative, open, and in tune with nature. If scientists could relearn how to talk to the trees, like their predecessors did, a lot of the malevolent science we have to live with today would cease to exist.

7. Warrior-Athletes. "Man's warlike instincts are ineradicable—therefore a state of perfect peace is unthinkable," Carl Jung wrote. "Morever, peace is uncanny because it breeds war," he said. "True democracy is a highly psychological institution which takes into account human nature as it is, and makes allowances for the necessity of conflict within its own national boundaries."[22]

What Jung is talking about is human nature, and especially the dark side or shadow element in all of us. When we try to make believe that we are holy, wonderful, and righteous, and that peace is simply something we will into being, ultimately an underlying element surfaces to destroy this kind of peace: carnal, physical violence. In each one of us there is a bear, a lion, a snake, and a tiger, as well as a dove. If the bear and the dove cannot learn to coexist, then the bear eats the dove. There is a new group called "Bullies for Peace," whose members run around saying they are aiding world peace by cramming their values down other people's throats. This kind of "peace making" ultimately breeds violence. Real peace arises more from working with all that is human in a constructive manner, rather than from practicing self-righteous denial.

Among traditional cultures, warriors are usually seen as being spiritually guided. In aikido, a Japanese martial art, the black-belt masters are such adept killers because they have attained a state of harmony with nature, but they express their lethalness only when serving a higher purpose. In terms of the military, Americans might seriously consider the mental-spiritual training regimens of other cultures who develop spiritual warriors. These regimens root their discipline, as well as their skills proficiency and obedience to a leader, in nature and God. Beyond the armed forces, today's warriors are athletes. The violence on the football field, the basketball court, and the wrestling mat is an honest expression of our shadow. Athletics serves as a creative and positive way to release aggressive tendencies and offers an avenue to transcendence. When athletes perform at their best, they are blending with nature and falling into a spiritual state of grace. This is why traditional cultures use sacred rites at spiritual places as part of their athletic training programs. Recall that the spirit of the Olympics originated with ceremonies performed at Delphi.

In our training and contests, Americans could and should work a lot more on developing the mental component of sports, especially on understanding how ritual and peak performance go together. We also need more sports which help us remember their origins and which preserve ecological awareness. I'd like to see a Stone Age Olympics, where participants compete in throwing spears, shooting archery with equipment made entirely from natural materials, kayaking and canoeing in boats made from skin and wood, casting nets and fishing lines for accuracy, and tossing large stones and poles, like at some Scottish games. Sport, ritual, and art were once all woven together. Today, athletes pay people to make high-tech equipment for them, forgetting the spirit which goes into the equipment and that participation is as important as time and score.

8. Spiritual Leaders. The purpose of religion is to preserve a sense of mystery, facilitate transcendence, and generate a sense of community. In terms of psychological health, William James said that transcendental experiences are the "root and center" of personal religion, but, as Walter Huston Clark has pointed out, a chief problem with religion today is that "it is probable that many who run the churches have either never known profound religious experiences, or if they have, they've forgotten it."[23]

In tribal societies, the core of religion is mystical experience, with the spiritual leaders being adepts at ecstasy as a result of intense personal training and study with accomplished masters of transcendence. In most traditions, including Christianity, such training has often included time spent alone in the wilderness. Returning from a vision quest on Bear Butte in the Black Hills of South Dakota, Brooke Medicine Eagle, the great-great grandniece of Chief Joseph of the Nez Perce, says, "Any of us can dream, but when you seek a vision, you do this not only for yourself but that the people may live, that life may be better for all of us, not only for me but for all life."[24]

Spiritual experiences, unlike religion, are nondenominational, especially when they occur in natural settings. For me personally, a vivid dream which helped me let go of my fears of shamanism came one night while I was working with the Klamath and Modoc tribes of Oregon. I had been deeply troubled about how to reconcile my growing interest in shamanism with Christianity, for I had been raised in the Episcopal church. In the dream I found myself standing in Saint James Church on Grosse Ile, Michigan. From behind the altar appeared Jesus. He looked at me with compassion, and then walked to a door and opened it. Out stepped a wizard, looking like Merlin himself. Then the church slowly dissolved away, and the wizard and I were standing on bare ground looking together at an oak tree.

"A fundamental element of religion is an intimate relationship with the land on which the religion is practiced," asserts Vine Deloria, Jr.[25] In the letter of apology from the Christian clergy of Seattle to the Native American people of the Pacific Northwest, there is a recognition of the spiritual significance of the land—a gift from the traditional religions to the modern ones. A common practice of cities is to adopt a city elsewhere as a sister city. I would advocate that each church, whatever its denomination, adopt a special place to love and protect and share with all others. More than one church could share the same place, and if Indians now use the place for spiritual purposes, the modern churches could help protect the practice of the traditions, possibly even using Indians to guide non-Indians about how to best work with the spirit of that place.

Most churches today are also created with little recognition of sacred design. A true place of religion is a microcosm of the macrocosm, which means that it is connected to the greater universe through its design. In earlier times, finding such alignments was the work of the geomancer, who is a blend of metaphysician and architect-contractor. The mountain within needs to be kept in harmony with the mountain without, and so in terms of designing an entire culture to work in alignment with nature, it is essential that modern people restore geomancy to its rightful central place in the order of human affairs, and drive out what Frank Lloyd Wright called today's "Cash and Carry Architecture."

THE ART OF FENG SHUI

Perhaps the most intact and successful geomantic system in the world is *feng shui*, which originated in China. Visitors to China today remark about the beauty, longevity, and design of the old Chinese tombs, temples, plazas, and palaces, not to mention the 1500-mile-long Great Wall. Rather than ignore or dominate the landscape, as is the custom of modern design, Chinese architecture seems to magnify the landscape. The enduring quality of the Chinese designs is in large part attributable to the old Chinese art of feng shui, which literally translates as "wind and water."

According to oral history, the first emporer, Fu Hsi, began the feng shui system when "looking upwards, he contemplated the images in the heavens; and looking downward he observed the patterns on earth." To set things in order for maximum harmony, he began to see how the two might work together, following a sentiment which has become a feng shui creed: "Heaven, it is said, requires the aid of man to carry out its scheme of justice. Earth requires the aid of man to bring about its products of absolute perfection. Neither heaven nor earth are complete in themselves, but leave the last finish to man."[26]

In the heavens, the sages saw patterns which called to mind mythic images based on the unique vibrations of each star and the harmonic chords struck as a result of the star groupings. From these images have come an Oriental astrology and astronomy which is described in the geomantic guide *Han Lung King*, which means "The Book for Shaking the Dragon." According to this system, the North Star and major constellations, including Ursa Major, or the Big Dipper, are important considerations in the heavens, as are the "nine fancied stars." These nine are listed below to show how they are said to each resonate with special earthly qualities and draw on the powers of natural harmonics[27]:

1. *Tun-lung*—the "covetous wolf," whose vibrations are attracted to the entrances of caves and waterfalls.
2. *Chu-men*—the "great door," which resonates with certain hills with flat tops and square sides.
3. *Lu-'tsen*—"rank preserved," which favors hills and people who wish to attain higher rank.
4. *Wen-'chu*—literally "windings," which likes water and serpent forms.
5. *Lien-cheng*—"purity and uprightness," which harmonizes with the fire element and mountaintops.
6. *Wu-chu*—"military windings," which harmonizes with metal and and lies in a constellation with the shape of an inverted pan.
7. *Po-kiun*—the "Breaker of the Phalanx," a metallic vibration from Ursa Major which is also attracted to hilltops.

8. *Tso-fu* — the "left assistant," which confers honor to people of position when properly honored.

9. *Yeu-pi* — the "right assistant," which likes flat places and whose influence is sought to help make decisions.

The Chinese believe people have two souls. The *shen* soul is associated with the heavens. The *kewi* soul relates to the Earth. In good feng shui, the design and orientation of a building or town should harmonize its occupants with those qualities in the heavens which are compatible with and supportive of the qualities which are desired on Earth. An army general, for example, might site his center on a sharp-peaked mountain, with a window in his decision-making chamber looking out on the "Wu-chu" or "Po-kiun" stars to aid his judgment in times of conflict.

The foundation for good decision making, health, and prosperity comes from the Earth. To plot out proper earthly alignments, the feng shui practitioner consults four dimensions:

1. *Chi* — the life-force energy, *chi*, composed of both yin and yang elements; the generative force in the universe. Cultivating its presence is essential to good feng shui as well as to health.

2. *Li* — the natural laws of the universe, including astrology, orientation according to the powers of the directions, and honoring the ancestors.

3. *So* — the mathematical relationships which explain the workings of nature.

4. *Ying* — the natural history of a place, especially its landforms and the behavior of animals.[28]

For each of these four components of the feng shui system, there are a number of elements. Putting them all together, the feng shui practitioner arrives at an assessment of each place — what its strengths and weaknesses are, and what can be done to enhance its potential. There also are a variety of approaches to the practice of feng shui, based upon different traditions and schools. The following is a generic, thumbnail sketch of the principles of feng shui to help one think more like a feng shui practitioner. I would strongly recommend two books by Sarah Rossbach — *Interior Design With Feng Shui* and *Feng Shui: The Chinese Art of Placement*, both published by E.P. Dutton—for more information.

THE ELEMENTS OF FENG SHUI

1. Chi. The Chinese concept of life is a combination of two words, *hsin* and *ming*. *Hsin*, meaning nature, has a quality of lightness of the yang masculine aspect. The pure yang element of the universe is called *shen* and it is colorless, odorless, shapeless, soundless, tasteless, and shadowless, but it possesses a spirit (*ling*) and, like air currents, it can be felt on contact. *Shen* together with its spirit is the root of life.

Ming means "life," and refers to the visible life which is formed when *shen* attaches itself to *ching*, the pure yin of the universe and the origin of physical things.

The energy of the Earth is yin, pushing upwards, giving nourishment to all things. It is symbolized by the white tiger. The energy of heaven is yang, and it filters downward, inspiring life to action. Its symbol is the azure dragon. Where the azure dragon and the white tiger come together with great force, there is a place of power.

Each place is a mixture of the yin and yang reflected in the nature of chi present there. A place with three-fifths yang and two-fifths yin, for example, is said to be a good place to live. Classically this would be a place like the foot of a gentle-sloping mountain, beside a gentle winding watercourse with some bamboo and other vegetation to trap chi and shield the house from the wind.

In the human body, chi travels through a vast network of channels called "meridians," moving in a circular manner beginning with the lungs, then outward to the extremities, then back inward to the next organ, and so on until the old chi is breathed out to be replaced by fresh new life force. As chi passes through the body, it activates each organ system, changing in quality according to unique nature of that organ. Should the chi not flow smoothly, imbalances can occur, and dis-ease results. Along each meridian there are special places or "points." Many of these points have creative names from nature which describe their activating vibration, for example "bubbling spring," "joined valleys," "ocean bottom," and "pond of the winds."

Feng shui practitioners believe that the Earth has chi meridians, just like the body. The interaction between the chi of a place and the chi in a person's body is of the utmost importance to health. To correct problems, chi of the Earth can be manipulated in a way similar to acupuncture treatments. Some methods of Earth acupuncture, like earth-moving and the erection of flag poles to bring chi up, are easy to fathom. Others methods of cultivating chi involve the use of mirrors, crystal balls, wind chimes, and flutes, and burning of certain colored candles.

2. Li. Nature is ordered according to various laws which play a direct role in creating the spirit of a place. The heavens produce vibrations which harmonize with certain conditions on Earth. Each of the directions has its alignments with seasons, colors, virtues, gods, and so on. The configuration of these forces is expressed through various symbols, one of which is the *ba-gua* (figure 14). This symbol is especially important to the Black Sect of Tantric Buddhism version of feng shui developed by Professor Thomas Lin Yun, the Grand Master of this sect.

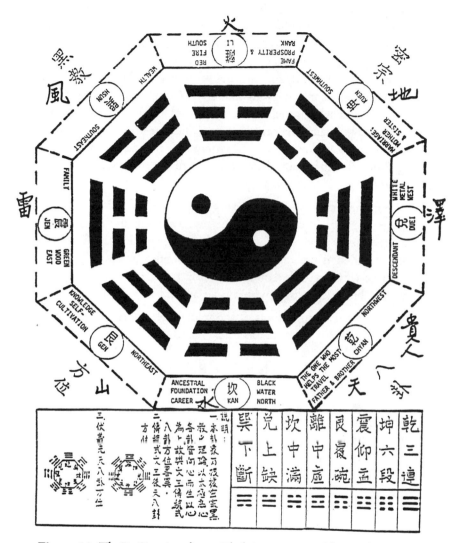

Figure 14. *The Ba-Gua According to Black Sect Tantric Buddhism. The Ba-Gua is used to orient design according to geographic direction in order to achieve the most favorable harmonies with the subtle forces of the universe. According to the Black Sect use taught by Master Thomas Lin Yun, the "mouth of the chi" or door of a room can be used as the north element for purposes of interior design, thus making the room configuration fall into place according to the "mouth of the chi" rather than actual geographic direction. Reprinted courtesy of Master Thomas Lin Yun and the Lin Yun Temple.*

The ba-gua is classically used to orient to the directions. However, for an interior space, according to Lin Yun the doorway is used as the "mouth of the chi" to determine orientation, as opposed to the points of the compass. My suggestion is to study his work and then experiment with changing around the interior of your house. Be ready for surprises when you do! His methods are used by places as diverse as banks in Hong Kong and Creative Artists Talent Agency in Los Angeles, and he has given advice to Pope John Paul. Lin Yun himself says he cannot totally explain why orienting one's home to the ba-gua works, but if this gets in the way of our using the system, he says that is modern society's problem. People should be more concerned with results than explanations in such matters, he feels.

3. So. The number of days in the monthly lunar cycle, the 365 days of the year, the four directions, the five elements, the mystical seven and nine, and so on, all have relevance to good feng shui. To help organize their calculations, some feng shui practitioners use a large compass surrounded by up to 28 concentric circles, each of which records a different vector. Included in this component of feng shui is Chinese astrology, which is an art and science in itself.

4. Ying. The relative proportions of the white tiger's presence and the azure dragon's presence at any place are intricately related to the shape of the landscape and the nature of bodies of water. The location of Lin Yun's temple in Berkeley, California, is a good example. He lives on Russell Street, which begins at San Francisco Bay and travels upward to the crest of the Berkeley Hills. The Lin Yun Temple is located almost at the top of the hills, but not quite, and on top of a small ridge. Lin Yun says this place was chosen because a dragon travels along Russell street from the Bay, going uphill. His head emerges at the ridge where the temple is sited, Lin Yun says. To be right on top of the hill would not be the best place to live, because it is too exposed and the winds would blow all the chi away.

In some cases, feng shui practitioners will engage in earth-moving to change landforms. They might cut off the top of a hill, for example, to control its chi from being too yang, or install fish ponds and groves of bamboo to capture chi.

Feng shui practitioners also believe that the land shapes the people who live on it. According to the Chinese book of wisdom the *Kuan Tzu*, fertile soil breeds handsome people, while ugly people are reared on poor soil. People who live on solid soil grow fat, while those who live on loose soil are tall, and dwellers on sandy soil are thin. In many ways, the feng shui practitioners were conservationists long before conservation was fashionable, no doubt because of their understanding of the land. In regard to good feng shui and resource use, the *Kuan Tzu* counsels:

Figure 15. *The White Tiger & the Azure Dragon Come Together at a Place of Power According to Feng Shui. Reprinted from an eighteenth-century woodcut, courtesy of the University of Washington library.*

If a human ruler likes to destroy nests and eggs, the phoenix will not rise. If he likes to drain the waters and take out all the fishes, the dragon will not come. If he likes to kill pregnant animals and murder their young, the unicorn will not appear. If he likes stopping the watercourses and filling up the valleys, the tortoise will not show itself.

Thus the [real] king moves only in accordance with the Tao, and rests only in accordance with the Li. If he acts contrary to these, Heaven will not send him long life, evil omens will appear, the spirits will hide themselves, wind and rain will not come at their usual times, there will be storms, floods and droughts, the people will die, the harvest will not ripen and domestic animals will not increase.[29]

The European Christian interpretation of dragons is that they are dangerous beasts which should be slain. In China, dragons are befriended. As the dragon is a symbol of the Earth force as well as of sexuality, much is implied by these varied myths and their relationship to conservation behavior.

Feng shui practitioners also insist that mythic symbols like dragons, lions, snakes, and birds are more than just metaphoric descriptions of the land. They are spiritual beings of power. If the birds are harmed, the phoenix will not rise, and the phoenix is the mythic carrier of rebirth. If the water is polluted and the fish killed, the dragon will not come, and people will not prosper. For each place there is a parallel spirit world, which in turn influences human affairs. Lin Yun says that if a sacred place is violated, curses will come upon the people who destroy the place. In earlier times in China, people sometimes took the feng shui practitioners' proclamations very seriously. In the late 1800s when Senator Amaral, the governor of Macao, built a road which violated a dragon and interfered with some tombs, he was ambushed and his head was cut off. The Chinese called this deed "the revenge of feng shui."[30]

Feng shui is a method of sensitively ordering human activity to attain harmony in all things. However, it is not the only approach to geomancy, and each geomantic style needs to grow from the Earth where it is needed. Humanity needs a new modern geomancy which can be readily applied to all cultural settings.

SACRED ENVIRONMENTAL EDUCATION

Any place can be sacred, but there are those places which are special. By honoring their presence, all else in life can become more vital and creative. Through multiple cultural elements, people collectively build a social system. The degree to which these elements are mutually supportive is often a direct indicator of the long-term success of that culture. The ecological problems of modern society are to a large extent the result of two factors: fragmentation within the cultural system and a lack of harmony with nature in social and personal behaviors. Sacred places are touchstones for personal and cultural renewal. Creating new social settings to reinvent the human species must include honoring sacred places as cornerstones of new ecological values. In this chapter I've suggested a number of ways people could rework their cultural links to each other and nature which would increase overall harmony. These ways involve looking at the potential harmonizing functions which social roles can play. The harmonizers listed here are meant to be examples of a way of looking at society to see what changes need to happen. You can think of many more. Just hold in your mind the image of sacred places as being like electric power plants, constantly sending out energies to charge our lives, perhaps as golden spiderwebs of vitality. See what new creative insights come to you about the problem of how to live in harmony with nature. Modern medicine is beginning to do this with its increasingly holistic approach. Now it is time for the fields of design, planning, business, science, and law to also take on more holistic approaches—ones that are rooted in nature.

Modern people will become better and better harmonizers as we learn to

Figure 16. *Feng Shui Geomancers at Work. Reprinted from* Environmental Design Primer *by Thomas Bender.*

model our minds after nature, rather than in ignorance of it. Because modern society has had compulsory education for so long, and nearly compulsory post-secondary education for an additional number of years, one of the primary places where people begin to increase their harmony with nature is through the content and process of education.

In the 1960s there was a push toward opening up schools to more freedom and experimentation. Then, in later decades, a "back-to-basics" movement reared its head, college entrance test scores became more important, and in some cases education moved back three steps for every one or two it had moved ahead.

When I consult in schools today, the constant feeling I get is one of pressure and anxiety among the kids, the teachers, and the administrators. This is reflected in increasing drug abuse, teen pregnancies, teen suicides, and gang violence. Schools have become a "worksheet wasteland," according to psychologist Thomas Armstrong, where the goal of teaching has become to get material covered so that the kids score high on tests, rather than much of anything else.[31] In response to the rising tensions in public schools, more and more people are taking their kids out of public school for either home or private schooling. In Mill Valley, California, where I live, if present trends continue, as of 1990 about half the school-age kids are not in public schools, a trend which is growing nationwide.

Maslow's research on self-actualization clearly shows that the real leaders of both past and modern times do not develop their zest for life and learning through conventional schooling. My own research on the development of environmentalist leaders confirms this. Environmental values arise from emotional experiences which serve as the generating forces for action. Schools can help people acquire skills, but unless what they offer is packaged in the right way and rooted to some healthy human motivation other than the fear of failure, they will soon become like dinosaurs going extinct.

Since the 1960s I have been working with the idea of what constitutes good environmental education. After some twenty years, my firm believ is that, while giving kids the facts about pollution and nature helps, what is best for kids and the environment is to provide experiences for kids which develop deep bonding with nature and an understanding of humanity's dependence upon the environment. An honest sense of harmony with nature arises from encounters with the natural world which touch people's primal roots, dispell needless fears of nature, and help people know who they are. Based on modern and ancient psychology, some of these experiences should include:

1. Survival Skills. Many children today grow up with the idea that food comes from the supermarket. It does not. Modern people are so distanced from the roots of existence that we have lost the sense of awe which comes from seeing our food grow, gathering it, killing it, and cooking it. I would propose that every school begin its environmental education by growing part of its own food, which the children can cultivate, cook, eat, and celebrate.

When modern society has a power outage, people panic, unable to deal with the loss of electricity, forgetting the simple beauty of life without it. At home and at school, periodically, people should have "energy fasts" when all electrical appliances and devices are turned off, making them more aware of how dependent they are on electricity. They would see that the world does not fall apart if the clocks, television sets, and electric lights don't run.

David Brower has suggested that much anti-environmental behavior is a result of the fear of nature. Bears can eat people, snakes can bite people, and mosquitoes can sting people, but with some common sense and practical skills, people can live close to nature as their ancestors did. I would suggest that more important to personal happiness than any SAT score is the ability to feel at ease in nature. Some of the best work along these lines is being done by Tom Brown, who learned to become a tracker by apprenticing himself as a child to an Apache Indian named Stalking Wolf.[32] Love of nature should be developed through a sequential program of experiences involving all senses. These can be planned and offered in a progressive manner and integrated with other curricula.

2. Isolation. For many people, the fear of being alone is one of their deepest fears. All their lives they have been surrounded by people, telephones, television, books, drugs, and buildings. Sometimes people avoid being alone in nature because they have specific phobias of bears, snakes, bees, and so on, but often wild places are avoided because they have the capacity to loosen people's ego boundaries and bare people's souls. Indians and Aborigines understand this and have developed careful educational programs to prepare people for spending time alone in nature. The purpose of this alone time is to help people discover who they really are, which is a very serious matter. The lessons of time show that the most meaningful solo experiences in nature come at sacred places. Like each church, each school should also have one or more places, in addition to the schoolgrounds, which it cares for as a regular part of the curriculum.

3. Ceremonialism. Recalling Joseph Campbell's warning that the chief sources of anxiety in our age are the loss of myth and ritual, schools offer a fantastic setting for creating rites to honor the passing seasons of the year and the power of place. "Men express in ritual what moves them most, and since the form of expression is conventionalized and obligatory, it is the values of the group that are realized," observes anthropologist Monica Wilson.[33] Already schools honor the passing seasons in art, and sometimes in festive activities at Halloween, Christmas, and Easter. They could do much, much more. If they grew their own foods, a planting and harvest cycle could become a major school theme of celebration, involving studying customs around the world in relation to local science and ecology. If the charge of bringing religion into the public schools becomes a problem, all religions could be brought in to see what they have to say about the seasons. Or, a seasonal cycle could be created with masks, plays, songs, and studies based on nature, and not called religion, even though it is. Science and math easily fall into practical application as part of a seasonal curriculum, taking their rightful place as methods to increase understanding, rather than as drudgery to get good grades.

4. Service. An education which avoids dealing with the reality of the school and the community from which it arises is an exercise in alienation. Kids do care about the places where they live and the quality of life. In this day of galloping technology, when powerlessness has become epidemic, people ought to spend as much time as possible in school helping kids learn how to think and solve problems. No child should graduate from high school today without knowing how to conduct an opinion survey, complain about community problems, and perform simple ecological monitoring exercises. William Stapp at the University of Michigan has developed numerous good ways to get kids out to gather data about their communities.[34] When the community becomes the classroom, learning becomes living. Kids can be a powerful force for increasing harmony with nature if they can just be given the chance to participate in making their education real.

5. Enchantment. The case for enchantment has been made throughout this book, and Carl Jung stands out as one of the all-time most salient minds on the power of the numinous. He says:

> As scientific understanding has grown, so our world has become dehumanized. Man feels himself isolated in the cosmos, because he is no longer involved in nature and has lost his emotional 'unconscious identity' with natural phenomenon. . . . Thunder is no longer the voice of an angry god, nor is lightning the avenging missile. No river contains a spirit, no tree is the principle of life in man, no snake contains the embodiment of wisdom, no mountain cave is the home of a demon. No voices now speak to man from stones, plants or animals; nor does he speak to them believing they can hear. His contact with nature has gone, and with it has gone the profound emotional energy that this symbolic connection supplied.[35]

As modern people, we have repressed our capacity for metaphoric thinking, which is part of what an Indian like Kenneth Cooper uses when he says he can go into the mountains and learn whatever he needs to know. We need to relearn how to talk to nature, and how to listen. Sacred places seem to have some of

If you wish to receive a copy of the latest BEAR & COMPANY catalogue and be placed on our mailing list, please send us this card.

Name _____ Date _____

(please print)

Address _____

City _____ State _____ Zip _____

Please check the following area(s) of interest to you:

1. □ Creation Spirituality   4. □ Healing/New Age
2. □ Medieval Mysticism   5. □ Native American/Mayan
3. □ Ecology/Sacred Sites   6. □ Other _____

BEAR & COMPANY
P.O. DRAWER 2860
SANTA FE, NM 87504-2860

Photo 24. *Machu Picchu, the ancient Inca city in the Andes of Peru. Photo © 1990 by Michael Powers.*

the strongest voices. As one way of beginning to develop an ability to work more closely with nature, try the following exercise.

Finding the Spirit of a Place

This is an exercise which I have done with thousands of people ranging in age from 7 to 90, usually with fascinating results.[36] Begin by finding a comfortable place, inside or outside, where you can sit or lie down and not be bothered for fifteen to twenty minutes. While this exercise is going on, I generally beat a drum with a steady rhythm to help people focus on their imagery processes and stabilize the local mind field. If you can't have someone present drumming, you may be able to take this journey without a drum, but if you want to do it alone, try using a portable tape recorder with earphones and listening to a shamanic drum journey tape. If you can't purchase such a tape in a local bookstore, then write to Institute for the Study of Natural Systems, P.O. Box 637, Mill Valley, CA 94942, as we sell several versions.

With or without the drum, close your eyes and take in a breath. Hold it for a minute, and then slowly let it out, imagining that your breath is going

Figure 17. *The Spirit of a Sacred Place. Reprinted from an eighteenth-century woodcut, courtesy of the University of Washington library.*

out from your feet into the earth. Do this several times, breathing away your tensions into the earth, until you feel relaxed.

Now think of a place which feels special to you. It could be a beautiful mountain meadow, a beach, a cave, or a special garden in a park. See yourself in this place. Feel the ground under your feet, the wind blowing in your hair, the sun or moon overhead, the lightness or darkness, the temperature. You may even smell things there. The more vividly and clearly you develop this picture, the better this exercise will work.

Now, either to yourself or out loud, begin to hum what you feel is the rhythm of this place. Reach out, entrain your mind with the ambiance of the place, and seek to harmonize with it. This is a song of power. As you are humming this song, in your hand appears a magical staff, the kind that wizards and shamans use to perform magic. Examine your staff. Get to know it and its power.

Now, raise up the staff in your hand, and strike it down on the ground. As you do, ask for the spirit of the place to come forth. Watch the land around you. What changes? It may be an animal, a plant, a stone, a cloud, a bird, or some ethereal form. Look for the spirit of the place to come forth.

Approach the spirit and ask it to speak its mind. What does it have to say? You may choose to ask it a question or two. Some people are able to carry on whole conversations with the spirit. When you've finished, say good-bye to the spirit, tap your staff on the ground again, and watch it disappear. Now let the place slip away, and return to the physical place where you are sitting or lying.

People doing this exercise report all kinds of fascinating creatures appearing as spirits. Sometimes the spirits say something simple and wise. Other times they give specific instructions about a place and what to do there. None of them have ever suggested littering, polluting, stripmining, or clearcutting. You may want to consult several different places and then draw pictures of the spirits of these places. Working with landscape planners and architects, I do this on sites where they are thinking of building. In some cases, I should warn you, spirits say not to build. If you let the land speak its mind, it may say no.

This exercise introduces you to a way of seeing which dates back to the earliest of times. It shows how mind and place can work together. It demonstrates on a small scale what kinds of things can happen to you at a sacred place. It is one more technique from a whole tool kit which people need to regain harmony with nature and pay their respects to the places on Mother Earth which are waiting for people to learn to use them. It is a way to engage nature as a planning consultant in the design of a new cultural system.

ENDNOTES

1. Mircea Eliade, *The Sacred and the Profane* (New York: Harcourt Brace Jovanovich Inc., 1959), p. 209.

2. A.R. Radcliffe-Brown, *The Andaman Islanders* (2d printing, London: Cambridge University Press, 1933), p. 233.

3. John Kneubuhl of the American Samoa Community College on Tutuila told me these stories one rainy afternoon in the islands.

4. Ananda Coomaraswamy, *The Rig-Veda As Landa-Nama bok* (London: Luzac and Co., 1935).

5. Rollo May, "Reality Beyond Rationalism," in *Agony and Promise: Current Issues in Higher Education*, ed. G.K. Smith (San Francisco: Jossey-Bass, 1969).

6. George Leonard, *The Transformation* (New York: Delacorte Press, 1972).

7. Carl G. Jung, *Civilization in Transition*, vol. 10 of *The Collected Works of Carl Jung* (New York: Pantheon, Bollingen Series 20, 1964), p. 49.

8. Joseph Meeker, *Minding the Earth Quarterly* (Rte. 2, Box 256A, Vashon Island, WA, 98070).

9. Lewis Thomas, *The Medusa and the Snail* (New York: Bantam Books, 1980), p. 73.

10. A. H. Maslow, *The Farther Reaches of Human Nature* (New York: Viking Esalen Press, 1971).

11. John Naisbitt, *Megatrends* (New York: Warner Books, 1982).

12. H. Kelman, "Processes of Opinion Change," *Public Opinion Quarterly*, 25 (Spring 1961), pp. 55-78.

13. Christopher Bird, *The Divining Hand* (New York: E.P. Dutton, 1979).

14. Idries Shah, *The Way of the Sufi* (New York: E.P. Dutton, 1970).

15. Joseph Campbell, *The Hero With a Thousand Faces* 2d ed. (Princeton, NJ: Princeton University Press, 1968).

16. Joseph Campbell, *Masks of God: Creative Mythology* (New York: Penguin Books, 1976), p. 92.

17. Donald Sander, *Navaho Symbols of Healing* (New York: Harcourt Brace Jovanovich, 1979).

18. Michael Harner, *The Way of the Shaman* (New York: Harper and Row, Inc., 1980).

19. William O. Douglas. This quotation is taken from study materials of the National Audubon Society Expedition Institute, N.E. Audubon Center, Sharon, CT 06069.

20. Yuri Rytkhen, "People of the Long Spring," *National Geographic* 163, no. 2, Feb. 1983, pp. 206-223.

21. David Bohm, *Wholeness and the Implicate Order* (London: Routledge and Kegan Paul Inc., 1980).

22. Carl G. Jung, *Psyche and Symbol* (New York: Doubleday and Co., 1958), p. 225.

23. W.H. Clark, "Selections from Religious Experience: Its Nature and Function in the Human Psyche," in *Advances in Altered States of Consciousness and Human Potentialities,* vol. 1, ed. T.X. Barber (New York: Psychological Dimensions, Inc., 1976), pp. 411-427.

24. Brooke Medicine Eagle, personal account of a vision quest reported in *Shamanic Voices,* ed. Joan Halifax (New York: E.P. Dutton, 1979).

25. Vine Deloria, Jr., *God is Red* (New York: Grosset and Dunlap, 1973), p. 296.

26. E.J. Etiel, *Feng Shui* (Cambridge, England: Land of Cokaygne Ltd., 1973).

27. J. Edkins, *Feng Shui* (Cambridge, England: Institute for Geomantic Sciences Research Occasional Paper no. 12, 1978).

28. E.J. Etiel, *Feng Shui.*

29. J. Needham, *Science and Civilization in China,* vol. 2 (Cambridge, England: Cambridge University Press, 1956), p. 272.

30. E.J. Etiel, *Feng Shui.*

31. Thomas Armstrong, *In Their Own Way* (Los Angeles: J.P. Tarcher, 1988).

32. Tom Brown, *The Tracker* (Englewood Cliffs, NJ: Prentice-Hall, Inc., 1978).

33. Monica Wilson, "Nyakysua Ritual and Symbolism" *American Anthropologist* 56, no. 2 (1954): p. 241.

34. William B. Stapp has developed a number of good guides for practical community ecological research, which are available through him at the University of Michigan, School of Natural Resources, Ann Arbor, Michigan 48109.

35. Carl G. Jung, *Civilization in Transition.*

36. James A. Swan, "Sacred Places in Nature: A Unitive Theme for a Transpersonal Approach to Environmental Education," *Journal of Environmental Education* 14, no. 4 (Summer 1983): pp. 32-37.

Photo 25. *Ancient spring, Roman masonry, Bath, England. Photo © 1990 by Cindy A. Pavlinac.*

SIX

The New Earth Paradigm

"Scientists are usually condemned to lead urban lives, but I find that country people still living close to the earth often seem puzzled that anyone should need to make a formal proposal of anything as obvious as the Gaia Hypothesis [that the earth is a living being]. For them it is true and always has been true."
JAMES LOVELOCK[1]

The first function of a culture's mythological system is to reconcile normal daily reality with the numinous, sacred mystery of life's spiritual dimension.[2] As I draw this examination of sacred places in nature to a close, it is appropriate to seek guidance from a mythic spirit whose functional power is to create order and synthesis in the world. The silvery white magician Poqanghoya of the Hopi creation myth resides at the icy cold, silent North Pole. He is an intelligence of perfect pitch with this need.

Let's imagine that we can look over Poqanghoya's shoulder as he sits in perfect stillness, breathing in and out with deep fullness, quietly chanting a magical mantra of crystalline perfection. From his breath arises the cold-cleansing north wind, which picks us up and carries us southward until the indigo-blue waters of the Arctic Ocean emerge from under the polar ice pack. We are transferred to a snowgoose, who then lifts us skyward on his back as he continues southward and finally comes to rest on the pancake-flat tundra plains of Alaska's northern shore, where he lets us off.

In three directions the world is like a billiard table, as far as the eye can see. Only further to the south is there any change in the landscape. There, the rugged Brooks Range mushrooms up into a formidable brown fortress of the nature spirit.

If people are shaped by the places where they live, then the circumpolar Inuit are the logical spokespeople of this place. The name "Inuit" means "the people," a meaning common to the titles of other indigenous tribes around the world. Their popular name, "Eskimo," is actually attributable to the early Christian missionaries, who heard Indians to the south speaking of the short people who lived in the north as the "Esquimaux," which translates as "the people who eat raw meat." We who worry about cholesterol in our diets should note that while Inuit eat a very high-fat diet, they suffer little incidence of cardiovascular disease when they live their traditional lifestyle.

Off to one direction, behind some low willows, we hear a drum beating. Upon investigating the sound, we discover that its gentle rhythm is coming from an Inuit shaman or *angakut*. In his cosmology, the people came into being in a place like this, babies popping up from the ground beside willows, which they wove into blankets to keep them warm.

Shamans are intermediaries for nature, fashioning their work according to local climate and geography and according to how they relate with human needs. Aside from healing abilities, which are universally possessed by shamans, the Inuit shamans have expertise in two areas particularly required for the Arctic: preventing madness and securing food. People are bothered by "cabin fever" when inclement weather keeps them indoors, amplifying tensions and anxiety. People in the Arctic spend several months with little or no sun in the sky, sub-zero temperatures, and winds gusting to 50 or 60 miles per hour. If we sat beside this shaman inside of his igloo or skin hut with his family, light would come from flickering seal-oil lamps, and we would dine on pickled eider duck eggs, whale blubber, seal steak, or, if luck was with us, some fresh sheefish or tasty Arctic char.

Under such close quarters, with the weather so inclement, people sometimes explode. They run outside, throw their clothes off, and shriek in wild hysteria. "Arctic madness" it's called: a dangerous condition to the afflicted and their close associates.

Inuit shamans treat such frenzied people by entering into deep trances to retrieve their troubled souls, which may have been taken over by evil spirits of the land or malevolent shamans seeking revenge or moved by greed. "We honor the good powers of places," one angakut told me, "because they have spirits which are allies to help us restore balance and health. We leave offerings there and perform ceremonies so those good spirits will be working with us."

In an age when mental illness is frequently treated with various chemical preparations to suppress symptoms, the paradigm of the Inuit shaman seems bizarre and frightening. "Normality," of course, is a relative term. More people in the world believe in spirits and shamanic states of consciousness than do not. While modern Western society may have unparalleled technological prowess, its views about what consciousness should be are a minority opinion.

One of the wisest books of the world, the *I Ching*, offers a paradigm concerning the power of place: "Heaven and earth determine the places. The holy sages fulfill the possibilities of the places. Through the thoughts of men and the thoughts of spirits, the people are enabled to participate in these possibilities."[3]

Modern medical research has enabled humanity to understand a great deal of how the brain works, but the mind remains a mystery. Most esoteric schools of psychology believe that the mind extends far beyond the physical body. Perhaps when shamans journey in their minds to visit special places, they are simply imagining things clearly, which is what conventional psychology says is the case. The shamans assert, however, that a part of them, a spirit body, actually undertakes this journey, transcending time and space in spiritual flight. It isn't too hard to see how the human creative faculties can conjure up a symbolic entity which is called a spirit. In less scientific cultures, however, spirits are beings of their own right that come from another dimension, perhaps part of what Carl Jung called the "collective unconscious."

The idea of a "big mind" or "Supermind," as the East Indian sage Sri Aurobindo called universal intelligence, is especially important to shamanic practitioners, for their powers arise from creating harmonies with forces in the big mind, enabling them to become conduits of power.[4] Stanley Krippner reports studies which suggest that sorcerer Carlos Castaneda is able to influence people's dreams without their being aware of what he is doing.[5] Rolling Thunder has performed successful rainmaking ceremonies and miraculous healings before public audiences at places like the Menninger Foundation, aided by the forces of nature and the Great Spirit. Elmer and Alyce Green, reviewing their years of study of the extraordinary powers of shamans, yogis, and dervishes, feel our definition of mind needs expansion:

> A unique energy field, a "field of mind," must surround the planet (expressed in some aspects as electrostatic, magnetic, and gravitational fields) and each individual mind with its extension, the body, must have the inherent capability of focusing energy for manipulation of both INS (inside the skin) and OUTS (outside the skin) events
>
> If we grant that most persons cannot perceive or control their own unconscious psychological processes, it is then understandable that most persons would be unaware of this field of mind.[6]

Using the Greens' expanded model of mind, it is possible to see that what happens at a sacred place is a blending of the personal mind with other mind fields. This blending allows extraordinary conditions or "siddhi" to manifest. Methods and techniques ranging from repetitive drumming and chanting to the taking of hallucinogenic drugs and the performance of rituals can be used to help merge these worlds. In the end, however, transcendence, which results in magical things happening, is beyond human control. This is why people pray. When people come to see that personal ego consciousness is not the ultimate seat of power, they surrender, let go, and ask that a force beyond the material plane hear their words. God only knows how many things in the world are spoiled when people get caught up in needing to be in control, instead of being concerned about results.

There is a danger in trying to explain sacred places in terms of modern science, because modern science may not be able to allow them to exist. The problem is with the scientific model. There is no Newtonian-Cartesian explanation for why shamanism works, but it does, which is much more important. Neither can science account for spiritual healing, psychokinesis, clairvoyance, prophecy, and karate chops which break bricks in two, but they all happen, daily. The "new science" which will guide humanity into the twenty-first century must be able to account for and work with such conditions as spiritual states of consciousness and the things which occur as a result of such states, because they are an integral and extremely important component of human existence.

One of the key elements of the new paradigm must be an acceptance of the existence and workings of life energies. All around the world, people assert that a life-force energy exists. It is called *chi, ki, prana, baraka, nerfesh, Skan, od,* orgone, bioplasm, bioenergy, and spirit. When it became clear that acupuncture was successful in treating various illnesses, Western theoreticians immediately said this was because it was a form of hypnosis.[7] Then, Korean professor Kim Bong Han decided to inject a radioactive isotope into areas of the body where acupuncture points were said to exist. Tracking the isotope, he found it flowed through the body along routes which could not be explained by any known circulatory pattern or system. These routes followed the places on acupuncture charts where energy meridians are supposed to be.[8]

Research such as Han's and others' from around the globe points to a new emerging theoretical model for explaining reality which contradicts some fundamental scientific assumptions about how things are supposed to be. For some time, physicist William Tiller at Stanford University has been studying the relationship between mind, spirit, and energy and the new emerging paradigm. He concludes:

> 1. From experiments on telepathy, psychokinesis (PK), manual healers, etc., we seem to be dealing with energy fields completely different from those known to conventional science.
> 2. From a large variety of experiments, we find indications for a level of substance in nature that exhibits (a) characteristics that are predominantly magnetic, as distinct from electric, in nature; (b) an organizing rather than a disorganizing tendency as the temperature increases (in seeming violation of the Second Law of Thermodynamics for the physical universe); (c) a radiation pattern or hologram of energy that acts as a force envelope for the organization of substance at the physical level.
> 3. From experiments on plants, animals and humans, evidence is mounting that there is an interconnection at some level of substance between all things in the universe.[9]

When most of us were in high school, we learned that there are three kinds of matter: solids, liquids, and gases. Today there is increasing evidence for a fourth condition of matter known as "plasma." Plasma is a mixture of subatomic particles, chiefly electrons and nuclei, without the formation of complete atoms. Plasma phenomena on Earth include such things as the aurora borealis or northern lights, ball lightning, and the unusual "lights" seen along earthquake fault lines. The Russian scientist Victor Inyushin takes things one step farther, suggesting that there is a fifth state of matter called "bioplasma." Inyushin proposes that bioplasma arises from the synthesis of many particle forms into a "biofield," such as the aura, or the energetic process which is captured in Kirlian photography.[10]

Fritz-Albert Popp, a West German chemist and physicist, has found that living things emit light energy ranging from the infrared to the ultraviolet during biochemical reactions. The source, he believes, is DNA. This means that all living things must produce a "light" as an expression of being alive. Confirming this, Herbert Pohl finds "faint, miniscule radio signals coming from living things."[11]

These data help me understand why, during a Rolling Thunder healing, six people in addition to myself independently saw a purple glow emanating from Rolling Thunder at the peak of the healing.[12] Spirit frequently seems to manifest as light when one is in the presence of spiritual people or sacred places. It may be that bioplasma is a manifestation of special places which will be reliably documentable when science develops reliable measures to monitor such a thing.

The point here is that if we encounter the sacred manifesting itself, as it does when we sit alongside an Inuit shaman on the North Slope of Alaska, this is not just a figment of our creative imagination. With drum, voice, and specially trained mind, shamans call together forces which are very real, causing things to happen which are contradictory to our normal reality, but which are perfectly normal within their paradigm. If we ask shamans their views about the Earth on which they are seated, regardless of whether they are in the Congo, Patagonia, Papua, New Guinea, or Siberia, their answer is always the same: "the Earth is alive." The reason why shamans around the world share this view of a living Earth may be the final key in coming to understand sacred places.

THE LIVING EARTH

The ancient Greek wise man Xenophon counsels in his treatise *Oeconomicus* (5:12): "Earth is a goddess and teaches justice to those who can learn, for the better she is served, the more good things she gives in return." The Greeks named their goddess of the earth "Gaia" and said that she was born when a great black bird, Nyx (night), hovering over a vastness "without form or void," laid a magical egg which, upon hatching, gave birth to the golden winged Eros (love). The eggshell cracked into two parts, one of which became Ouranous (sky) and the other of which became Gaia (Earth). Gaia then manifested her offspring as the powerful forces of nature, the Titans, who lived along the boundaries of the Earth. The Titans were subdued by the divine acts of Zeus himself, making Earth truly habitable for mortals.

Up until the 1500s, the concept of a living Earth was fairly widely accepted by people of reason. Then Kepler and Copernicus turned their telescopes to the heavens and showed that the Earth was not the physical center of the universe, and explorers including Columbus destroyed the myths of the Titans and the flat Earth. At this point, the living-Earth thesis was placed on a shelf marked "superstition," along with dragons, unicorns, alchemy, and wizardry. The sacred groves became profane spaces, and the popularity of magic began to wane in favor of objectivity and logical proof.

Modern science then roared into being, demonstrating the powers of objective methods and rational thought, and seeking balance after so many years without rationality. Time, of course, is both a linear and a cyclical process, and so the Hopi, who could see the coming juxtapositions of new cycles, offered prophecies which have proved to be all too true. In 1970, people suddenly found themselves looking at a picture of the Earth from space and realizing that it was all they have to live on, shocking their consciousness into a new awareness. This new symbol unearthed old regions of the psyche paved over by the Newtonian-Cartesian thought suppressors.

Earth Day 1970 was like a giant can opener on consciousness, enabling a whole new set of ideas and concepts to be spoken and put into practice. After taking a back seat to astronauts and engineers for so many years, biology and ecology were suddenly recognized as being able to save our lives. One of the most popular voices raised at that time was that of Lewis Thomas, who captured the feelings of millions of people who had seen the space photos of Earth when he said, "Viewed from the distance of the moon, the astonishing thing about the earth, catching the breath, is that it is alive."[13]

The mark of a good writer is the ability to sense what is emerging in people's minds, and then to say it in a way which helps to crystallize their thoughts, advises my neighbor George Leonard. While Thomas described what people felt, at a modest country cottage in England, James Lovelock was collaborating with several other bold thinking scientists to offer the living-Earth thesis as a scientific truth as well as a metaphoric statement. In 1975, Lovelock and Sidney Epton published this theory in New Scientist magazine, offering a choice between the following two premises:

1. Life exists only because material conditions on Earth happen to be just right for its existence; and

2. Life defines the material conditions needed for its survival and makes sure that they stay there. [14]

The first premise—that life exists on Earth because of some marvelous "accident" of chemistry—is the view commonly held by most scientists. It is an easy position to take, especially if one holds that religion is something that happens only on Sunday morning to cleanse the soul of the week's sin while one shows off the new clothes and car—compartmentalized myopic thinking.

The second premise is subversive. It states that the primary characteristic of living organisms is that they are capable of organizing the raw stuff of the universe into entities that express life. According to this position, life then exists whenever and wherever this organizing force is operative, which could mean that the entire universe is alive, as Nobel Prize-winning biologist George Wald believes.

Lovelock came up with this second premise after being hired by NASA to develop methods of detecting life on other planets. During the project, as others were arguing about which chemical and physical tests were going to be put on board a space shot to Mars, Lovelock raised a more difficult question: "What is life?" NASA wasn't ready for this question and, returning home, Lovelock pondered the fact that modern science has not really defined what life is. Thanks to inspiration from the nearby sacred place of Brentor and from friends including Lynn Margulis and Sidney Epton, Lovelock later advanced the idea that the chief property of living entities is self-regulation or homeostasis.

An atmospheric scientist with a self-confessed "almost pathological curiosity about things," Lovelock came to conclude that homeostasis was the primary defining principle of life. At the same time, he realized that the entire Earth was not just a network of systems, but was in fact behaving in the fashion of a living organism, for it contained a myriad of interacting biochemical and physical systems. Lovelock one day shared this idea with his neighbor novelist William Golding, and it was Golding who said that such a theory should be named in honor of the ancient Greek Earth goddess, Gaia. Thus, the "Gaia Hypothesis"—that the entire earth is a living being—was born.

Prior to 1975, the massive computer files of the University of California at Berkeley's library system contained virtually no entries in the scientific literature under the title of "living Earth." The smattering of articles and the one or two books which bore this subject heading, when carefully examined, showed that the use of the phrase "living earth" in their titles was poetic, rather than a proposition of a new scientific paradigm.

After publishing their thesis in *New Scientist* magazine in 1975, Lovelock and his friends continued to publish articles about the Gaia Hypothesis over the next few years, substantiating their claim that the entire planet is a living being because it exists as the result of interacting self-regulatory systems. Reactions to this thesis from the scientific community, especially at first, were skeptical and negative.

Then, in 1979, Lovelock published a full-length book, *Gaia: A New Look at Life,* presenting an in-depth argument for the Earth being alive, based upon a careful evaluation of its various systems and cycles, especially those involving carbon, nitrogen, and the oxygen/carbon dioxide group.[15] Suddenly, within the next couple of years, like mushrooms after a warm spring rain, articles about the Earth being alive cropped up everywhere. By 1985, the library showed 33 books and too many articles to count appearing under the "living Earth" heading. Millions of American television viewers have watched David Attenborough's captivating "Living Planet" series, and NOVA has tackled the living-Earth issue head on in an hour-long feature, "Goddess of the Earth." Since then a whole new movement called "Gaia Consciousness" has emerged, seeking to articulate the implications of the living-Earth thesis in terms of psychology and philosophy. Some proponents want to rename this planet Gaia.

Some skeptical critics of the living-Earth thesis consider the Gaia Hypothesis to be naive. Scientifically, however, there is no problem with seeing the Earth as being alive. Science is not a collection of facts to be memorized, although schools serve it to students this way. It is a dynamic process of inquiry in which everything should be open to question to allow for new insights to emerge. Like trying on new shoes for the best fit, people search for theories which are the best fit for the data on hand. Much of what has been used for a working scientific paradigm is not the right fit for reality. It's time for a change, and in many ways Lovelock's model of a living Earth works better than what has been used so far, because it is based on a recognition of systems as the fundamental characteristic of life.

Scientists can and will debate the living-Earth thesis for years to come, jousting about how to decide if such and such a thing is alive or not. Psychologically, however, the living-Earth thesis is a breath of fresh air long overdue. Carl Jung pointed out that in the psyche, everything is alive.[16] Seeing the Earth as alive is an affirmation of what the human unconscious mind has always believed. The "Earth mother" archetype is one of the most powerful symbols in human consciousness. To see the Earth as being alive strikes a harmonic chord between the Earth within and the Earth without, which enables energy to be exchanged and the feminine principle in life to emerge more clearly and powerfully.

Lovelock arrived at the Gaia Hypothesis from studying atmospheric chemistry. Boston University biologist Lynn Margulis supports the same concept from her work in cellular biology. She compared the Earth's biochemical cycles to those in tiny cells and noted the similarities between the Earth's self-organization and cellular homeostasis.[17] Louise Young makes an equally compelling case for the

Earth being alive based on her studies of the oceans.[18] Physicist Jerome Rothstein of Ohio State University agrees, suggesting that life can be seen as a process
of energy flow and application. In Rothstein's view, life exists when a Carnot
cycle (a thermodynamic cycle consisting of four reversible changes in the opera-
tion of an ideal heat engine working at optimal efficiency) is created from the
actions of living systems.[19] To these views, Lewis Thomas adds his further support of the Earth being alive:

> Although it seems at first glance to be made up of innumerable separate
> species of living things, on closer examination every one of its working parts,
> including us, is interdependently connected to all the other working parts.
> It is, to put it in one way, the only closed ecosystem any of us knows about.
> To put it another way, it is an organism.[20]

In science, proof is a slippery thing. It is possible to prove that something
does not happen or cannot work easily, but certifying that it *does* is very difficult. One of the strongest scientific proofs is "concurrent validity": when two
or more independent sources arrive at the same conclusion. The living-Earth thesis
is now being supported by atmospheric scientists, biologists, physicists, and
chemists, as well as psychologists, philosophers, and shamans. Few concepts in
human history have found such widespread cross-cultural and cross-disciplinary
support.

Tucked away in Lewis Thomas's explanation of why he feels the Earth is
alive is a profound statement: "On closer examination every one of its working
parts, including us, is interdependently connected to all other working parts."
People talk about everything being connected to everything else in poetic
imagery, but when this idea is applied to humanity, red lights go on in the con-
servative computer. Skeptical scientists comment that one cannot say the Earth
is alive, for if it is, it must have a communication system, and everyone knows
the Earth cannot talk. But it can talk. This is precisely what the research on sacred
places shows. People go out to certain places and engage in interactions with
nature in which information is exchanged. The Earth may not speak in English,
but if we allow our minds to perceive through dreams, intuitions, animal messages,
and voices that speak to us in the silence, the Earth is talking to us in words
that are strong and clear. It is telling us to get our act together and stop polluting
the world and denying ourselves of who and what we are. All around the world,
people are getting the same message, and it is about time we started taking the
Earth seriously.

Telepathy, or mind-to-mind communication, works best when two people
or organisms are in sympathy. If we allow the Earth to be alive within us, then
we will be more able to have dialogues with the Earth outside us. Yogis know
this. That is why they retreat to caves: to hear the Earth talk. Pueblo Indian

children learn to listen to the Earth talking while sitting in kivas in the silence for long periods of time. Shamans and saints have done this for centuries, honoring the power of silence as great source of wisdom.

Jim Lovelock points out that his neighbors who farm and raise livestock have always considered the Earth to be alive, because they can feel it. If people forget the arguments and let their bones do the thinking, the Earth will feel as alive to them as they know it to be in their unconscious.

Just how is this organism called Gaia or Earth special? One way is that it has these special places where people are more able to transcend. What could be their purpose? The answer, which seems to come so clearly, is that these sacred places are organs for the Earth to communicate with us. Like a mother's breasts, the sacred places nurture us by enabling us to step into states of consciousness in which we realize wisdom, truth, health, and inspiration. Transcendence is normal at sacred places, and love, whether it be the brotherly variety of "agape" or the passionate "eros," cannot exist without transcendence. Sacred places, then, are not just places of power, they are places where we can and do find love from our second mother, the Earth. Many people describe their special experiences at sacred places as feeling the deepest love they have ever known. And love seems to be the correct word to describe what goes on at sacred places when all things are in accord, because the power of love is to move us to become what we truly are, as Joseph Campbell reminds us:

> Set apart from all spheres of historic change, the Venus Mountain with its crystalline bed has been entered by lovers through all the ages, from every order of life. Its seat is in the heart of nature—nature within and without— which two are the same.[21]

There is a definite difference between the ephemeral passion of eros and the carrying on of a loving relationship. Lovers experience ecstasy when they first meet, which may serve the purpose of psychologically bonding them for a relationship. This happens as well between people and sacred places. Loving relationships are rooted in trust, truthful communication, and mutual respect. Our relationship with the Earth can also be described in these terms. Shamans around the world assert that we can befoul sacred places with our thoughts and actions, just like loving relationships can be destroyed by negative intentions and words. All pollution starts in the mind, and corruption of the relationships we have with places by the power of our thoughts is a form of pollution we can all do something about.

This idea is not that far out. The view that the power of thought can influence the ambiance of place may be supported if the theory of "morphogenic fields" advanced by plant physiologist Rupert Sheldrake can be verified. Sheldrake says that a common quality of living things is the establishment of enduring patterns which have neither mass nor energy as we know them, but which nonetheless act to organize and direct the course of life. "Systems are organized in the way they are because similar systems were organized that way in the past," Sheldrake maintains.[22]

Sheldrake illustrates his theory of morphogenic fields by noting the work of people like Harvard psychologist William McDougall, who in the 1920s found that successive generations of rats seemed to learn a task like running a maze more quickly, even without knowledge from previous generations which had mastered such a task. According to his theory of "Formative Causation," the first generations of rats had somehow set up a morphogenic field pattern which successive generations of rats attuned to, thus learning more quickly. Sheldrake feels that this patterning principle applies to all biological and physical systems.[23]

Transferring Sheldrake's thesis to sacred places, the behavior of shamans as they approach and interact with sacred places become more understandable. Showing proper attitudes of respect and humility, the shamans project sentiments which favor establishing rapport with the places. Their performance of rituals at the sites not only helps these ritual masters, it also helps the places. Good rituals cleanse the psychic vibrations of the past by creating harmonies with spiritual dimensions which overpower negative memories and drive them away, thus enabling clearer communication with the places and their forces to occur.

A number of people I spoke with who reported special experiences at sacred places talked about recognizing the memories of those places. One radio talk-show host admitted that while visiting Mount Olympus in Greece with some friends when he was in the Navy, they were drawn into a state in which they were almost compelled to engage in an evening of wild drinking and dancing on this mountain, which is so often linked with Dionysus. Sensitive Ann Armstrong reported visiting a nearby ancient building which apparently had been used to house temple prostitutes. The experiences of the former residents of this place filled her mind and body, and she said later that she felt as though she understood now what it would be like to participate in an orgy.[24]

Sheldrake's thesis also seems supported by work I once did on littering behavior. While I was observing public behavior in a variety of parks and recreation areas, it became clear that people were most likely to litter if others before them had done so. There is a feel about a place where people have been habitually littering which makes it more likely for others to do so. There are other places which feel so special that littering seems to be a very difficult act.

"Our species has been shaped by the earth and we feel guilty and somewhat incomplete when we lose contact with the forces of nature and the rest of the living world," scientist-humanist René Dubos observed.[25] His views would find support from shamans all around the world. Not that many years ago, the scientist and the shaman were one and the same, and subjectivity and objectivity were two ways of working together toward the same goal.

As mentioned earlier, one of the Hopi prophecies says that a new age will begin when the white-robed person from the East dances in the sacred circle with the blue-star kachina. The language of visions and dreams is subject to reinterpretation. In the last century, a number of holy people from India and the East have come to the United States wearing white, which some people could interpret as fulfilling this prophecy. But most of these visitors came from the direction usually considered to be the west. The east, where the sun rises, is the direction of Europe, where the scientists have come from. Scientists wear white coats and represent priests also. Americans cannot go back to the Stone Age nor transplant a foreign culture on American soil and hope for it to solve all problems. People have to work with what is, and seek to create a new dynamic synthesis of science with spirit to make the world safe, sane, peaceful, and ecologically sound.

When scientists dance in the sacred circle with the blue-star kachina, a new science will be born which honors and integrates the sacred and the profane into a new whole. In the Four Corners area, as they dance around the leaping flames of brother fire, they are being watched. From the north, Mount Hesperus sees them with the crystal-clear cold eyes of the north wind. To the west, in the San Francisco Peaks, the eyes of all the kachinas are on them, while the thunderbeings watch from a higher balcony. In the south, with passionate eyes, Mount Taylor sees them and hopes for wisdom and insight to occur. And in the east, the direction of the rising sun, an eagle circles Mount Blanca, his piercing call sending a prayer to the Great Spirit that a new age of peace on Earth begins with science and spirit agreeing on what is right and true.

ENDNOTES

1. James Lovelock, *Gaia: A New Look at Life on Earth* (New York: Oxford University Press, 1979), pp. 10-11.

2. Joseph Campbell, *The Masks of God: Creative Mythology* (New York: Penguin Books, 1968), p. 4.

3. Richard Wilhelm, trans., *I Ching* (Princeton, NJ: Princeton University Press, 1959).

4. Sri Aurobindo, *The Mind of Light* (New York: E.P. Dutton, 1976).

5. Stanley Krippner and Alberto Villoldo, *The Realms of Healing* (Albany, CA: Celestial Arts, 1976).

6. Elmer Green and Alyce Green, "Afterword" in Doug Boyd, *Rolling Thunder* (New York: Random House, 1974), p. 272.

7. J.F. Chaves and T.X. Barber, "Needles and Knives: Behind the Mystery of Acupuncture and Chinese Meridians," in *Advances in Altered States of Consciousness and Human Potentialities*, vol. 1 (New York: Psychological Dimensions, Inc., 1976), pp. 285-290.

8. The original research was published in Korean journals which are hard to find. The best source is in endnote 9 by William Tiller.

9. William Tiller, "Some Energy Observations in Man and Nature," in *The Kirlian Aura: Photographing the Galaxies of Life*, eds. S. Krippner and D. Rubin (New York: Doubleday, 1974), pp. 92-136.

10. Inyushin, V.M. "Bioplasma: The Fifth State of Matter" in *Future Science*, eds. S. Krippner and J. White (Garden City, NY: Anchor Books, 1977).

11. S. Krippner, *Human Possibilities* (Garden City, NY: Doubleday, 1980).

12. James A. Swan, "Rolling Thunder at Work," in *Shamanism: An Expanded View of Reality*, ed. Shirley Nicholson (Wheaton, IL: Theosophical Society Publishing House, 1987), pp. 145-158.

13. Lewis Thomas, *The Lives of a Cell* (New York: Viking Press, 1974).

14. James Lovelock and Sidney Epton, "The Quest for Gaia," *New Scientist* (1975).

15. James Lovelock, *Gaia: A New Look at Life on Earth* (New York: Oxford University Press, 1979).

16. Carl Jung, *Civilization in Transition*, vol. 10 of *The Collected Works of Carl Jung* (New York: Pantheon, Bollingen Series 20, 1964).

17. Lynn Margulis, *Symbiosis in Cell Evolution: Life and Its Environment on the Early Earth* (San Francisco: W.H. Freeman and Co., 1981).

18. Louise Young, *The Blue Planet* (New York: Little, Brown and Co., 1983).

19. J. Rothstein (Paper presented at the "Is the Earth a Living Organism?" symposium, Amherst, MA, August 1-6, 1985, under the sponsorship of the National Audubon Society Expedition Institute).

20. Lewis Thomas, *Discover* (February 1984): p. 34.

21. Joseph Campbell, *The Masks of God: Creative Mythology*, p. 184.

22. Rupert Sheldrake, from an interview in *Investigations* newsletter, vol. 1, no. 1 (Sausalito, CA: Institute of Noetic Sciences, 1983).

23. Rupert Sheldrake, *A New Science of Life: The Hypothesis of Formative Causation* (Los Angeles: J.P. Tarcher, Inc., 1982).

24. Anne Armstrong, "On Being a Psychic" (Taped interview, Big Sur Recordings #4770, Big Sur, CA—available from the Esalen Institute).

25. René Dubos, *The Wooing of the Earth* (New York: Chas. Scribner's Sons, 1980), p. 17.

Photo 26. *Sleeping Bear Dunes in northern Michigan, a legend site. Author photo.*

EPILOGUE

Visiting a Place of Power

You may feel moved to seek out one or several sacred places in the hopes of gaining some new and important experiences or inspiration. The magic of sacred places, it seems, has a will of its own. Rest assured, if the place you choose has some soothing, hot, artesian mineral springs to bathe in, a spectacular setting, unusual artifacts, or lush vegetation, you will be refreshed and inspired from your visit. These kinds of experiences represent what anyone would hope to receive from a good outdoor recreational outing, and they make the visit worthwhile regardless of whatever else happens.

"Care for the place and it will care for you," don Juan told Carlos Castaneda. This is sound advice. While you're visiting a special place, pick up litter. If a branch has fallen across your path from a windstorm the night before, toss it to the side of the path. Leave the place cleaner than you found it. It will look better for others and yourself, and prevent animals from getting injured by things like plastic six-pack holders which get stuck on the necks of birds and mammals. Also, if you believe in them, the spirits will be pleased.

Before setting foot on a place which you know to be sacred, try to find out if there is any continuing usage of the place by indigenous Indian tribes. If ceremonies or rituals are in process, leave them alone unless you're invited. If you are a member of a church-going religion, imagine how you would feel if you walked into a church, kneeled down, and began to pray, and suddenly a tour bus pulled up and people began taking pictures of you, their flash bulbs popping off like popcorn. Mount Taylor in New Mexico and Bear Butte in the Black Hills of South Dakota are both good examples of places with long-standing histories of Indian use for sacred ceremonies. I personally wouldn't go to either of these places unless I had an invitation from the medicine people who use them. Places like these, I think, should be given back to the original people who have used them for centuries, so they may keep them preserved and use them in much the same fashion that Buddhist priests in Nepal tend shrines at sacred places there. If the Earth has a mind, the keepers of the sacred places have a very important part to play in aiding the stability and vitality of humanity's consciousness, as well as the Earth's and their own.

If the place has a long-standing record of traditional use but is still open to everyone, like Sorté Mountain in Venezuela, which is a national park, try to make contact with some of the people who have been using and protecting the place to show your respect and thanks. You might, for example, stop at a trading post and buy something before going to visit an Anasazi ruin in the American Southwest. Even a cup of coffee at an Indian restaurant before going up on Mount Rainier or exploring Chaco Canyon is a gesture of recognition. It's not the amount of money you spend that is important so much as the attitude you have in doing it.

When you park your car and first set foot on the earth at this special place, stop and look around. Don't rush off to the top of the mountain. Get a sense of the place. Let its ambiance sink into your mind so you can walk gently on your pilgrimage.

As you set off in the direction that feels correct, stop, say a prayer, and leave a little food like cornmeal. It doesn't have to be much, but the gesture of sacrifice is essential to demonstrate your attitude and purpose for being there.

Move slowly as you walk along the trail. Watch for animals and plants which seem to stand out, not by their beauty necessarily, but because they feel like nodes of power. At Point Conception near Santa Barbara, California, the trumpet-shaped white flowers of Jimson Weed or *Datura stramonia* are apparent, although not necessarily the most beautiful plants. On the Olympic Peninsula in Washington State, the giant red cedars express a presence which should not be ignored. The behavior of the animals and the growth of the plants can tell you a lot about the use of the place, and how much harmony exists there.

Religion is a personal matter. If you feel moved to say prayers at some place, do what feels right to you; don't just copy what the Indians have done. If you want to conduct some kind of ceremony, let it be one that honors the place. If you use fire, even lighting a match to smoke a pipe or light a candle, be aware of any fire hazards. Building a fire is a touchy matter in many places, as fires are often restricted to special fire rings. In lieu of building a fire, I often use a single white candle. Fire is the essence of transformation, symbolic of the purification of the soul in spiritual development, and a statement of matter becoming spirit. Honor its power.

If you plan to stay at a certain place for much time, you may want to mark off a special area for yourself. Spreading a blanket on the ground marks an area as being different, and provides boundaries for your special spot. Many people mark off each direction of the compass with an object or stone. The purpose of this is to create a microcosm of the macrocosm, and to draw in power during this special time of unity. If you use anything from the place, like rocks, return them to their original places when you finish unless you have permission to build a more permanent shrine.

"The sacred always manifests itself as a reality of a wholly different order," counseled Mircea Eliade.[1] When you visit a sacred place, you cannot predict what will happen. Even shamans who have used a place for decades say they ask for the spirit to be with them, but that what the spirit will do is beyond their control. It may be that animals will seem to speak to you, clouds will take on unusual shapes, rocks will talk to you, visions will pop up from the ground, an angelic chorus will serenade you, and Bigfoot will suddenly walk out of the bushes. You may feel deep emotions bubbling up to the surface. Many modern people cry at sacred places because living in the rest of the world requires emotional suppression. All these things may happen, or nothing out of the ordinary may occur. Whatever happens is right if your behavior and attitudes are respectful.

People get excited about mystical experiences associated with sacred places, and rightfully so. When the spiritual world decides to show itself, beauty, peace, truth, bliss, wonder, and awe can manifest in the most extraordinary ways. The real reason for going to a sacred place, however, is not just to get high. The purpose is to come into harmony with the greater unity of all life so that you can become who you are and then serve others according to who you are. The greatest power in life comes from surrendering to a higher force, not from gaining control of people and things. You seek power, but it comes to you of its own nature and in its own forms.

After I go to a sacred place and do whatever I feel moved to do, there is an "answer" for me. Sometimes, shortly after I do a ceremony, I feel a rush of energy which seems to be nature giving back to me what I have given to it. In honoring the power of a place, you set things into harmony and thus seek the way or path for you based on higher intuition. However, when you go to the sacred and seek balance, harmony, guidance, and a higher purpose, remember that you get back what you need, not necessarily what you expect or want.

The first time I seriously undertook a ritual at a sacred place, I went on a vision quest in the North Cascades. Marie Norris of the Klamath tribe had given me instructions about seeking visions in the mountains. The experience itself was awesome. Animals approached me, vivid dreams came, and I cried a lot. Some months later I met an older woman named Olgamaria Galambos, who lived in Eugene, Oregon. Olga was a female don Juan who made her money as an astrological counselor, but confessed to me that her charts really just gave her structure to help her be psychic. She was a Transylvanian countess by birth who had been tutored by her gypsy nursesmaids, and was somewhat of a folk heroine during the Second World War when she used her psychic abilities to guide people away from falling bombs. When she came to the United States she became one of the principle disciples of the Indian saint Yogananda.

At the advice of a friend, I went to Olga for a reading, and found her to be the most perceptive person I'd ever met. In little over an hour she told me everything about myself that I had come to know through years of workshops, counseling, psychological testing, and much, much more. After my reading, we sat and talked. Suddenly, she looked at me with the large dark eyes of gypsy wisdom and said, "Jim, you need to go on a vision quest for the material world."

I told her about what I had done in the mountains, and she said that was fine, but that now it was time to get down to business. She suggested that I go to the top of Skinner's Butte, which is a small butte in a park in downtown Eugene, right beside the Willamette River, and conduct a short, simple ceremony. The ritual she suggested consisted of much of what I've suggested here, with the provision that I was to stand, facing the sun, and say out loud that I was ready to accept my life's purpose.

It sounded easy enough, and so a couple of days later, as the new moon was beginning, I rode my bike to Skinner's Butte and performed the ceremony she suggested. Nothing out of the ordinary happened. A couple of birds sang, a car drove by, and so on, but nothing special happened.

Dejected and angry, I went home. To make matters worse, I got a flat tire on my bike and so I had to walk. At that time I was living in a communal housing arrangement. I felt like I wanted to be alone, and so I stalked off to my bedroom. When I got there, lying on my bed was a pile of very expensive, beautiful clothes. There were cashmere sweaters, Palm Beach slacks, and a couple of handmade dress shirts. I tried them on, and they all fit.

I walked out into the hall and started asking my housemates where these clothes had come from. Finally, I discovered their source. It turned out that one of the women in the group was dating a man who was an actor in Hollywood. He had come to visit her, and had brought the clothes along with him. They had been given to him and didn't fit him. He said the clothes were his brother-in-law's. I asked him who that was. Dean Martin, he replied.

I put on one of the suits and went to see Olga. She chuckled when I told her my story. She then told me that Yogananda, after her years of study with him, one day held graduation exercises. As a present to her upon graduation, Yogananda gave her a carton of cigarettes. Several disciples questioned how he could do such a thing. He replied simply that tobacco was a good herb for her and that because she was so psychic, smoking would help ground her.

Some fifteen years later, even though she smoked two packs of cigarettes a day, doctors could find no trace of damage to her lungs, for she also did daily routines of yoga and breathing exercises.

Within six weeks after my ceremony on Skinner's Butte, Olga introduced me to the lady who is now my wife. Nine months later I quit the university system, moved to Seattle, and became a writer and a therapist—a dramatic switch for someone who had been a full-time resident in unversity systems for fifteen years.

I had assumed that the Dean Martin clothes simply meant that I should not live like a hippie, but should relate to more of mainstream society. However, as I found myself drawn more and more into shamanism, my dreams took on two forms: mythic settings of numinous qualities and specific suggestions about performing on stage. Around Earth Day in 1970, I played folk music at teach-ins and coffee houses, but I had given up any thought of doing anything professional along those lines, so the second form of dream was puzzling. Then I was introduced to Native American chanting, and suddenly I found new qualities to my voice that I had never known before. I began chanting, and people liked it. I chanted on one interview show in 1982 in Vancouver, British Columbia, and soon found myself with fifteen minutes on CBC prime time doing chants. Shortly thereafter, dreams led me to move to the San Francisco Bay Area, where I have lived ever since.

Since moving to the Bay Area, I have found my life slowly moving into the entertainment world, frequently inspired by dreams and visits to sacred places. Following a ceremony on Mount Tamalpais, I had a dream which told me to begin reading the *Marin Independent Journal*, as I would find things in it that would help my earlier dreams come true. Not long afterward there was an ad for people to act in the Lucasfilm movie "Tucker." I showed up along with 1500 other people and got selected for the movie. That appearance has led me since to appear in the "Midnight Caller" and "Jesse Hawkes" television series, as well as in local theater productions and benefits.

Traveling to sacred places to work on this book, I often had vivid dreams. Some of the dreams provided imagery for songs which I now perform, such as "Skeletons of Memories" which was written about an abandoned gold mine in the Sierra Nevada mountains in California. Camping out near the mine, I had a series of dreams about the skeletons of the miners who had died in a mine disaster. Upon finishing the song, I had a dream in which the skeletons were dancing to its beat!

I have been a folk musician since the 1960s, but the songs that come following contact with sacred places and the shamans who serve them are of a very different kind. Following a ceremony led by the Peruvian shaman Don Eduardo Calderón, I had a vivid dream of a giant condor. This was at the time when the last wild California condors were being trapped to try to preserve the breeding stock in captivity. The dream was so energetic that it woke me up, and I sat down and wrote a song, "Keepers of the Dream," about the last California condors—sort of a cheer for them to breed in captivity so they wouldn't vanish like the passenger pigeon and the great auk. The first time I played the song in public, a lady walked up to me after the song was finished and handed me a giant black feather that she had found that afternoon. I think it was a vulture feather, not a condor feather, but vultures are close cousins of the condor and the spirit of the bird felt like it came right with that feather.[2]

The point of telling these stories is to underscore that the power that can be contacted through sacred places is the spirit of self-actualization. It is not something one can capture and predictably use. A person must go to the place with humility, perform his or her acts of respect, and then see what happens. Surrender, not control, is the bottom line. Poet Michelle Berditschevsky went to Mount Shasta with the conscious purpose of writing poetry, but what the mountain asked her to do was to organize a campaign to prevent a ski area from being built at a sacred place. As Vine Deloria, Jr., says, when you go to the top of the mountain seeking guidance, you have to be prepared to follow through with what comes to you, if you want to have the power of that place working in you and through you—and what comes to you is what you *need*, not necessarily what you *want*.

Rolling Thunder, who has been my guide for much of this journey, finds my story very understandable. He sometimes kids me for being a college professor for so long. "Jim, what you folks call 'paranormal' is really what is normal to Indian people," he chuckles. "Maybe it's the modern white man's world that ought to be called paranormal."

May the sacred places be your friends, and you theirs. They are there to help people find out who they are and become themselves, in service to the Earth and all its creatures.

ENDNOTES

1. Mircea Eliade, *The Sacred and the Profane* (New York: Harcourt Brace Jovanovich Inc., 1959), p. 10.
2. These songs are available on the album, "Nature Spirits," which is available through ISNS, P.O. Box 637, Mill Valley, CA 94942.

APPENDIX

A Regional Guide to Some Sacred Places of the United States

Ｉn the United States, sacred places are found throughout the 50 states and in all U.S. territories. Their nature varies from spectacular mountains to bubbling hot springs, crystal caves, nondescript plains and hills, and silent burial mounds. Some are well known, but many are kept secret. This book presents a case for honoring sacred places because they are touchstones for human inspiration and renewal, as well as areas where people can converse with the living Earth and spiritual forces.

The following list of places represents sacred sites which are set aside for public use on federal or state lands, and where there are no significant controversies about use which concern Indians not wishing white people to be present. It's not a complete list by any means, but it is a start. Each place has a teaching all of its own to share and, like experiencing the great books of the world, each needs to be appreciated in its own right.

Northeast Region

MOUNT KATAHDIN. From north-central Maine's rugged white birch and dark green spruce forests arises the 5,268-foot pinnacle of Mount Katahdin, the highest point in the state and the "Greatest Mountain," according to the Abenaki Indians. Located in Baxter State Park, Mount Katahdin's massive granite body is supposedly guarded by Pomola, a spiritual being with the head of a bull moose, the wings of an eagle, and a human body. Pomola presides over weather of that region, and has a spirit helper, "the storm bird," which appears as tiny birds who can foretell storms if you watch and listen to them.

STONEWORKS. Professor Barry Fell has written a controversial book, *America B.C.*, which reports substantial evidence that people of Nordic or Celtic origin and possibly some Inuit lived in or visited the United States long before Columbus. Some Indian legends agree, but regardless of who built the stoneworks near Danbury, Connecticut, South Woodstock, Vermont, and Mystery Hill, Vermont, there are old stone dolmens, altars, crypts, and underground rooms which will move you. If you want more information about special places in this part

225

of the world, stop by the national headquarters of the American Society of Dowsers in Danville, Vermont.

Southeast Region

ASSATEAGUE ISLAND. Assateague Island is a beautiful low-lying sandspit island stretching along the Maryland and Virgina coasts. Preserved as a national seashore, and best known for its wild horses, this picturesque area is said to be the Eastern Gate—a balancing point for Point Conception in California—and a portal for souls to enter and exit the Earth plane.

EVERGLADES. Too many people go roaring through the Everglades west of Miami, not stopping to spend some time with the Seminole Indians or to go for a ride in a canoe or an airboat. Get back in the Glades, far away from any outside noises, and sit in the silence. The sounds, especially at night, are a priceless symphony, and strange forms sometimes seem to stalk the woods.

OKEFENOKEE SWAMP. Another enchanting marshy area of a different character is the Okefenokee Swamp of Georgia. A number of people who have explored the swamp in canoes tell me that a very "strong spirit" lives there which "changed their life."

MOUNDS. It would take a lifetime to spend a day at each of the mounds which are scattered throughout the southern and eastern part of the United States. Many are small burial mounds, but others are temples, effigies, and shrines left behind by the Hopewell, Mississippian, and Adena peoples. Some of the most famous and accessible include Etowah Mounds, Georgia; Crystal River Mounds, Florida; Moundville, Alabama; Ocmulgee National Monument Park, Georgia; Moundsville, West Virginia; Indian Temple Mound, Florida; and Emerald Mound, Mississippi. If you come upon burial mounds, please treat them with great respect, and report anyone you see trying to dig them up. All the deceased deserve the same respect.

PILOT MOUNTAIN. Pilot Mountain, North Carolina, at the foothills of the Appalachians, sits all by itself and is a state park. The Cherokees say the spirit of the place is Jomeoki, and that the place was once used for initiation rites. Rose quartz is found nearby, and ravens which live there are supposed to be very alive. UFO hunters say it's a good spot for alien watching.

Midwest Region

MOUNDS. The Moundbuilders pushed up from the Southeast into the Midwest. As many as 10,000 mounds of Indian origin have been recorded in the Ohio River Valley alone. By far the most spectacular is the Serpent Mound in southern Ohio, close to Locust Grove. Not far away is Seip Mound, also a state historic park. Other prominent mounds of the Midwest include Temple Mounds, Wisconsin;

Norton Mounds, Michigan; Effigy Mounds National Monument, Iowa; and Mounds State Park in Indiana.

PIPESTONE QUARRY. The sacred red-sandstone quarry of northern Minnesota, source of medicine-pipe bowls and stone for other ceremonial purposes, is preserved today as Pipestone National Monument. There is an excellent museum on the grounds, and watch for the two rocks which are said to be the spirit women who guard the quarry.

SLEEPING BEAR DUNES. Along the eastern shore of Lake Michigan, not far from Traverse City, is the sprawling golden-sand mountain called the Sleeping Bear. According to an Ojibway legend, this is actually a giant mother bear waiting for her cubs—two offshore islands—to finish swimming across the lake. This is a national lakeshore with some beautiful wild areas, if you don't mind walking in sand.

The Great Plains

BLACK HILLS. The Black Hills of South Dakota contain many jewels of power and beauty. Mount Rushmore is the most famous, and Bear Butte is the most controversial, but try hiking through Custer State Park, climbing around Devil's Tower, or visiting Wind Cave to catch the spirit. To the Sioux, this is their Sistine Chapel.

BIGHORN MEDICINE WHEEL. Perched on the lofty shoulder of Medicine Mountain between Lovell and Sheridan, Wyoming, the Bighorn Medicine Wheel is an American Stonehenge. It's located at an elevation of 9,640 feet and is snow free only during the summer. It is also is surrounded by a fence, but no fence can stop the spirit of a place. A controversy swirls around the Bighorn Medicine Wheel as of 1990, for the U.S. Forest Service has made public plans to put in a road right to the site, with a parking lot next to it. They also have proposed to allow exclusive Indian use of the medicine wheel only at sunrise and after sunset, which is a little ridiculous for a solar observatory. Personally, I would not go there around the summer solstice unless I was invited by a tribe who uses this site. According to John Eddy, there are some 50 of these medicine wheels scattered throughout the northern Plains. One of the most striking is a giant turtle-shaped medicine wheel found near Minton, Saskatchewan.

MOUNDS. Just across the Mississippi River from St. Louis, Missouri, lies Cahokia Mounds State Park, which protects the remains of the ancient Mississippian village of Cahokia. Monk's Mound, some 1000-feet long, 700-feet wide, and 100-feet high, is the largest prehistoric earthen construction in the world. On the western side is a group of wooden poles called Woodenhenge, which apparently was used for astronomical sightings.

Southwest Region

SAN FRANCISCO PEAKS. According to the Hopi, these snow-capped peaks are the home of the kachina spirits. All other tribes which can see these majestic Arizona mountains agree that they are sacred.

ANASAZI RUINS. Mesa Verde National Park in Colorado and Hovenweep National Monument in Utah, along with Chaco Canyon National Cultural Park and Gila Cliff Dwellings National Monument in New Mexico, are among the most prominent ruins of the ancient Anasazi. At Mesa Verde, go to the Sun Temple, which has a spectacular view of the gorge below. In Chaco Canyon, the astronomical observatory nicknamed the Sun Dagger is on top of Fajada Butte, which is off-limits to the general public and also the home for lots of rattlesnakes.

MOUNT TAYLOR. In south-central New Mexico, Mount Taylor, or *Tso'dzil* to the Navajo, is the prevailing spirit. There are some unusual "breathing caves" near its base which send out negative-ion-rich air.

SHIPROCK. In northwestern New Mexico, the 1500-foot-tall dark volcanic spire of Shiprock juts out of the desert like a castle from science fiction movie, and no doubt has been the inspiration for some. It is located on the Navajo Reservation.

CHIMAYO. Not far from Española, New Mexico, is the simple sanctuary which is called the "Lourdes of America" for its healing earth. Also look for springs nearby.

WUPATKI BLOWHOLES. At Wupatki National Monument in western Arizona, the ground breathes through caves which vent winds up to 30 miles per hour of negative-ion-rich air.

CAPITOL REEF NATIONAL PARK. The blood-red rocks and other natural mosaics in stone at Capitol Reef in Utah are unforgettable. However, seek out the petroglyphs and pictographs tucked under an overhang not far off the main road. They are special.

GRIMES POINT ARCHEOLOGICAL AREA. Traveling along Highway 50 in western Nevada, east of Falton you go through an area marked "earthquake fault area" on some road maps. In this region, where old lake beds are trying to turn into dry mountains, is Grimes Point Archeological Area, which is a whole tribe of gray and black stones set amidst the sagebrush. It doesn't look too spectacular from the road, but the rocks are covered with very old rock art. Speculation has it that once this was a hunting-increase ritual site for the Shoshonean peoples. This is one of those places that isn't immediately obvious in physical form, but sit on one of those stones for an hour or so when no one else is around and watch what your imagination does. Morphogenic fields!

INDIAN HOT SPRINGS. In Hudspeth County south of El Paso and north of Big Bend National Park, this group of 22 artesian hot springs described by Pat Ellis Taylor's *Border Healing Woman* deserves personal inspection. They aren't easy to get to, and the resort there is very modest, but their power is strong.

GRAND CANYON. The Grand Canyon of the Colorado River is an awesome cavern which has stirred many minds. At the bottom of the canyon lies Havasupai Falls, which is accessible and has been recognized as a sacred place for as long as minds have known this part of the world existed.

West Coast Region

DESERT GEOGLYPHS. The Nazca markings of Peru have received considerable attention, but the United States has an equally astounding set of giant earth etchings in the desert region where California, Arizona, and Nevada come together. These are best seen from the air, but are distinguishable from the ground. Some are a half mile in length. Walk, don't drive, to them. If you see people driving on them, report them to the Bureau of Land Management, which manages the area.

ESALEN HOT SPRINGS. At Big Sur, California, where the fabled growth center the Esalen Institute is located, there is a strong center of power where the creek tumbles into the ocean and where there are nearby hot springs baths. Esalen is not open to the general public like a hotel, as the general program is one of seminars; however, you often can get in to use the baths after midnight if you aren't a regular seminarian. Check at the gate and enjoy.

POINT CONCEPTION. Just north of Santa Barbara, California, where Highway 1 turns inland from the ocean, lies the Western Gate, a sacred portal to the Chumash tribe. There is a state park and beach on the south side and a road which goes out onto the point; however, the road may be closed by a gate. A few miles away in the hills to the south you can drive to within 50 yards of a vision cave whose walls are covered with beautiful pictographs. The cave, however, has a fence across its mouth, and there is often litter around it. Help keep this place clean and safe from vandals.

HIGH COUNTRY OF THE SISKIYOU MOUNTAINS. Along the Oregon-California border, where the Klamath River slips into California, lies the "high country" which Peter Matthiessen has brought to national attention through his essay "Stop the G-O Road." Beautiful stands of trees, wise old rock ledges, and rugged little canyons with tumbling streams—some with gold in the stream bottoms—fill the area just east of Highway 1.

VOLCANIC MOUNTAINS. All the major volcanic mountains of the West Coast are sacred to Indian tribes near them. The Panther Meadows area at Mount Shasta may be developed into a ski area, despite the fact that it has been used for ceremonies and sweat lodges for a long time. Mount Adams now belongs to the Yakima tribe, so be sure to honor their ancestral values with this sentient being. One of my favorites is Mount Lassen, which is actually the ruins from what was once the biggest volcanic peak in the whole area. There are steam vents on the mountain which have evocative artistic qualities, and on the northeast slope there is a section along a small stream, which was a traditional summer camp for Indians, that feels very special to me. Ishi came from this area, and it's not hard to see how a whole tribe of Stone Age people could survive in some of the rugged areas around Lassen. Don't miss the Indian Ways nature trail at the visitor's center at the north entrance.

MOUNT TAMALPAIS. Marin County's Mount Tamalpais is probably the most visited sacred mountain in the world, since it lies just north of San Francisco and the Golden Gate Bridge. You can drive to within a few hundred yards of the top if you like heights, or slip down into the giant redwoods at Muir Woods on the west slope. Many trips to Mount Tamalpais helped make this book happen.

RING MOUNTAIN. Also in Marin County, California, is the Coastal Miwok tribe fertility stone on the summit of Ring Mountain in Tiburon. The best access is from the north on Paradise Drive, just before you come to the Marin County Day School.

VISION CAVES. I already noted the Chumash caves in the hills above Santa Barbara. Another cave is located just north of Spokane, Washington, and you can drive right up to it. Here again, chainlink fences are necessary to protect this place. When you see the abuse of such priceless treasures, you see why there should be citizens groups responsible for watching such places.

MYSTERY SPOTS. All across the United States there are mystery spots or "vortex" tourist attractions. Two of the best known are located at Gold Hill, Oregon, and Santa Cruz, California. I can find no Indian legend that says these were sacred places, but you ought to go visit them to see what you think. Strange things seem to happen there. Some professional skeptics say it's all by suggestion and funny angles, which I think is absurd. If you go to one of these places, close your eyes and "see" with your body. I think they're magnetic anomalies, probably due to some geological anomalies. Animals don't seem to like to be around them, which is the best measure I know of that something is strange there, although just what it is, I'm not certain.

Alaska

MOUNT McKINLEY, or DENALI. The tallest mountain in North America, the "wild one," *Denali*, is an awesome giant whose slopes are populated by grizzly bears, dall sheep, moose, and caribou. To preserve some element of wilderness, this National Park's main road is only open to tour buses during the summer, accommodating 3,000 visitors per day over a 96-mile bumpy trail. This is fragile tundra, which couldn't handle many people if they were allowed to run free like lemmings, but still you can camp and hike in some pretty awesome places with the mountain in plain sight.

CAPE KRUSENSTERN. You can only get to Cape Krusenstern by boat, but there is a fine visitors' center in Kozebuk. These rolling dunes, slipping into the Arctic Ocean and the Bering Land Bridge National Preserve to the south, look out toward Siberia, which is just a raven's flight away. If ancient people came to North America from Asia, this was one of their entry points. Just to the east lies Gates of the Arctic National Park, which has a number of ancient sacred places and some hot springs, if you can get there. Definitely not a place for greenhorns!

Hawaii

KAIWAINUI MARSH. Most people come to Oahu first when they come to Hawaii, and it is known as the "meeting place." On the north side of the island, near Kailua, lies the green gem of Kaiwainui Marsh, the largest freshwater marsh in the islands. Behind the YMCA is a large black volcanic-stone platform *heiau*, built on the edge of the marsh, with a great view. The magical Krider's Rock lies across the marsh but is difficult to get to, as a large sanitary landfill for Honolulu is just across the road. Also on the north shore you will find the Valley of the Temples, Waiahole Beach Park, and the "sacred falls" near Kahana Valley State Park. Look for the quiet places. You can still hear the drums beating at some of them.

VOLCANOES. The volcano goddess, Pele, is said to live at Kilauea Crater in Hawaii Volcanoes National Park on the big island of Hawaii. One park ranger I interviewed said she had seen Pele once, and it "scared the hell out of [her]," because the goddess looked so real before she vanished in a split second.

CITY OF REFUGE. Traditional Hawaiian culture set aside certain places where people could find sanctuary, one of which is preserved today on Hawaii as the City of Refuge National Park. Kahunas were very concerned with place, and did ceremonies to help mark special places, which is why so many people seem to slip into altered states around the sacred places of Hawaii. At the Pu'uhonua o Honaunau National Historic Site, you can see a reconstructed village, old *heiaus*, and a sanctuary.

KAHO'OLAWE ISLAND. A group of Hawaiians have banded together to save Kaho'olawe Island, which is a traditional sacred island inhabited today only by goats, because the Navy has been using it for bombing practice. Now the Navy is restricting bombing there, and is letting Hawaiians go over on special days. Ask around if you want adventure, as they do allow others to come and help sometimes, for they are trying to rebuild the old shrines and reclaim possession of the island using the American Indian Religious Freedom Act.

American Samoa

It's too bad more people don't go to visit American Samoa, because you can still see why Margaret Mead wrote such an enthusiastic book about this place and its people. On the main island of Tutuila, by all means go to see Shark and Turtle Rock in the village of Vaitongi. You may or may not see the mythic shark and turtle, but you will see awesome blowholes created by the surf pounding into black volcanic rocks when the tide is just right. Having whetted your appetite, then take a small twelve-passenger plane 63 miles away to the Manua group, where Mead wrote her book. You can stay in village guest homes and get fat on heaps of local fresh food for next to nothing. Samoans say the greatest chiefs come from Manua, and that to even say this word in conversation is considered a blessing.

RECOMMENDED READING

$\int$ ome other books which provide important information about sacred places include:

God Is Red, Vine Deloria, Jr., Grosset and Dunlap, 1973. A brilliant and eloquent accounting of American Indian religion and the weaknesses of Christianity that supports the creation of a new Earth-based religion.

Living The Sky, Ray Williamson, Houghton-Mifflin Co., 1984. A thorough and readable, detailed presentation of Indian astronomy and its links to sacred places.

A Song from Sacred Mountain, Anita Parlow, Oglala Lakota Legal Rights Fund, P.O. Box 354, Pine Ridge, SD, 1983. The Lakota people tell their story of why Bear Butte is a sacred place of power with moving words which bring tears to the eyes.

Cry, Sacred Ground: Big Mountain U.S.A., Anita Parlow, Christic Institute, 1988. The people of the Four Corners area tell the story of Big Mountain in words and photos, accompanied by an in-depth study of the Indian land law of that area.

Chuchama and Sacred Mountains, by W.Y. Evans-Wentz, edited by Frank Waters. Swallow Press, 1981. A moving treatment of the power of sacred mountains east and west, inspired by Chuchama or Tecate in California.

Indian Country, Peter Matthiessen, Viking Press, 1984. A vivid documentary of a journey around the United States describing today's Indian life in the author's award-winning dramatic narrative style.

The Way of Animal Powers, Joseph Campbell, Harper and Row, 1984. In pictures, mythic tales, and pure poetic wisdom, the master mythologist of the twentieth century guides the reader to see the reverence which can be expressed for place. This is a coffee-table-size presentation which is almost a modern holy book.

INDEX

ABOUT THE AUTHOR

J ames A. Swan, Ph.D., as a young faculty member at the University of Michigan in 1970, helped produce the nation's largest Earth Day college teach-in and appeared at 22 other teach-ins as a speaker and singer. Feeling a need to probe the psychological roots of the ecological crisis more deeply, he helped found the modern field of environmental psychology and then engaged in more than fifteen years of cross-cultural work and study with Eskimos, American Indians, and Polynesian peoples. He also spent the years between 1975 and 1982 practicing as a transpersonal pyschotherapist.

Swan is the producer of the Spirit of Place symposium, a contributing editor to *Sufism* magazine, a member of the editorial advisory board of *Shaman's Drum* magazine, a developer of the "Great Gardens" PBS television series, and a faculty member at the California Institute of Integral Studies. He has produced the National Audubon Society's "Is the Earth a Living Organism?" symposium and is a director of Full Circle music and media productions. He has also published over 100 articles in popular magazines and appeared frequently on radio and television. His education includes a bachelor's degree in conservation education, a master's degree in resource planning, and a doctorate in environmental psychology, all from the University of Michigan.

Author at the Miwok fertility stone on Ring Mountain in Tiburon, California. Photo © 1990 by Cindy A. Pavlinac.